DRONE STRIKE!

UCAVs and Unmanned Aerial Warfare in the 21st Century

Bill Yenne

SPECIALTY PRESS

Specialty Press
838 Lake Street South
Forest Lake, MN 55025
Phone: 651-277-1400 or 800-895-4585
Fax: 651-277-1203
www.specialtypress.com

Edit by Mike Machat
Layout by Monica Seiberlich

ISBN 978-1-58007-238-0
Item No. SP238

Library of Congress Cataloging-in-Publication Data
Names: Yenne, Bill, author.
Title: Drone strike! : UCAVs aerial warfare in the 21st century / Bill
    Yenne.
Other titles: UCAVs aerial warfare in the 21st century
Description: Forest Lake, MN : Specialty Press, [2016] | Includes index.
Identifiers: LCCN 2016028846 | ISBN 9781580072380
Subjects: LCSH: Uninhabited combat aerial vehicles. | Uninhabited
    combat aerial vehicles–Government policy. | Drone aircraft. | Air warfare.
Classification: LCC UG1242.D7 Y463 2016 | DDC 358.4/14–dc23
LC record available at https://lccn.loc.gov/2016028846

Written, edited, and designed in the U.S.A.
Printed in China
10 9 8 7 6 5 4 3 2 1

Front Cover: *A striking view of the General Atomics RQ-1 Predator Unmanned Aerial Combat Vehicle that no enemy ever wants to see. (USAF)*

Front Flap: *A Northrop Grumman X-47B makes an arrested landing aboard the aircraft carrier USS Theodore Roosevelt (CVN-71) in November 2013. The ship was the third carrier to be involved in tests of the X-47B. (U.S. Navy photo by Mass Communications Specialist Seaman Anthony Hilkowski)*

Front Endpaper: *Advanced U.S. Army MQ-1C Gray Eagle Unmanned Aerial Combat Vehicle flies over the National Training Center at Fort Irwin, California. (General Atomics)*

Title Page: *An MQ-1B Predator and an MQ-9A Reaper unmanned combat air vehicles assigned to the 432nd Aircraft Maintenance Squadron remain ready for their next mission at Creech AFB, Nevada. The two aircraft have flown intelligence, surveillance, and reconnaissance, as well as most of the unmanned strike operations during Operations Iraqi Freedom, Operation Enduring Freedom, and other 21st Century conflicts. (USAF photo by Staff Sergeant Vernon Young Jr.)*

Contents Page: *An artist conception of a U.S. Air Force MQ-1B Predator firing an AGM-114 Hellfire air-to-surface missile. In the background are a U.S. Navy MQ-4C Triton and a U.S. Army MQ-1C Gray Eagle. (DOD)*

Back Endpaper: *Inflight view of Genera; Atomics Predator B Multi-mission maritime patrol aircraft, variant of the combat-proven Predator B Reaper. (General Atomics)*

Back Cover Photos

Top: *Preparing a U.S. Air Force MQ-9 Reaper for flight during exercise Combat Hammer in 2014. The unmanned combat air vehicle is armed with GBU-12 Paveway II and AGM-114 Hellfire munitions. (USAF photo by Staff Sergeant Nadine Barclay)*

Bottom: *A British Royal Air Force Reaper armed with a full complement of two GBU-12 laser-guided bombs and four AGM-114P Hellfire air-to-surface missiles seen operating over Afghanistan during Operation Herrick. (Photo by Tam McDonald, Ministry of Defence)*

Distributed in the UK and Europe by:

Crécy Publishing Ltd
1a Ringway Trading Estate
Shadowmoss Road
Manchester M22 5LH England
Tel: 44 161 499 0024
Fax : 44 161 499 0298
www.crecy.co.uk
enquiries@crecy.co.uk

TABLE OF CONTENTS

The scariest, most intimidating message for the Taliban, at any level, from fighter to Taliban senior leadership, is anything to do with drones or aerial bombings. The Taliban has no way to defend against them and they are certain to end in absolute destruction of whatever their target is.

— *"Ahmad," a senior Taliban detainee, during a debriefing (2013)*

The F-35 [manned multi-role strike fighter], as much as we need it, as much as we want it, as much as we're looking forward to having it in the fleet, should be and almost certainly will be our last manned aircraft.

— *U.S. Secretary of the Navy Ray Mabus,*
speaking of unmanned combat air vehicles operating from aircraft carriers (2015)

ACKNOWLEDGMENTS

I thank all of the people who assisted me with this project, especially Erik Simonsen, late of Boeing Phantom Works, who has shared his extraordinary photo illustrations with me through the years, and who did so here. At General Atomics Aeronautical Systems, Incorporated, I was aided and cordially received onsite by Christopher Ames (Rear Admiral, USN, retired) GA-ASI's regional vice president for international strategic development, Europe; Kimberly Kasitz, GA-ASI's public relations and communications manager; Scott Nyberg; and Robert J. Walker, GA-ASI's director of strategic development. My appreciation also goes out to all of the people who have licensed photography under Creative Commons and have thereby shared a wealth of imagery with the rest of the world. And finally, for his encouragement and steady hand, a tip of the hat is due the editor on this project, Mike Machat.

— Bill Yenne

ABOUT THE AUTHOR

Bill Yenne (BillYenne.com) is the author of more than three dozen nonfiction books, mainly on military and historical topics. These include an earlier book on unmanned aerial combat published by Specialty Press titled *Birds of Prey: Predators, Reapers and America's Newest UAVs in Combat*.

His books on military aviation have included *Convair Deltas* from Specialty Press, as well as his profiles of such legendary aircraft as the B-52 Stratofortress and the B-29 Superfortress, the latter coauthored with General Curtis LeMay. His books on aviation and military history have included his dual biography of Dick Bong and Tommy McGuire, *Aces High: The Heroic Story of the Two Top-Scoring American Aces of World War II*, which was described by pilot and best-selling author Dan Roam as "The greatest flying story of all time."

Yenne has written histories of America's great aircraft manufacturers, including Convair, Lockheed, and McDonnell Douglas, and has been praised for his recently updated *The Story of the Boeing Company*. He has also written histories of the U.S. Air Force and the Strategic Air Command. Mr. Yenne has contributed to encyclopedias of both world wars and has appeared in documentaries airing on the History Channel, the National Geographic Channel, the Smithsonian Channel, and ARD German Television. His book signings have been covered by C-SPAN.

His work has been selected for the official Chief of Staff of the Air Force Reading List, and he is the recipient of the Air Force Association's Gill Robb Wilson Award for his "most outstanding contribution in the field of arts and letters." He was described as "a prolific airpower author whose works have shaped how thousands of Americans understand and appreciate airpower. His accessible writing style and broad focus have kept the value of airpower in the public eye."

INTRODUCTION

Until just a decade or so ago, unmanned aerial vehicles were merely a footnote in the big picture of military history. The concept and the hardware have been around in one form or another since before World War I, but their names were certainly not household words. In listing the important aerial weapons of 20th-Century wars, including those of the Cold War, hardly any historian or combat commander would have ranked unmanned aerial vehicles (UAV), or remotely piloted vehicles (RPV) as they were known mid-century, as being among even the remotely significant.

Suddenly, with the Global War on Terrorism (GWOT), this changed. Beginning with Operation Enduring Freedom in 2001, unmanned aerial vehicles played a much bigger role in battlefield doctrine, not only an important role, but an *essential* role. Unmanned aerial vehicles (or "drones" as popular culture likes to call them) emerged as the signature new weapons system in the skies over the modern battlefield.

Meanwhile, they have become established as icons of both battlefield doctrine and popular culture well beyond what had earlier been imagined. The word "drone" has long since become a household word.

It was not the first time this had happened with aerial vehicles. Just as most military commanders in the first decade of the 20th Century had a hard time imagining how to use airplanes, so too did most military commanders at the end of that century have a hard time seeing unmanned aerial vehicles as anything more than observation platforms. When the world celebrated the end of the millennium on the last day of 1999, few people outside a mere handful within the armed forces of a few countries recognized the potential of *arming* unmanned flying machines.

The idea of the armed, combat-configured unmanned aerial vehicle entered the 21st Century much as the idea of military airplanes had entered at the threshold of the 20th Century, as an untried and untested concept that was soon thrust into the spotlight in an unexpected global war.

Just as unmanned aerial vehicle technology and applications have evolved unimaginably since the turn of the century, unmanned *air combat* vehicles have become the signature new warplane of the 21st Century. Armed drones have turned heads and earned themselves a permanent place on the modern battlefield just as military airplanes did a century earlier.

Likewise, they now occupy that peculiar niche in popular culture in which they are cast as both heroes and villains, depending upon the perception of their nemesis. While most people see drones as the antagonist of the truly nefarious villains of our time, a cottage industry has flourished within the counterculture that deems their use as "unfair" because of collateral damage. Such a strange focus upon drones as a signature evil is mystifying, certainly given that the blast radius of a 20-pound Hellfire missile warhead circumscribes far fewer civilian casualties than that of a 500-pound or 1,000-pound bomb dropped from a conventional aircraft.

Meanwhile, the voices of concern within the cottage industry are generally mute on the fact that "civilian" deaths in drone strikes are usually among people who know that they are liable to be attacked. They are either willing groupies in a terrorist entourage or innocent people with whom the callous jihadist masterminds (indifferent to the obvious dangers) deliberately choose to surround themselves.

A U.S. Navy X-47B unmanned combat air vehicle demonstrator aircraft banks over the main runway at Edwards AFB, California. (Northrop Grumman)

A General Atomics Predator of the Royal Air Force, armed with AGM-114 Hellfire missiles, prepares to take off on a mission from Kandahar Airfield in Afghanistan. (Ministry of Defence)

WHAT ARE THEY CALLED?

This book borrows the term "drone" embraced by popular culture, but what should these vehicles be called? By definition, a drone is a male honeybee without a stinger who produces no honey; hence he is an idler with nothing to contribute. In the aeronautical sense, the unflattering term was applied in the middle of the 20th Century to passive target drones, whose function was simply to be intercepted and shot down. As drones in the original aeronautical sense were adapted for other uses, the name migrated with them, now being applied not only to *passive* vehicles, but to vehicles *actively* involved in missions such as reconnaissance and even combat. Today, the term immediately conjures up the image of a very active aerial vehicle. The languid bee is largely forgotten.

Many technical terms for these vehicles have come and gone over the years, driven by the winds of the times. In the second quarter of the 20th Century, they were the "Remotely Piloted Vehicle" (RPV). This name also applied to radio-controlled (RC) model aircraft used by hobbyists. Indeed, the two had common roots. Reginald Denny, who made and sold RC models in Hollywood, started the Radioplane Company, which manufactured most of the target drones built in the United States in the 1940s and was later absorbed by Northrop Corporation.

By the latter part of the century, the term "Unmanned Aerial Vehicle" (UAV) came into almost universal use, though there was briefly a trend toward the modification "Uninhabited" Aerial Vehicles. When the United States Defense Department launched its Unmanned Air Combat Vehicle program at the turn of the century, the acronym UCAV came into widespread usage to describe armed UAVs generically.

Early in the 21st Century, the United States Defense Department coined the replacement terms "Unmanned Aircraft System" (UAS) and "Unmanned Combat Aircraft System" (UCAS), also seen as "Unmanned Aerial System," to describe the aircraft. These terms implied that the aircraft was more than just an aerial *vehicle*, it was hardware integrated into a broad ground control and data download infrastructure, which is often called a "system of systems."

This term was adapted to a limited extent by the industry and the technical media, but UAV remained in use. In the second decade of the 20th Century the terms "Remotely Piloted Aircraft" (RPA), "Remotely Piloted Aerial Vehicle" (RPAV), and "Remotely Piloted Aircraft System" (RPAS) were all entering the lexicon.

In this book, we use the terms "UAV" and "UCAV" to refer to *vehicles* because they are still widely used, and because we find it confusing to refer to a vehicle as a system when it is merely a *part* of the larger system.

An X-47B aircraft is loaded aboard the aircraft carrier USS Harry S. Truman at Norfolk, Virginia on November 26, 2012, ahead of its early carrier-borne flight testing. Once the X-47B would have been an "Unmanned combat air vehicle," then it was an "unmanned combat air system," and later it was a "remotely piloted aircraft system." (DoD photo by Petty Officer 3rd Class Lorenzo Burleson, USN)

America's first military unmanned aerial vehicle was Charles Kettering's Aerial Torpedo, best remembered as the "Kettering Bug." It first flew (albeit not well) in 1918 and was being considered for deployment overseas when World War I ended. It remained top secret for decades. (USAF)

Members of the 451st Expeditionary Aircraft Maintenance Squadron unit push an MQ-1B Predator toward a hangar for a routine maintenance inspection shortly after landing at Kandahar Airfield, Afghanistan. (U.S. Air Force photo by Senior Airman Nancy Hooks)

As the 21st Century began, the dimensions of the doctrine and policies guiding the uses of drones in combat were entirely tactical and technical and not yet cloaked in such political nuances. As with any weapon (as with any tool) if it was technically and practically appropriate to the operational situation, the drone was the weapon to use.

How then, is this weapon used?

In discussing the operations of drones in combat, Scott Meyers of General Dynamics Robotic Systems famously said that they were appropriate for three types of missions: "the dull, the dirty, and the dangerous." These include long, dull, repetitive reconnaissance missions; missions into a battlefield environment made dirty by chemical or biological weapons; or missions against targets that are very dangerous for human pilots.

In the first decade of the 21st Century, the emphasis was on the dull. The dirty had yet to materialize, and the dangerous, as defined by penetrating sophisticated air defenses, did not exist over places such an Afghanistan, Yemen, or Somalia.

However, it was discovered that UAVs were an ideal platform for combat against a new type of foe and a new type of warfare that was emerging in Afghanistan and Yemen. In the new century's second decade, the Defense Department summarized in its *Unmanned Systems Integrated Roadmap* that "unmanned systems continue to prove their value in combat operations in Afghanistan, where military operations are planned and executed in extremely challenging environments. Indeed, adversaries are fighting using increasingly unconventional means, taking cover in the surrounding populations, and employing asymmetric tactics to achieve their objectives. In future conflicts, we must be prepared for these tactics as well as for a range of other novel methods of opposition, including so-called 'hybrid' and A2/AD approaches to blunting U.S. power projection. Unmanned systems will be critical to U.S. operations in all domains across a range of conflicts, both because of their capability and performance advantages and because of their ability to take greater risk than manned systems."

In looking at the origins of military UAVs, we see them serving in World War II as target drones for training operations. Two decades later, it occurred to planners that such vehicles could be used as reconnaissance aircraft. The United States led the way by adapting the Ryan BQM-34 Firebee family of target drones for high-speed, jet-propelled, unmanned photoreconnaissance. During the 1960s and beyond, aircraft of this family, including the related Ryan Model 147 series Lightning Bugs, were widely used by both the U.S. Air Force and the CIA for missions into the hostile air space of North Vietnam and China, where risking the lives of human pilots was not an option.

Airmen attached to the 324th Expeditionary Reconnaissance Squadron perform a preflight inspection on an MQ-1 Predator unmanned aerial vehicle in October 2013. (U.S. Navy photo by MC2 Brian T. Glunt)

In the 1970s and 1980s, it was Israel's turn to lead the way, this time with *low-speed* reconnaissance drones. The Israel Aircraft Corporation (IAI) Hunter and Pioneer vehicles were developed in response to a need for an aircraft that could loiter high above a battlefield like a soaring hawk, quietly observing. They were much slower, less sophisticated aeronautically, and easier to deploy than the fast jets, and they were much better suited to the tactical requirements of the battlefields upon which Israel was engaged.

In turn, the simple twin-boom, pusher-prop configuration of the Hunter and Pioneer defined the look of the late 20th-Century tactical surveillance drone, a configuration that was widely copied (and is *still* being copied) by dronemakers throughout the world. Indeed, it is the configuration of today's IAI Heron, discussed in Chapter 11, which in turn was adapted as France's Harfang, discussed in Chapter 9.

In 1994, General Atomics Aeronautical Systems Incorporated (GA-ASI) of Poway, California, rolled out the RQ-1 Predator reconnaissance UAV, a vehicle nearly twice the size of a Hunter and three times that of the Pioneer. It had a straight wing, an inverted V-tail, and was powered by a Rotax four-cylinder engine. It was nearly the last aircraft that anyone would think of as a warplane. That is, until surveillance operators looked at the enemy remotely through a Predator's video feed and wished they could direct a strike against the target they were watching.

During the Balkan Wars of the 1990s, U.S. Air Force General John Jumper served in the dual roles of commander of U.S. Air Forces in Europe (USAFE) and commander of Allied Air Forces Central Europe (AFCENT) for Operation Allied Force/Noble Anvil in the Balkans. He was there when they field-modified RQ-1s with a laser designator and rangefinder system, a Raytheon AN/AAS-44(V) sensor turret, or

"laser ball," that could "laze" an enemy tank so that an F-16 with laser guided munitions, such as a GBU-24 Paveway III, could then find and destroy the "lazed" target.

As Jumper later described it, this transition was "a breakthrough." As he said, the laser ball "turns the Predator from just a pure surveillance system into something that actually . . . directs weapons on the targets."

And then there were those who looked at the enemy remotely through a Predator's video feed and wished they could take a shot themselves.

At Jumper's next job, as the commander of Air Combat Command, came the next idea for the Predator: to arm it. However, the Predator was never designed to be armed. Its total payload capacity is less than 500 pounds, the weight of the lightest standard "dumb"

At the turn of the century, General John Jumper was the driving force in moving the U.S. Air Force toward arming its unmanned aerial vehicles. (USAF photo by Master Sergeant Jim Varhegyi)

The U.S. Air Force RQ-4 Global Hawk High Altitude Long Endurance (HALE) unmanned aerial vehicle is used for very long-range intelligence, surveillance, and reconnaissance missions. (Northrop Grumman)

bomb. Laser-guided GBU-24s weigh four times that. The solution was the laser-guided AGM-114 Hellfire, an air-to-surface, anti-armor missile that had been designed for use aboard Army and Marine Corps attack helicopters. They weigh about 100 pounds each.

As Jumper described it, the Hellfire was ideal for "fleeting, perishable targets that don't require a big warhead that we can just go ahead and take care of." The first tests, which came early in 2001, proved successful.

John Jumper became Chief of Staff of the U.S. Air Force on September 6, 2001, less than a week before the United States found itself thrust into the GWOT. He came to the post as a combat commander who'd had direct experience with UAVs in a combat theater. The Predators were among the first aircraft to go to war, and by 2007, they were joined by the larger and more capable General Atomics

MQ-9 Reaper. The rest, of course, is history.

Just as Israel's first generation of small surveillance drones inspired a world of imitators, so too have the Predator and Reaper. As we will see in later chapters, there is a growing number of near-clones of the General Atomics design around the world. These unmanned combat air vehicles include Turkey's Anka and Iran's Shahed 129, as well as the CH-4 and Pterodactyl I in China.

Another class of unmanned aerial vehicle that deserves mention in this introduction consists of the large, long-endurance reconnaissance drones that are described as Medium Altitude Long Endurance (MALE) or High Altitude Long Endurance (HALE) aircraft. HALE originated as the DARPA research program in the United States in the 1980s that produced the record-setting Boeing Condor with its 200-foot wingspan, a ceiling of 67,300 feet, and an endurance

During the early 21st Century, efforts toward developing a pan-European Medium Altitude Long Endurance (MALE) unmanned aerial vehicle devolved into confusion and delays, so the European Aeronautic Defence and Space Company (EADS) teamed with Israel Aerospace Industries (IAI) to develop an "interim" MALE program called Système Intémaire de Drone MALE (SIDM). The result, based on the IAI Heron, was the Harfang (Snowy Owl). It is seen here, probably, at Istres-Le Tubé Air Base in southern France. (Airbus Defence and Space)

U.S. Air Force crew chiefs of the 49th Aircraft Maintenance Squadron conduct routine work on an MQ-9 Reaper unmanned combat air vehicle in August 2014 at Holloman AFB in New Mexico. (USAF photo by Airman 1st Class Aaron Montoya)

A 2015 delivery celebration for Turkish Bayraktar TB2 Medium Altitude Long Endurance (MALE) unmanned combat air vehicles at Kesan Airport in Turkey. A Medium Altitude Long Endurance (MALE) class system, the Bayraktar was originally developed for tactical reconnaissance and surveillance missions, but it is also armed with Turkish-made Roketsan UMTAS ground attack missiles. (Baykar Makina)

In May 2013, an X-47B unmanned combat air vehicle demonstrator, aboard the USS George H.W. Bush (CVN-77), became the first unmanned aircraft successfully catapult launched from a carrier flight deck. (U.S. Navy photo by Alan Radecki)

Taranis unmanned combat air vehicles at the BAE Systems hangar at Warton in Lancashire, England. The aircraft is named after the Celtic god of thunder. (BAE Systems)

The X-47B unmanned combat air vehicle demonstrator seen here at the threshold of the flight deck of the aircraft carrier USS George H.W. Bush was the first unmanned aircraft to be launched from a carrier at sea, and the first to execute touch-and-go landings at sea. (U.S. Navy photo by Mass Communications Specialist Seaman Brian Stephens)

beyond 80 hours. In turn, the HALE concept is represented for the future by the Boeing Phantom Eye, a demonstrator that evolved from the Condor, first flew in 2012, and which may lead to a larger HALE warplane (see Chapter 7).

Currently, the HALE concept is perhaps best described operationally by the Northrop Grumman Global Hawk, which is in service with the U.S. Air Force as the RQ-4A and with the U.S. Navy as the MQ-4C Triton. It was also operated by the German Luftwaffe and NATO as the EuroHawk, though these were mothballed for cost reasons. The Global Hawk has a 130.9-foot wingspan, a ceiling of 60,000 feet (plus), and a proven endurance beyond 30 hours.

Generally, the much more common MALE unmanned aerial vehicles have a ceiling of around 30,000 feet and an endurance of up to 48 hours. MALE drones are important in the context of this book because many of them were deliberately built as unmanned combat air vehicles and others have a payload capacity that allowed them to easily be armed.

The Predator has sufficient endurance to be classed as a MALE vehicle, as do the Anka and Shahed 129. Turkey's Bayraktar also fits the category, as does India's Rustom (Warrior), while in Israel, both the Hermes 900 and Heron are MALEs.

Earning a great deal of media attention since the turn of the century have been a class of advanced, jet-propelled stealth attack aircraft with delta or flying wing configurations. As discussed in Chapter 7, this concept originated at the end of the 20th Century as an alternative to using high-performance manned aircraft to attack targets protected by heavy enemy air defenses. The goal was a high-performance *unmanned* aircraft for this mission, and in

the United States, the Defense Advanced Research Projects Agency's Unmanned Combat Air Vehicle (UCAV) program was born.

Two specific stealthy flying wing UCAV demonstrator aircraft were produced, the Boeing X-45A for the U.S. Air Force, and the Northrop Grumman X-47A Pegasus for the U.S. Navy. They made their respective first flights in May 2002 and February 2003. In the beginning, both the U.S. Air Force and U.S. Navy identified their aircraft as UCAVs, but later in 2003, the UCAV program was renamed the Joint Unmanned Combat Air System (J-UCAS) program.

In 2006, more advanced and capable UCAVs (to use the generic term) were in the pipeline. Boeing was beginning work on the X-45C and Northrop Grumman on the X-47B. However, under its Quadrennial Defense Review, the Defense Department pulled the plug on the whole program. The X-45C was canceled outright, but the X-47B continued to evolve and is discussed in Chapter 16.

Perhaps the most important legacy of the UCAV/J-UCAS program was that it inspired a whole new class of sophisticated, high-performance, stealthy flying wing UCAVs, including the British Aerospace Taranis and the Dassault Neuron, which are discussed in Chapter 9, not to mention the X-47B, discussed in Chapter 16.

In the United States, which has led the way in the operational deployment of unmanned combat air vehicles, the numbers of aircraft, or aircraft types, and of operational missions dependent upon them has grown exponentially, as has their importance and proportion in the overall defense establishment. The Defense Department's *Unmanned Systems Integrated Roadmap* observed that "as unmanned systems have proven their worth on the battlefield, DOD has allocated an increasing percentage of its budget to developing and

On April 22, 2015, the U.S. Navy's X-47B unmanned combat air vehicle demonstrator became the first unmanned aircraft refueled in flight. (U.S. Navy photo)

The Neuron is a European unmanned combat air vehicle that developed from a collaborative program led by Dassault in France. The configuration is similar to that of the American X-47B or the British Taranis. (Dassault Aviation)

acquiring these systems. With the transition from a handful of innovative experimental systems to normalized program developments, unmanned systems have received their share of inclusion in Congressional direction and are influenced by many acquisition initiatives and departmental policies."

UAVs and UCAVs are having a significant effect not only in acquisition initiatives but also in battlefield doctrine. Indeed, the 21st Century battlefield is a far different place and unmanned systems have become integral for both tactical and budgetary reasons.

In their article "An Air Force Strategic Vision for 2020–2030," published in *Strategic Studies Quarterly*, General John Shaud and Adam Lowther, both of the Air Force Research Institute at Maxwell AFB, wrote that "with the F-22 and F-35 likely to serve as the nation's principal air superiority platforms until 2030 and a reduction in the purchase of F-35s likely, relatively inexpensive force multipliers such as autonomous unmanned platforms, human-computer enhancements, and cyber-attack capabilities may become more important."

Meanwhile, as those in the UAV and UCAV world evaluate operating environments in the context of system performance flexibility, they are considering a broader than previously imagined spectrum of technologies in the fields of automation, maneuverability, and communications options that are needed to accomplish an expanding portfolio of mission profiles.

In the first decade of the new century, the principal role and value of unmanned aerial vehicles (operations in hostile skies without compromising the lives of pilots) became routine. In the second decade and beyond, this continues to expand, and the place of unmanned aerial warfare in the annals of military history has been assured.

Sailors move a Northrop Grumman X-47B unmanned combat air vehicle demonstrator onto an aircraft elevator aboard the aircraft carrier USS George H.W. Bush. *(U.S. Navy photo by MC2 Michael Smevog)*

Chapter 1

IN THE HOME OF PERSISTENT SITUATIONAL AWARENESS

The Ikhana remotely piloted aircraft is a General Atomics Predator B Reaper that was acquired by NASA's Suborbital Science Program. It has been used for monitoring wildfires as well as a variety of scientific missions. It is seen here in 2014 operating as part of the Air Collision Avoidance System project. (Photo by Carla Thomas)

There is no better place in the world to begin a look at the state of the art in unmanned aerial combat than with the makers of the aircraft that have accounted for around 90 percent (if not more) of the combat actions conducted by unmanned aerial vehicles in the 21st Century.

General Atomics Aeronautical Systems Incorporated (GA-ASI) of Poway, California, created the Predator vehicle in the last years of the 20th Century and has greatly expanded its portfolio in the first decades of the 21st with the Reaper and Avenger vehicles, and with many interoperable variations on these aircraft.

When this author visited the home of General Atomics in the spring of 2016, its production lines were filled with a substantial number of MQ-9 Reapers, with a scattering of other craft among them. Meanwhile, in another vast room, lines of Advanced Cockpit Ground Control Stations were taking shape and marching toward completion.

As I sat down with Christopher Ames, the company's regional vice president for international strategic development in Europe, he acknowledged all of this. However, the retired rear admiral and former naval aviator was quick to add that *the* lead products at General Atomics are persistent surveillance and persistent situational awareness.

Indeed, the consistent and reliable delivery of these, whether one considers them products or services or an amalgam of both, is at the core of what General Atomics is about and what its customers depend upon it for. Indeed, the company motto positions the company as "leading the situational awareness revolution."

Ames called General Atomics aircraft the most reliable products of their kind in the international market, proudly referencing a

90-percent mission-ready rate for the MQ-9 with the U.S. Air Force, the highest of any aircraft used by that service.

Integrated into operations and, indeed, into the corporate culture at General Atomics is an insistence on quality that one recalls from the golden age of American industrial prowess in the middle of the 20th Century. Around the company we hear mention of the "secret sauce," a blend of quality control and "ingrained reliability."

In April 2016, as we spoke, the company had delivered 755 aircraft and 342 Ground Control Stations, but it was clear from my stroll down the production lines that those numbers were due to change within a few days. Ames mentioned an aggregate flight time for the General Atomics fleet of 3.8 million hours, but the fact that half a million of those hours had come in just the preceding year makes the numbers in this paragraph a mere point of reference on a continuing timeline.

Like many of the great American industrial success stories, that of General Atomics Aeronautical Systems is one of modest beginnings, of near bankruptcy, of singular vision, and in no small measure of being in precisely the right place at precisely the right time.

This story began with Abraham Karem, an immigrant from Iraq by way of Israel, who started building remotely powered aircraft in his Los Angeles garage in the 1980s. The story is reminiscent of that of Reginald Denny, who started the Radioplane company in a Los Angeles garage four decades earlier. Karem's breakthrough came when the Defense Advanced Research Projects Agency (DARPA) contracted with his company, Leading Systems Incorporated, to build a demonstration UAV, an aircraft that he called *Amber*, and which evolved by 1989 into the GNAT-750. By then, however, consolidation and truncating of U.S. military UAV programs led to diminished funding, and to hard times for Leading Systems. In 1990 the nucleus of the company was acquired by General Atomics.

General Atomics, meanwhile, had originated in San Diego in 1955 as the nuclear physics component of General Dynamics Corporation. After being owned by a succession of oil companies after 1967, it was acquired in 1986 by the present owners, brothers James Neal Blue and Linden Stanley Blue. The company remains active in both fusion and fission nuclear energy research and development, as well as in advanced electromagnetic technology. In 1994, the company's UAV business was spun off as the affiliated General Atomics Aeronautical Systems. In that same year, the Predator, derived from the GNAT-750, made its first flight. Just a year later, the first RQ-1 Predators were serving with the U.S. Air Force in the Balkans.

By the turn of the century, the Predator had taken on a life that could not have been imagined when it was first introduced. Retrofitted to deliver AGM-114 Hellfire missiles, the multi-role variant was designated as MQ-1A, and soon, improved Predator systems with updated data links and other equipment, such as the AN/AAS-52 Multi-Spectral Targeting System, joined their predecessors under the RQ-1B and MQ-1B designations.

In 2007, General Atomics rolled out its larger, higher performance Predator B, which was acquired by the U.S. Air Force under the designation MQ-9 and given the name "Reaper," an appellation by which it is best known, and by which international users know it. Whereas the Predator could carry a Hellfire missile under each wing, the Reaper carries a total of four, in addition to two 500-pound GBU-12 Paveway II laser-guided bombs, or a pair of 500-pound GBU-38 Joint Direct Attack Munitions (JDAMs). In addition to these six underwing hard points, the MQ-9 can also carry ordnance on a seventh hardpoint beneath its fuselage centerline.

Together, the Predators and Reapers amassed far more flight time as operational unmanned *combat* air vehicles than all other such aircraft worldwide combined. They proved to be an ideal weapon for the battlefields of the Southwest Asia wars because they could linger quietly in the airspace above potential targets, watching and waiting, a mission unsuited for an F-16 or an F/A-18.

With the prosperity that flowed from the success of the Predator and Reaper, the once-obscure component of General Atomics grew substantially. From a handful of employees at the turn of the century, the workforce expanded to 2,000 by 2006, and to 7,000 a decade later, with more than 30 being added each month.

Manufacturing is concentrated in northern San Diego County, from the main complex near Scripps-Poway Road in Poway to Rancho Bernardo a half-dozen miles to the north. Aircraft are in turn trucked out for flight testing at locations such as the company-owned Gray Butte Flight Operations Facility near Palmdale, California, and more recently, to the Castle Dome Heliport, a UAV operating location within the U.S. Army Yuma Proving Ground in Arizona.

The company has also recently opened a UAV training academy adjacent to Grand Forks AFB in North Dakota, where General Atomics aircraft are operated by U.S. Customs and Border Protection, as well as by the North Dakota Air National Guard.

Electronic components being assembled at General Atomics. In addition to aircraft, the company also produces systems such as the Lynx multi-mode radar and Claw 3, an intelligence, surveillance, and reconnaissance integrated sensor payload control and analysis software package. (General Atomics)

This is one of nearly a dozen states in which the Air National Guard operates Predators or Reapers. Export sales have seen Predators going to Italy, Morocco, Turkey, and the United Arab Emirates. Reapers, meanwhile, have gone overseas to France, Italy, Spain, and the United Kingdom.

The Predator and Reaper have each spawned a family of variants. The U.S. Army ordered a Predator variant as a replacement for its RQ-5 Hunters. Designated as MQ-1C, it was initially called "Warrior," but was renamed "Gray Eagle" in 2010. The Predator XP, which made its debut in 2014, is an unarmed reconnaissance aircraft with an endurance in excess of 40 hours, which was specifically designed for export sales to a broad range of countries.

U.S. Customs and Border Protection operates several Predator B aircraft, which are based at Grand Forks to watch the Canadian border, while the Mexican border is observed from several bases, including Fort Huachuca in Arizona and NAS Corpus Christi in Texas. The Predator B variants include the multi-mission maritime patrol aircraft that is called "Guardian" rather than "Reaper." It is equipped with Raytheon SeaVue multi-mode maritime radar and Raytheon MTS-B electro-optical/infrared sensors, and is distinguishable by the large antenna located beneath the rear fuselage.

Two specially configured Predator B airframes have been operated by NASA. Under its Environmental Research Aircraft and Sensor Technology (ERAST) program, NASA operated both a civilian variant of the Predator called "Altus" and the third Predator B airframe, which the agency called "Altair." The Altair was notable for its 86-foot wingspan, 30 percent greater than a standard Predator B. Since 2006, NASA has operated a second Predator B as part of its Suborbital Science Program. Named *Ikhana* (the Choctaw word for "Awareness"), it flies out of Edwards AFB and has been used to observe and monitor California wildfires and the reentry of Orion space capsules. Through the winter of 2015–2016, *Ikhana* was being used in NASA's Air Collision Avoidance System project to develop "Detect and Avoid" technologies that would allow unmanned aerial vehicles to be integrated into the National Airspace System in the United States.

In August 2015, meanwhile, the U.S. Air Force became operational with the Reaper Extended Range (Reaper ER). As described by the company, the Reaper ER is an MQ-9 that has been equipped with "a field-retrofittable modification package consisting of two wing-mounted fuel tanks which significantly extend the aircraft's maximum endurance."

The description continues, adding that "the Reaper's original external payload carriage configuration remains unchanged, providing the aircraft with a 'mix and match' capability that allows it to carry both [external] fuel tanks and an assortment of external payloads. To increase thrust and improve takeoff performance at higher gross weights, an alcohol/water injection system and a four-bladed propeller were incorporated, along with a heavyweight trailing arm landing gear system that enables safe ground operations at the heavier gross weight."

The General Atomics Predator B Guardian multi-mission maritime patrol variant of the Predator B Reaper, equipped with Raytheon SeaVue radar in its dorsal pod. (General Atomics)

A further advanced iteration of the MQ-9 is the Reaper ER Long Wing, which made its first flight on February 18, 2016, at Gray Butte. The new long-endurance wing, which spans 79 feet, provides greater internal fuel capacity as well as additional hard points for carrying external stores, provisions for leading-edge de-ice, and integrated RF antennas. Developed by General Atomics with its own Internal Research and Development (IRAD) funds, the new aircraft has an endurance that has increased from 27 hours in the standard Reaper to more than 40 hours.

As Linden Blue, the CEO of General Atomics Aeronautical Systems, puts it, the new wing not only boosts the aircraft's endurance and range, but it "also serves as proof-of-concept for the next-generation Predator B aircraft that will be designed for Type-Certification and airspace integration. The wing was designed to conform to STANAG 4671 [NATO Airworthiness Standard for RPA systems] and includes lightning and bird strike protection, non-destructive testing, and advanced composite and adhesive materials for extreme environments."

It should also be pointed out that the later Predator B aircraft have greatly increased electrical power capabilities designed to accommodate the requirements of present as well as future electronic systems.

Beyond the Predator B, General Atomics has also been developing its jet-propelled Predator C, also known as Avenger, which is discussed in Chapter 7.

There is more to the portfolio of the world leader in unmanned combat aircraft than just its aircraft platforms. Heading the list of sensors developed at General Atomics is the Lynx multi-mode radar, which provides high-resolution imagery of photographic quality and precision accuracy. Lynx possesses wide-area search capabilities through clouds, smoke, and other atmospheric contaminants. It was designed with a UAV in mind, consuming minimal size, weight, and power. Members of the Lynx family include the AN/APY-8 Block 20, the AN/APY-8A Block 20A, and the AN/DPY-1 Block 30 radar systems.

Technical features of Lynx include Synthetic Aperture Radar (SAR), Ground/Dismount Moving Target Indicator (GMTI/DMTI), and a Maritime Wide Area Search (MWAS) mode. The GMTI mode provides for quick location of moving vehicles, while the DMTI allows operators to spot very slow-moving vehicles and people on foot. The latter is useful both to air forces and to border protection services. The Lynx MWAS can detect ship and boat traffic in various sea state conditions, and integrates Automated Identification System (AIS) data to identify targets.

Among the other General Atomics sensor systems is Due Regard Radar (DRR), an air-to-air radar developed with company funding to "meet the requirements envisioned to enable Remotely Piloted Aircraft to fly in International Airspace." DRR comprises a two-panel Active Electronically Scanned Array (AESA) Antenna and a Radar Electronics Assembly (REA) that give the pilot the ability to detect and track aircraft across the same field of view as a manned aircraft. DRR is seen as a key component of the General Atomics Detect and Avoid architecture for its Predator B for operations within the U.S. National Airspace System.

Heading the list of General Atomics Intelligence, Surveillance, and Reconnaissance (ISR) exploitation systems is Claw 3, described as "a highly sophisticated yet user-friendly integrated sensor payload control and analysis software package originally developed with a point-and-click, intuitive Graphic User Interface (GUI) for the Lynx." Claw provides image data integration, payload feedback

A large number of MQ-1 Predators undergoing systems integration on the General Atomics factory floor at Poway, California. The early-generation Predators have since moved on, their place having been taken mainly by MQ-9 Reapers and a growing number of Predator XP aircraft. (General Atomics)

The General Atomics Predator B Guardian multi-mission maritime patrol variant of the Predator B Reaper, equipped with Raytheon SeaVue radar in its dorsal pod. (General Atomics)

and diagnostics, and enables sensor data post-processing analysis. It is used in both manned and unmanned aircraft.

General Atomics has also developed its System for Tactical Archival, Retrieval, and Exploitation (STARE), a self-explanatory, Google-Earth compatible, data management setup used to process information for users at the strategic and tactical level.

The company is also developing long-range, solid-state lasers, including its Airborne Laser Communication System (ALCOS). The General Atomics Trident is a compact laser rangefinder/designator designed for tactical airborne applications, supporting "precision strike with either laser-guided or coordinate-seeking munitions from long standoff ranges." The High Energy Liquid Laser Area Defense System (HELLADS) program is aimed at a laser weapon system.

Recalling that the nomenclature of Unmanned Aerial Vehicles (UAVs) was once changed to Unmanned Air Systems (UAS) to underscore their being part of a system of systems that includes the operator on the ground, we next turn to what can be described as the keystone of the General Atomics product line.

Ground control stations are obviously the "cockpits" for aircraft that do not have them, and as with manned aircraft, these cockpits are developed in parallel with the aircraft and are integrated with them every step in the process. Each of these is a two-person cockpit, with a place for a pilot and a sensor operator.

From the original "small-screen" stations, General Atomics has migrated to the Advanced Cockpit GCS. This multi-screen console wraps around the controller chairs, providing a 270-degree horizon

Heavy fabrication work at the General Atomics facility using a Hurco PH90-30 90-ton hydraulic press brake. (General Atomics)

field of view in high-definition video on wide-screen graphic overlays, complete with three-dimensional graphics and moving maps. Multi-source data (Link 16, Blue Force Tracking) is fused into a Common Operational Picture (COP) on a single display.

Testing a wingspan prior to assembly. (General Atomics)

The Advanced Cockpit GCS incorporates touch-screen technology, and is described as being easy to switch between automated "point and click" and manual "hands on" flight operations. The latter involves Hands on Throttle and Stick (HOTAS) mechanization for greater ease of aircraft and sensor control, "inspired" by the cockpits of manned aircraft such as the F-16 and F-35 with which pilots may be familiar.

On the assembly line, this author saw Advanced Cockpit GCS units being tested live with an MQ-9 Reaper, but the system incorporates NATO STANAG 4586 architecture to "facilitate interoperability" with a variety of other unmanned aircraft.

Each of the Advanced Cockpit GCS units has the appearance of (and is compared internally to) an extremely elaborate home entertainment system, though it would take up roughly half of an average living room or home media room. In turn, multiple consoles are installed in heavily reinforced shipping containers.

Though the converging production lines at Poway are replicated at locations around the world (from Europe to the Middle East to China), General Atomics is confident that the hardware and the situational awareness that it delivers is second to none in terms of quality and reliability. The historical record of combat operations spanning two decades bears this out.

In a scene reminiscent of the General Atomics production line, airmen from the 849th Aircraft Maintenance Squadron disassembling an MQ-1B Predator for shipment. At the factory, the aircraft are assembled, ground tested, and then disassembled for shipment to flight test facilities and end users. (USAF photo by Staff Sergeant Anthony Nelson Jr.)

As at the factory, the right wing is removed from a General Atomics MQ-1B Predator by air force personnel prior to its being packed for shipment and reassembly. (USAF photo by Staff Sergeant Anthony Nelson Jr.)

An extended-range variant of the MQ-9 Predator B Reaper with external fuel tanks, as well as with its complement of AGM-114 ground-attack missiles. (General Atomics)

Two elaborate consoles for Advanced Cockpit Ground Control Stations take form on the floor at General Atomics in Poway. When the electronic components are installed, the screens and all of the user interface hardware will be added. (General Atomics)

Improvements found in the General Atomics Advanced Cockpit Ground Control Station include intuitive interfaces that are designed to make potentially hazardous situations easier to identify and to improve the decision-making process generally. Among the features are improved synthetic video with 3D graphics and moving maps, a 270-degree horizon field-of-view on multiple wide-screen graphical overlays, data link integration, collision avoidance, and terrain avoidance. It is easy to switch between automated "point and click" or manual "hands on" flight operations. (General Atomics)

Airmen from the 849th Aircraft Maintenance Squadron move a "casket" through the hangar to begin packaging a disassembled Predator for shipment. These fiberglass containers, in which the aircraft were originally packaged when factory delivered, are also known as "swimming pools" at the General Atomics factory. (USAF photo by Staff Sergeant Anthony Nelson Jr.)

Whether it is called a "casket," a "swimming pool," or something else, the original fiberglass shipping container follows the General Atomics aircraft from the factory to wherever it may go, and is used for packing and shipping whenever it is moved. (USAF photo by Staff Sergeant Alice Moore)

A Block 5 variant of the General Atomics Predator B Reaper aircraft. (General Atomics)

A General Atomics Predator C Avenger jet-propelled unmanned combat air vehicle takes off at sunrise. (General Atomics)

The final assembly floor at General Atomics in Poway shows three MQ-9 Predator B Reapers with their wings installed and final work being done to them. In the background, several Reaper fuselages are being assembled prior to wing mounting. When completed, each Reaper will be disassembled and packed into its "swimming pool" like the one in the foreground. (General Atomics)

Chapter 2

EVOLVING SYSTEMS TECHNOLOGY

As the technology of unmanned aerial vehicles grew in sophistication during the first decade of the 21st Century, so too did the complexity of their operating environment. With that came both technical and management challenges that affected the systems of which the aircraft are mere components.

For example, the Defense Department's *Unmanned Systems Integrated Roadmap* cited five specific areas of ongoing interest involving "the use of unmanned systems in today's world environment." These included (1) autonomy, (2) data protection, (3) data exploitation, (4) selective innovation, and (5) the emerging tactical doctrine of Manned-Unmanned Teaming (MUMT), aka Manned-Unmanned System Teaming.

Autonomy is an obvious component to evolving unmanned tactical doctrine. Most unmanned aerial vehicles are operated by a controller, but research and development in the field are gradually moving from automatic systems requiring human control toward autonomous systems able to make decisions and react *without* human interaction.

Defense Department planners recognize that reducing cost through the use of technology to decrease or eliminate specific human activities presents great promise, while they also realize that challenging questions are raised when applying automation to certain actions or functions where human judgment seems critical.

An autonomous reconnaissance drone is one thing. An autonomous attack vehicle is another. When a remotely controlled unmanned combat air vehicle prepares to take a shot at an enemy target, it is a human who makes the judgment call. When an autonomous drone calculates the pros and cons of taking the shot, the questions "extend quickly beyond mere engineering challenges into legal, policy, or ethical issues."

Celebrating the promise of technology, General John Shaud and Adam Lowther observed in their article, "An Air Force Strategic Vision for 2020–2030," in *Strategic Studies Quarterly* that "developing unmanned platforms that are enhanced by artificial intelligence (enabling autonomous operation) will support the Air Force conventional power projection mission."

The second item on the checklist, data protection, was a virtual non-issue at the turn of the century when communications technology was less sophisticated, and when most of the modest number of people with handheld devices owned "flip-phones." However, in the second decade of the 21st Century, the numbers, capability, and malevolence of "black hat" hackers has increased

Staff Sergeant Tyler Groff, a 451st Expeditionary Aircraft Maintenance Squadron dedicated crew chief, checks the propeller of an MQ-9 Reaper before a flight on August 27, 2013, at Kandahar Airfield, Afghanistan. Members of the 451st are responsible for maintenance, launch, and recovery of both MQ-1 and MQ-9 aircraft. (USAF photo by Senior Airman Jack Sanders)

beyond anything that could reasonably have been imagined as late as 2010.

Even the proverbial teenager in his mother's basement is more skilled than many turn-of-the-century nation states. Today's nation states (from Iran to China) who are energetically intruding into American cyber secrets have developed an intrusion capability that is never more than a step or two behind American efforts at cyber security. This is not to mention the myriad of "black hat" hackers and hacker collectives (including the Islamic State's "Cyber Caliphate") that are proliferating worldwide.

Encryption of unmanned systems communications and data links is essential for protecting the operations, and it is a job that is *never* done.

In the second decade of the 21st Century, there is an emphasis on staying abreast of state-of-the-art technology and the use of NSA Suite B Cryptography, developed under the NSA's Cryptographic Modernization Program, which better enables the protection of classified information and allows faster product certification. The future will see higher data rate cryptography, and hardware consolidation through single chip and coprocessor encryption modules that will make routine cryptography both faster and feasible for smaller systems.

Data exploitation is enhanced by an increasing number of sources and by sensors with increased resolution, but it is challenged by the increasing volume of data, the ability to process and exploit in a timely manner, and the requirements that it be downsized for transmission. In turn, there is a requirement for an increasing number of analysts to "draw conclusions for the decision-makers."

The Defense Department reports that it is endeavoring to make ongoing improvements in ground-based "intelligence production" systems, in the networks of ground station families, in its attack and Joint Architecture for Unmanned Systems (JAUS) programs, and throughout the elements of its unmanned systems infrastructure.

Shaud and Lowther pointed out that improvements to battlefield situational awareness necessitate a "metamorphosis into a tightly organized and dynamic force that realigns its assets for global as well as regional coverage."

They recommended that "overhead capabilities must be planned and executed in coordination with the National Reconnaissance Office (NRO) because surveillance is increasingly becoming a stand-off capability," and that automated technologies should be exploited to "improve data analysis so that human analysts are employed in the highest-order tasks."

They also advocated "accelerated development of translation software, artificial intelligence, and electronic means to process raw data (signals and electronic intelligence) is the most practical approach to managing this glut of data and should become an Air Force funding priority."

At the U.S. Defense Department, both national military strategy and joint concept documents talk a great deal about utilizing technical innovation for the improvement of future capabilities. They do so aware that this will be done under the shadow of shriveling budgets and that future mission requirements will be met only when funding is balanced between improvements and existing systems.

Within the budget morass, unmanned systems are seen as exceptional because, when compared to manned systems, they are smaller,

Deputy Defense Secretary Bob Work meets with a group of people including Tim Chung, the deputy director of the consortium for robotics and unmanned systems, education, and research, and assistant professor of systems engineering, during a visit to the Naval Postgraduate School in Monterey, California on June 19, 2015. (DOD)

A soldier prepares the InstantEye II Small Unmanned Aerial System to conduct surveillance over a ridgeline during a combined arms live-fire exercise in May 2015. The exercise included the integration of two emerging technologies, Robotic Human Type Targets to provide a moving threat signature and the InstantEye II. The latter provides real-time, full-motion video to both support-by-fire and assault elements. (DOD)

Paratroopers learn how to interface with the feeds from unmanned aerial vehicles at the Joint Readiness Training Center at Fort Polk, Louisiana, in January 2012. (DOD)

lighter, more manageable, faster to develop, and often cheaper. The Defense Department notes that "the ability of unmanned assets to take risks that would not be taken with manned assets opens up new CONOPS [Concepts of Operations], such as low-cost, expendable systems that trade armor and stealth for quantity. In other words, a fleet of low-cost, disposable platforms could survive through attrition rather than through expensive, exquisite capabilities."

Manned-Unmanned Teaming falls under the heading of an emerging technology that will play an increasingly important role as those two types of operations are tactically integrated in the skies over future 21st-Century battlefields. MUMT is essentially the practice of having an unmanned aircraft fly as a wingman to a manned aircraft, with the unmanned aircraft controlled either from the ground or from the manned aircraft. Under its Aviation Restructure Initiative, the U.S. Army began teaming AH-64 Apache attack helicopters with either MQ-1C Gray Eagle or RQ-7B Shadow unmanned aerial vehicles.

Lieutenant Colonel Steven Van Riper of the Army Acquisition Corps (late of the 101st Airborne Division) wrote in *Army Magazine* in September 2014 that the service had fielded two MUMT systems to combat training centers within and outside the continental United States, and that they had "also been deployed [to Afghanistan] in support of Operation Enduring Freedom."

Explaining in detail, he added that "the first system fielded is the MUMT Level of Interoperability (LOI) 2 (MUMT-2). It is a data link for the AH-64D that provides a fully integrated multi-band, interoperable (LOI 2) capability that allows pilots to receive off-board sensor video streaming from different platforms in non–Tactical Common Data Link (TCDL) bands. The MUMT-2 data link can retransmit Unmanned Aerial System (UAS) or Apache Modernized Target Acquisition Designation Sight full-motion sensor video and metadata to another MUMT-2-equipped Apache. It can also transmit to ground forces equipped with the One Station Remote Video Terminal.

"The second system, the UAS Tactical Common Data Link Assembly (UTA) for the AH-64E, provides fully integrated LOI 3 and 4 with ranges exceeding 50 km. The UTA system is currently compatible with TCDL-equipped UAS. It provides Apache aircrews with increased situational awareness and net-centric interoperability while significantly reducing sensor-to-shooter timelines. This combination results in increased survivability of Apache aircrews and ground forces by decreasing their exposure to hostile fire. It also allows for earlier identification of key decision points."

Van Riper pointed out that during AH-64E operational testing in 2013 at the National Training Center at Fort Irwin in California, a Gray Eagle had transmitted real-time, full-motion video to an AH-64E

Sergeant Rebecca Hatfield (left), an instructor with Field Training Detachment 26 of the California Air National Guard, explains the components of an MQ-1B Predator to Sergeant Carlos Barrera (center) and Sergeant Alex Bush, both crew chiefs with the 163rd Reconnaissance Wing. (USAF photo by Val Gempis)

Marine Corps Sergeant Cynthia Zermeno (left) watches Navy Petty Officer 3rd Class Nathalia Londono land an unmanned aerial vehicle during a UAV course at Camp Pendleton, California. (U.S. Marine Corps photo by Lance Corporal Keenan Zelazoski)

Aurora Flight Sciences program manager J.C. Lede with a Golden-Eye 100, one of the company's family of Small Unmanned Aircraft Systems tailored for use in urban or crowded environments. They are designed to be lightweight, easily portable, deliver long endurance on quiet electric power, and provide multi-domain autonomous operation. (Aurora Flight Sciences)

Airmen attached to the 324th Expeditionary Reconnaissance Squadron perform a preflight inspection on an MQ-1 Predator unmanned aerial vehicle. (U.S. Navy photo by MC2 Brian Glunt)

While Secretary of the Navy Ray Mabus (in red shirt) was at Marine Corps Air Station Cherry Point in North Carolina on May 6, 2015, he took time to inspect a ScanEagle unmanned aerial vehicle. The ScanEagle is a small, long-endurance vehicle developed by Insitu of Bingen, Washington, which has been a subsidiary of Boeing since 2008. In addition to the marines, the ScanEagle serves with the navy, the air force, and the National Oceanic and Atmospheric Administration. (U.S. Navy photo by MC2 Armando Gonzales)

U.S. Navy Captain Clay Allen (left), the ScanEagle Theater Chief for the Guardian 8 Site at Kandahar Airfield in Afghanistan, explains the ScanEagle Skyhook Recovery System to Rear Admiral Luke McCollum, Vice Commander of U.S. Naval Forces Central Command. The Skyhook employs the use of a boom assembly with a vertical capture rope in tension to pull a ScanEagle out of the air. Catapult launchers impulsively launch or fire the vehicle down a rail or tube, similar to the action of a spear gun or crossbow. (U.S. Navy photo by Lt. Kristine Volk)

This ScanEagle unmanned aerial vehicle at the Guardian 8 Site at Kandahar Airfield in Afghanistan was launched by Rear Admiral Luke McCollum on June 25, 2015. Normally, the Vice Commander of U.S. Naval Forces Central Command does not launch UAVs. His job is to train, advise, and assist the regional CENTCOM component at Kandahar. (U.S. Navy photo by Lt. Kristine Volk)

Apache cockpit display over a distance of more than 60 miles. He reported that the Apache crew used the streaming video from the Gray Eagle to identify a target and to coordinate artillery fire to destroy it without even leaving their assembly area. Technology has taken several leaps since then.

In March 2015, the U.S. Army established its first MUMT squadron. As Beth Stevenson reported in *FlightGlobal*, Apaches were teamed with RQ-7B Shadows in a heavy attack-reconnaissance unit within the 1st Armored Division's Combat Aviation Brigade at Fort Bliss, Texas. Initially designated as the 1/501st Aviation Battalion, it later became the 3rd Squadron of the 6th Cavalry Regiment.

In September 2015, Science and Engineering Services, a prime contractor to the Apache MUMT infrastructure, issued a subcontract to L-3 Communications to "deliver high-speed transmit and receive capability of wideband video and data" for an upgrade program called MUMT-X. Mark Pomerleau reported in *Defense Systems* that "based on the company's MUMT-2 system, which is in use in the Army, the MUMT-X communications suite incorporates new equipment, including a ROVER 6 modem, multi-band radio frequency equipment, and a directional antenna capable of relaying multiple video streams back to the command center."

A September 2015 L-3 company statement adds, "MUMT-X significantly increases the Apache aircrews' situational awareness and combat effectiveness, while shortening decision-making timelines."

Two months later, it was revealed that the U.S. Army was conducting Manned-Unmanned Teaming exercises over the Korean Peninsula, operating out of Kunsan AB, 150 miles south of Seoul, where the United States has had a significant military presence since 1951.

During the exercise, MQ-1C Gray Eagles streamed video and metadata via a line-of-sight data link directly to an Apache helicopter, from which it was retransmitted to field commanders at a Tactical Operations Center on the ground.

Thinking broadly, the Defense Department has determined that "technological advances and military adaptation" will permit the integrating of manned with unmanned systems on the ground and at sea, as well as in the air. Again, technology has taken several leaps since then.

The DOD sees MUMT as an essential part of a shift of geographical priorities from the Middle East to the Asia-Pacific region, which is in keeping with a broader strategic outlook that minimizes the importance of the threats active in the Middle East.

Meanwhile, the United Kingdom conducted a series of operations over Afghanistan in 2014 in which tactical targeting data from a British Army Thales WK450 Watchkeeper reconnaissance UAV was passed to a Royal Air Force MQ-9 Reaper unmanned combat air vehicle.

The Lockheed Martin Stalker is a small, silent, unmanned aerial vehicle that provides unprecedented long-endurance imaging capability for Special Forces throughout an array of environments. A unique droppable payload compartment allows the precise delivery of small payloads from the air. The Stalker is powered by a proprietary Hush Drive electric system. (Lockheed Martin)

An MQ-1C aircraft in the Gray Eagle Unmanned Aircraft System Modeling, Navigation and Integration Lab at the Redstone Arsenal in Alabama in January 2016. (U.S. Army)

A General Atomics MQ-1C Gray Eagle undergoing maintenance. (U.S. Army)

MQ-1C Gray Eagles await maintenance at the maintenance facility at Fort Hood, Texas. The aircraft serve the U.S. Army Intelligence and Security Command and the U.S. Special Operations Command formations. (U.S. Army photo by Staff Sergeant Christopher Calvert)

A U.S. Army MQ-1C Gray Eagle over the National Training Center at Fort Irwin, California. (General Atomics)

Colonel Thomas von Eschenbach, the capabilities manager for unmanned aircraft systems at the U.S. Army Training and Doctrine Command discusses the future of Manned-Unmanned Teaming at the 2014 meeting of the Army Aviation Association. (U.S. Army photo by David Vergun)

Chapter 3

COMMUNICATIONS AS THE KEYSTONE OF UAV OPERATION

Communications is the keystone, and arguably the Achilles' heel, of all unmanned aerial vehicle operations. In one aspect, communications technology is its own worst enemy. The volume of transmitted data has increased exponentially since the turn of the century, and so too has the number of communications platforms that exist within the tactical hierarchy and the communications grid. The infantry platoon now has the communications capability that once resided at the brigade level.

Meanwhile, interoperability challenges have made it hard for parallel platforms within the same grid to communicate with one another. Conversely, as noted in Chapter 2, the proliferation and sophistication of 21st-Century hacking has rendered the entire grid vulnerable to attack.

For the United States, where operators at Creech AFB in Nevada control Predators and Reapers worldwide, and where crews at Beale AFB in California operate RQ-4 Global Hawks around the globe, the whole spectrum of communications (command and control, uplink, and downlink) is a necessarily well-honed art and science.

The Defense Information Systems Agency (DISA) is the U.S. Defense Department agency for global command, control, and communications. It is based at Fort Meade, Maryland, as is OPS 2A, the headquarters of the National Security Agency (NSA). Among other avenues, DISA operates via the Defense Information Systems Network (DISN), which manages the military and civilian communications and relay centers that connect unmanned systems back to their operators, while forwarding real-time data from unmanned aerial vehicle reconnaissance and combat missions.

DISA's Unified Video Dissemination Service (UVDS) was established to support global real-time distribution of high-bandwidth data such as full-motion video. The Defense Department uses the Common Data Link protocol that encompasses a family of waveform specifications and allows terminals to operate in S, C, X, Ku, and Ka bands with encryption capability.

Long-distance communications not involving landlines within Defense Department operations are mainly via three families of communications satellites with uplinks generally in the extremely high-frequency Q band and downlinks within

This illustration depicts the high-tech, futuristic soldier on the battlefield communicating with an unmanned aerial vehicle which is presumably linked to a vast archipelago of communications nodes spanning the entire planet. (DOD)

the super high-frequency Ka band. The oldest is the Defense Satellite Communications System (DSCS), dating back to the first DSCS II launch in 1971. An additional 14 DSCS III satellites were launched between 1982 and 2003, but they have been gradually taken off line.

Milstar, the Military Strategic and Tactical Relay system, consisted originally of a half-dozen satellites launched between 1994 and 2003 to provide secure and jam-resistant worldwide communications to the United States armed forces. The next-generation system is the high-capacity Wideband Global SATCOM (WGS). Each of the WGS spacecraft have as much bandwidth as all of the DSCS satellites combined. The first of three Block 1 WGS satellites was launched in 2007, followed by the first launches of the more capable Block II WGS satellites in 2012 and 2013.

Meanwhile, the Defense Department concedes that the National Geospatial Intelligence Agency (NGA) and the National Security Agency (NSA) are the functional combat support agencies for imagery and signals intelligence, and they maintain the authority and responsibility for data storage and dissemination.

In global combat operations during the first decade of the 21st Century, as unmanned aerial vehicle warfare and the use of reconnaissance drones proliferated, so too did issues (some of them unanticipated) with intrasystem and intersystem line-of-sight and beyond-line-of-site communications.

Looking forward, the expectation for unmanned aerial systems is that they will be able to process a larger and larger number of high-bandwidth data streams. This will be done through evolving and improving routers that can process such information and accurately route it to the appropriate end user in real time. This will be a challenge to existing and future systems, especially in the heightened tension of live combat operations, often in the presence of hostile electromagnetic and cyber countermeasures.

Among the key challenges that are cited by the United States Defense Department in its internal strategic evaluations are the availability of communication links, the quantity of data that the communication links support, the assignment of spectrum allocations, and the resilience of all radio frequency subsystems against interference, such as electromagnetic and cyber disruption.

When it comes to data transmission, the Defense Department has articulated that it is vital for there to be a process for the distribution of operational control and mission data flowing to and from active unmanned systems, especially non-autonomous systems. For some Unmanned Ground Systems (UGS), Unmanned Maritime Systems (UMS), and Unmanned Undersea Vehicles (UUV), these types of information exchanges can use a landline, but for mobile unmanned operations, especially aerial vehicles, it must involve a data stream transmitted by way of the electromagnetic spectrum (EMS), or through optical or acoustical transmissions, i.e., sight and sound. Of course, operational systems employ various EMS frequency bands, communication gateways, and relay sites, as well as varying types of data and data dissemination centers.

These issues are being built into the design of future systems. With the exception of purely autonomous unmanned vehicles, this has affected, and will continue to affect, all unmanned systems, whether aerial, maritime, or ground-based.

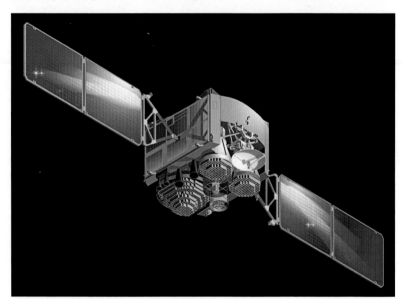

The U.S. Air Force Defense Satellite Communications System (DSCS) B12 satellite, built by Lockheed Martin, exceeded 20 years on-orbit, double its operational design life. It is part of the DSCS III military communications satellite constellation. (Lockheed Martin artist rendering)

Airman 1st Class Stephen Parker, a 32nd Aircraft Communications Maintenance Squadron ground control station maintainer at Creech AFB, powers a ground data terminal used to transmit signals needed to fly both the MQ-1B Predator and MQ-9 Reaper unmanned aerial vehicles. (USAF photo by Airman 1st Class Christian Clausen)

Tech Sergeant Manuel Quiñones-Figuero, the 432nd Aircraft Communication Maintenance Squadron NCO in charge of the formal training unit, teaches Tech Sergeant Thomas Diest basic post-flight procedures for the MQ-1B Predator and MQ-9 Reaper at Creech AFB. The 432nd ACMS is the only unit of its kind in the Air Force dedicated to maintaining the communications network for the Air Force's UAV establishment. (USAF photo by Airman 1st Class Christian Clausen)

At Creech AFB, the 432nd Maintenance Group ensures that ground control stations, Predator Primary Satellite Links, and a globally integrated communications network are fully capable to support operations. (USAF)

Staff Sergeant Spenser Amos, part of the infrastructure team that maintains all the communications cabling and telephone switches for the 628th Communications Squadron at Joint Base Charleston in North Carolina. (USAF photo by Senior Airman George Goslin)

Senior Airman Brendan Kennedy, a 1st Combat Communications Squadron satellite communications technician, calibrates an L3 Panther Manpack Portable very small aperture terminal (VSAT) two-way satellite ground station at Powidz Air Base, Poland, during Baltic operations in 2015. (USAF photo by Senior Airman Michael Battles)

The global electromagnetic spectrum is utilized by the Defense Department in parallel with both international commercial users and foreign military users, and is highly regulated on the national and international level by the National Telecommunications and Information Administration and the International Telecommunication Union. Therefore, Defense Department usage of specific bandwidth is often subject to an approval process because United States military operations occur in many parts of the world where an adequate spectrum is not available for sensor and data link systems. Because of this, there is an ongoing demand for increased spectrum efficiency, and unmanned systems must compete with other systems.

To meet such concerns, DARPA initiated its "Wireless Network after Next" (WNaN) program to investigate the achievability of Dynamic Spectrum Access (DSA), which would allow operators to change frequency band based on whether or not Spectrum Dependent Systems were using adjacent frequencies at the moment. Of course, issues such as susceptibility to countermeasures and the cost of integrating WNaN systems with existing systems will have to be addressed.

The prevailing school of thought at the U.S. Defense Department is that downloaded sensor data from operational missions should "instantly reside on globally accessible data centers that enable users worldwide to find, obtain, and consume real-time and non-real-time Intelligence, Surveillance, and Reconnaissance (ISR)."

There is therefore an ongoing requirement between the branches of the United States armed forces, and between them and allied services, to enhance global connectivity and interoperability to meet the needs of combat commanders in the field, and in all fields. In the acronym-intensive vernacular of the Defense Department, such requirements are called a "Joint Urgent Operational Need" (JUON). As has long been demonstrated in modern warfare, the whole command, control, communications, and computers (C4) infrastructure should be interoperable with or without unmanned systems, or in operations involving both.

Specifically, it has been noted that there were situations involving insufficient capacity to distribute high-bandwidth data, such as full-motion video, from unmanned vehicles. Because most of the operational hardware and most of the tactical users of unmanned systems are in or focused upon the Middle East, it has been found that there is little left over for operations elsewhere in the world.

In the second decade of the 21st Century, as the overall U.S. defense budget has declined, much of the funding for global unmanned vehicle communications hardware

The Defense Information Systems Agency (DISA), the U.S. Defense Department agency for global command, control, and communications, is headquartered at Fort Meade, Maryland, which is also home to OPS 2A, the "black cube" main building of the National Security Agency. (U.S. Government photo)

The Advanced Extremely High Frequency (AEHF) system provides vastly improved global, survivable, protected communications capabilities for strategic command and tactical personnel operating on ground, sea, and air platforms. The first launch was in August 2010. (Lockheed Martin artist rendering)

and satellite communications in general has had to come through short-term Overseas Contingency Operations (OCO) budgets, which have declined as the overseas commitment of United States forces, especially in the Middle East, has itself declined.

Ironically, this whole crisis in the downsizing of command, control, and communications capability comes at a time when demand is *growing*. This is true throughout the Defense Department, but especially in unmanned operations, because most of the overall unmanned systems infrastructure was born and built during the 21st Century.

In contrast to the way similar satellite communications were handled in the Cold War era, the dramatic downsizing of American

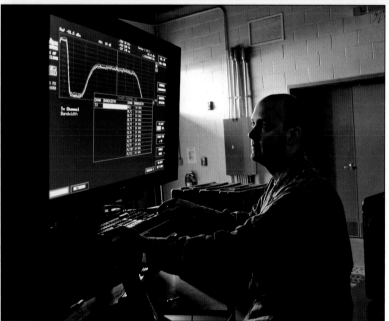

Master Sergeant Carl Champagne disrupts an adversary's communications by using spectrum monitoring tools during a simulated satellite communications electronic attack exercise. Champagne is a telecommunications specialist for the 263rd Combat Communication Squadron. (U.S. Air National Guard photo by Master Sergeant Patricia Moran)

armed forces capabilities at home as well as abroad has meant that most communication bandwidth is purchased by DISA through contracts with commercial operators. Because the leases for each system are separate, budgets are often inflated through a costly duplication of effort.

Meanwhile, the commercial operators have naturally developed "vendor proprietary solutions" that are specific to individual programs. This prevents them from communicating with one another. Because the technology and the applications are vendor proprietary, interoperability suffers. Interoperability is further cursed by "stovepiping," meaning that those within a specific program may communicate up and down within the program chain of command, but they do not communicate with other programs outside their narrow stovepipe. This may be well and good during a program's development, but it is very counterproductive after a program becomes operational.

In an environment of limited resources, the interoperability of unmanned systems and associated communications systems will necessarily be guided by open standards and interfaces, which will theoretically provide both improved interoperability and budgetary savings through information sharing.

Another difficulty in the seamless transmission of data comes when remote locations supporting unmanned systems are outside the coverage area of satellite ground stations. It is like an individual being unable to get cell service while backpacking in the mountains. To deal with this situation, DISA must work through commercial satellite channels to establish access for encrypted "black" DISN data. Indeed, communications systems, whichever the operator, need to support both commercial Ku band and military Ka band transmissions.

Transmitter and receiver system technology is migrating gradually toward connectivity with both commercial Ku band and military Ka band transmissions, which would be less expensive and more adaptable in the long term, but which have steep initial development costs. Examples of programs that are biting the bullet and installing the versatile hardware are those around the U.S. Army's MQ-1C Gray Eagle and the U.S. Navy's MQ-4C Triton.

Meanwhile, communication with highly mobile systems requires specific equipment designed with an emphasis on simplicity and ruggedness rather than complexity. During operations in Afghanistan, a joint urgent operational need compelled the development of relay systems to support the transmission of high-volume sensor traffic. In this case, the Defense Department admits that "the corresponding C4 infrastructure took more than a year to build and deploy."

Technology continues to evolve, with phased array antennas offering an alternative to traditional dish antennas. Phased array antennas are capable of receiving signals over a broad range of frequencies, while being frequency selective. In remote locations, though, they require concessions resulting in less than optimal size, weight, and power. The improvements include replacing gallium arsenide solid-state power amplifiers with those made with gallium nitride, which provide more than double the efficiency and increase the operational bandwidth of the amplifiers.

Airman 1st Class Ashley Kellar, a 432nd Aircraft Communications Maintenance Squadron radio frequencies technician, patches in a ground control station for unmanned aircraft communications at Creech AFB, Nevada. (USAF photo by Airman 1st Class Christian Clausen)

U.S. Army Chief Warrant Officer 2 Michael Lyons, a Joint Tactical Communications Office communications operator, at a work station inside the Combined Air and Space Operations Center at Nellis AFB during a Red Flag exercise in 2014. (USAF photo by Senior Airman Brett Clashman)

The drive toward simplicity is leading toward communications systems in which a single operator will have an improved ability to handle an increased level of "real-time analysis of multiple situations," while an unmanned aerial vehicle or other unmanned system performs many of its assigned functions autonomously. The Defense Department is on a trajectory toward a future in which communication equipment will be in the form of progressively simpler to operate plug-and-play hardware that is uncomplicated and (in the best possible world) rapidly modified, updated, or upgraded in the field.

Within U.S. Defense Department acquisitions, there has always been frequent mention of saving money through buying "off-the-shelf" hardware, and this is an example. Under the Mobile Technologies Initiative, an effort is being made to integrate tablets and smart phones, as well as a 4G cellular infrastructure, for disseminating data, intel, and voice communications.

Another next-generation of communications technology for tactical unmanned aerial vehicles and unmanned aerial combat vehicles is in the world of Free-Space Optical Communication (FSOC), an optical technology utilizing light in "free space" to wirelessly transmit telecommunications or computer data. As defined in this context, free space involves the use of empty space within or outside the atmosphere as a transmission medium in the same way that wires, cables, fiber optics, or other solid forms are used. FSO can also be used to provide increased target detection capabilities and improved anti-jam performance.

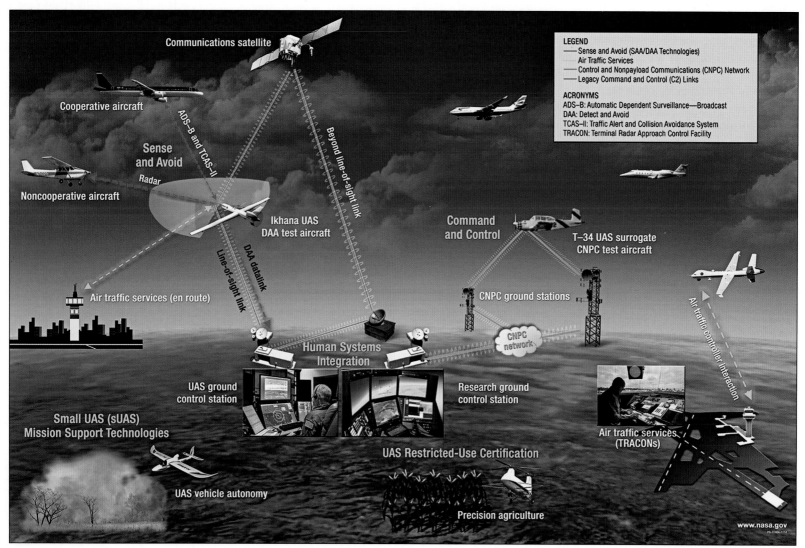

This diagram shows some of the complex communications issues involved in the integration of unmanned aerial vehicles into the National Airspace System (NAS) of the United States. NASA's Aeronautics Research Mission Directorate manages a project designed to help integrate unmanned air vehicles by reducing technical barriers related to safety and operational challenges associated with routine unmanned access to the NAS. Note the General Atomics Predator B Ikhana on the far right. (NASA)

Optical routers are seen as being potentially practical in operations involving high-flying unmanned aerial vehicles such as the Northrop Grumman RQ-4 Global Hawk, the Boeing Phantom Eye, or the Boeing X-37B spaceplane. While optical communication systems are inhibited by atmospheric conditions, they do provide increased bandwidth capability.

The FSOC concept was evaluated as part of the DARPA Free Space Optical Experimental Network Experiment (FOENEX), which conducted its final field tests at Naval Air Weapons Station China Lake in the California desert. The experiment was a continuation of development work by the Air Force Research Laboratory (AFRL) and the Naval Research Laboratories (NRL) with DARPA funding. FOENEX, which issued its final report in July 2012, demonstrated an air-to-air range of 125 miles with data rates up to 6 gbps, and an air-to-ground range of 80 miles at 9 gbps.

"Free-space optical communications (FSOC) links provide an appealing and complementary enhancement to current radio frequency (RF) systems because of their inherent benefits of high-bandwidth and directional communication," wrote L.B. Stotts of DARPA's Strategic Technology Office. "Though FSOC systems can be inoperable through clouds or thick fog, employing them in a hybrid RF/optical link configuration can yield a system that can operate under most weather conditions and provide high-bandwidth, secure, jam-resistant communications under most conditions. Beyond attenuation effects and line-of-sight limitations, FSOC link performance is primarily driven by optical turbulence along the beam path, which leads to severe fluctuation of the communications channel and distortion of the signal wavefront. Many methods have been either modeled or field-tested to reduce this fading with varying degrees of success."

During the second decade of the 21st Century and beyond, the driving forces in unmanned systems communication infrastructure are interoperability, cost reduction, and integration (the word "centralized" is also used) of the management of command, control, communications, and computing. The Defense Department sees this as a path to "network redundancy, resilience, and path diversity for sensor platforms" that will move the system away from stovepiping.

All of this, of course, occurs against the backdrop of protecting the unmanned systems communication infrastructure from intrusion by hackers.

Master Sergeant Paul Edwards establishes satellite communications for the joint operations center at Senghor International Airport in Dakar, Senegal, in support of Operation United Assistance in October 2014. (U.S. Air National Guard photo by Major Dale Greer)

Chapter 4

DATA TRANSMISSION AND THE KILL CHAIN

In 21st-Century unmanned combat, just as in combat throughout ages, the essence of warfare is in losing the projectile, in taking the shot, whether it involved a stone axe or a Hellfire missile. And in taking the shot, the intrinsic precursor is the *decision* to do so.

With unmanned aerial vehicles operating from control centers half a world away from the actual aircraft, commands being given by the operator must be transmitted via satellite link to the vehicle. In this process, multiple technical factors enter into the equation, notably the dimensions of time and bandwidth. Time is a fixed dimension, while bandwidth is not. Take as an example the aerial vehicles operating over Afghanistan and Pakistan. They are controlled at Creech AFB in Nevada, 7,500 miles away, and there is a time delay between the command and execution that ranges from a half second to 1.2 seconds depending on the position of the satellite carrying the telemetry.

Bandwidth, the rate of data transfer, is measured both in volume and in rate of transfer, or bitrate, and calculated in bits per second. Requirements for bandwidth by the United States armed forces, once inconsequential, have increased tremendously in the 21st Century.

Writing in *MilSat Magazine* in 2012, David Furstenberg of NovelSat observed that United States military bandwidth demands from Operation Desert Storm in 1991 through Operation Iraqi Freedom in 2003 rose by nearly 4,000 percent, from 100 megabits per second to 4 gigabits per second. To run a modern war, he noted, the Defense Department would need approximately 16 gigabits per second of satellite bandwidth to support a large joint service operation, compared to only 2 gigabits per second available in 2003.

Of course, the same factor is also present on the commercial side with the proliferation of "bandwidth-hungry" technologies such as high-definition television.

How do unmanned aerial vehicle operations fit into the picture? They are, to coin a phrase, "bandwidth hogs." For example, a single RQ-4 Global Hawk demands 500 megabits per second of bandwidth. The situation is magnified by the fact that so many remotely piloted vehicles are being operated simultaneously. According to a report in *Defense News*, "some 20 gigabits per second is needed to cope with the growing number of UAVs, which are swamping the current Ku-bandwidth available on satellite communications links."

One solution involves potential innovations in satellite modulation technology that have come on line during the second decade of the 21st Century, and which could potentially boost satellite capacity

Lieutenant Colonel James Curry, commander of the 62nd Expeditionary Reconnaissance Squadron, remotely pilots an MQ-9 Reaper operating from Kandahar Airfield in Afghanistan. (USAF photo by Senior Airman Nancy Hooks)

by 20 percent or more by replacing 36 MHz transponders with 72 MHz wideband transponders.

Earlier in the 21st Century, there were issues with the quality of data at high bitrates. U.S. Air Force Major Julian Cheater points out that during early tests at a 2.5 gbps transmission rate, "a temporary fade in the optical link caused by the atmosphere could translate into a large data loss rate measured in the mbps range. However, inertial sensors kept the laser pointing at the receiver for up to 3 seconds, which was longer than the fade duration and therefore minimized the possibility of data loss."

A further consideration entering into the problems of data link transmission in unmanned aerial warfare is *operational* time. It may take as little as a half second for an unmanned aerial vehicle operator in Nevada to trigger a Hellfire missile in Pakistan, but how long does it take between target identification and the order to fire? That length of time is referred to as the decision cycle or "kill chain."

Operational 21st-Century unmanned aerial vehicle combat missions begin with an Air Tasking Order (ATO) identifying the goals of the mission and the parameters within which the operator may conduct the mission. However, if an unanticipated target of opportunity emerges, the operator must request an authorization to engage that target. The goal is for authority to be granted in 10 minutes or so, although it frequently takes up to 45 minutes, and often it takes *hours* in sensitive counter-insurgency operations.

Requests to engage must be routed up the chain of command to the level where someone is willing to take responsibility, often against the backdrop of *political* rather than operational concerns, for specific actions. It may, though usually it does not, go all the way up to the White House. Many planners are still haunted by the sighting by a Predator of the infamous "tall man in white robes" near Kandahar on September 27, 2000. The man was almost certainly Osama bin Laden. For political reasons, he was not targeted that day.

After 2001, procedures were put in place to prevent such a missed opportunity from occurring again.

Today, the kill cycle consists of a series of steps, beginning with the initial identification and tracking of the target. Next, the request for authorization to engage begins its climb up the levels of the chain of command, where it is evaluated by a team assigned to time-sensitive targets, and the order denied or given, often with restrictions. Adding to the time is the possibility that at any level, the routing may take the request sideways into parallel chains of command which may have a tactical or political interest in the target or the area where it is located.

Once the order to engage has been given, it is handed back down the chain to the operator. In the aftermath, a battle damage assessment takes place to determine whether or not the target was taken out or must be targeted again.

In 20th-Century wars, with the notable exception of Vietnam, rules of engagement usually allowed combat pilots to make their own decisions and to react to situations as they were encountered. In 21st-Century conflicts, as in Vietnam, there has been a desire on the part of the upper levels of the command authority to micromanage combat operations. As the speed of communications has improved, this has become technically possible to a greater degree, though it still often remains as impractical today as it was in Vietnam.

The obvious downside to this aspect of the kill chain is that emerging targets are usually time-sensitive, and they often escape before targeting authority is granted. Collateral damage may be prevented by this delay, but the target may no longer be within sight by the time a green light shines upon the order to engage. Reducing the

A crew assigned to the 91st Attack Squadron remotely operated an MQ-9 Reaper during a training mission at Creech AFB. (USAF photo)

At the top of the kill chain, Joint Chiefs of Staff Chairman Admiral Mike Mullen (left), National Security Advisor General James Jones (center), and Secretary of Defense Robert Gates (right) wait for President Barack Obama before starting a meeting in the Oval Office in 2010. (Official White House photo)

time that it takes a request to work its way up, and for authority to work its way back down, is an operational challenge and the Achilles' heel of the cycle.

As Lieutenant Colonel Wes Long, formerly Chief of Offensive Combat Operations at CENTCOM's Combined Air Operations Center, noted to Major Cheater "no matter how quickly we can find, fix, track, and target, the decision to engage (assuming there is a human in the loop) will probably take longer than all the rest of the cycle combined."

Echoes of the lessons that were learned in Vietnam, and apparently forgotten, are heard in Cheater's Air War College paper on the acceleration of the unmanned aerial vehicle kill cycle when he writes that "by acting more rapidly than the enemy, the U.S. military can drive the fight instead of reacting to the adversary. Many [unmanned aerial vehicle] missions today follow a model of centralized control and centralized rather than decentralized execution."

Other problems within the kill chain involve the nature of the parties who are "read in" to the levels of the chain. As with military intelligence throughout the ages, the more people who are briefed on a secret, the more likely that the secret will be betrayed to the enemy. In May 2013, Michael Boyle, a former Obama counterterrorism adviser, told Kelly McEvers of

National Public Radio, "You have a situation under which if you contact the Pakistani government to tell them you want to conduct an operation or engage in a strike, you often run across the problem that the information gets out to the target."

While improved sensors will help unmanned aerial vehicles speed up target identification and target acquisition, Cheater notes "advances in autonomy, intelligent control, and microprocessing

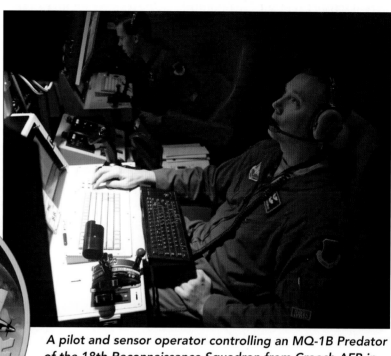

A pilot and sensor operator controlling an MQ-1B Predator of the 18th Reconnaissance Squadron from Creech AFB in July 2015. (USAF photo by Tech Sergeant Nadine Barclay)

Lest there be any doubt about the function of the MQ-9 Reaper; this nose art was created by Ken Chandler. (USAF)

At the other end of the kill chain, aircraft armament systems specialists assigned to the 62nd Expeditionary Reconnaissance Squadron walk past the MQ-9 Reapers at Kandahar Airfield, Afghanistan, in August 2014. (USAF photo by Staff Sergeant Evelyn Chavez)

will allow future [unmanned aircraft] to quickly gather accurate data and conduct a comprehensive onboard analysis. This analysis includes rapidly cross-checking collected data against stored memory to produce valid target identification."

Elements of the target engagement process that are being automated include attack axis, weapons selection, fusing, and estimated and weapon time of flight. If the slowest part of the kill cycle is to be automated, Cheater suggests that it will have to accurately process data related to collateral damage estimates, cross-checks against the restricted and "no-strike" target lists, locations of friendly forces, and rules of engagement. Ideally, this will reduce the time from 10 minutes to mere seconds.

Cheater goes on to say that Jon Park, senior functional analyst for the U.S. Air Force Command, Control, Intelligence, Surveillance, and Reconnaissance (C2ISR) Center, has noted that the Air Force has been "working to reduce the decision cycle time now by using a common machine-to-machine language [using] XML tags to leverage the Global Information Grid (GIG) via the NIPRNET or SIPRNET." The approval process, as Cheater describes, can be likened to the time-sensitive target team conducting internet searches for information related to targets, and the goal of the C2ISR Center is to shorten the time that it takes via automation.

Student sensor operators from the 6th Reconnaissance Squadron practice tactical operations during an MQ-1 Predator super sortie simulator mission at Holloman AFB. Super sortie missions allow two student crews to be trained simultaneously. Student sensor operators learn a variety of missions, including raid over watch, route clearance, target development, and close air support. (USAF photo by Senior Airman Bree-Ann Sachs)

President Barack Obama and Vice President Joe Biden hold a meeting with combat commanders and military leadership in the Cabinet Room of the White House on November 12, 2013. (Official White House photo)

However, Cheater adds that "the reality is that decision-makers and not technology will often be the limiting factor in reducing the time it takes to kill a target. The decision-maker will rarely have all the necessary information but instead will likely have to make a very difficult call. [By the third decade of the 21st Century] technological improvements in autonomous [unmanned aerial vehicle] operations and communications will quickly provide most of the information required but strict ROE can prevent weapons release. Until the United States improves technically and changes culturally, its kinetic capabilities will exceed its abilities to quickly decide, slowing the kill chain, and providing its enemies with opportunities to escape."

A Reaper sensor operator from the 138th Attack Squadron aims a laser onto a target during the 432nd Wing's Wing Hunt exercise at Creech AFB in June 2014. (USAF photo by Tech Sergeant Shad Eidson)

Senior Airman Bethany Lamb and Tech Sergeant Travis Wheeler of the 849th Aircraft Maintenance Squadron load an inert AGM-114 missile onto an MQ-1 Predator during an exercise at Holloman AFB in 2013. (USAF photo by Airman 1st Class Michael Shoemaker)

President Barack Obama is briefed on the situation in Libya during a secure conference call with National Security Advisor Tom Donilon, right, and White House Chief of Staff Bill Daley in Rio de Janeiro, Brazil, on March 20, 2011. (Official White House photo by Pete Souza)

An 18th Reconnaissance Squadron sensor operator (foreground) and pilot direct a remotely piloted MQ-1B Predator at Creech AFB in support of Red Flag 15-3 in July 2015. (USAF photo by Tech Sergeant Nadine Barclay)

Former B-1B Weapons Systems Officer Maj. Bishane Whitmore remotely pilots a 432nd Wing MQ-9 Reaper from Creech AFB. (USAF photo by SSgt. Vernon Young Jr.)

President Barack Obama receives a briefing from General Joseph Dunford, Commander of International Security Assistance Force and United States Forces-Afghanistan, at Bagram Airfield in Afghanistan on May 25, 2014. Seated across the table from left are James Cunningham, U.S. Ambassador to Afghanistan, and Jeff Eggers, Senior Director for Afghanistan and Pakistan, right. (Official White House photo by Pete Souza)

Chapter 5

EXCEPT ON A CLOUDY OVERCAST DAY

The success of "drone strikes" and the unmanned aerial vehicles that execute them is perhaps best calculated in the impact they have made on the morale of the enemy. It is measured in their instilling within terrorist warlords the fear that the end could come at any moment. Unlike the suicide bombers whom these warlords are happy to dispatch to their deaths in the name of martyrdom, the terrorist leaders do *not* want to die.

In 2016, the Office of the Director of National Intelligence released a collection of documents that had been snatched from the files of Osama bin Laden. Among them is a 2010 memo from bin Laden to al-Qaeda sub-lieutenant Atiyah Abd "Shaykh Mahmud" al-Rahman, complaining that in northwestern Pakistan, "air strikes [are] a major and long-standing issue. . . . I insist on the brothers [being] advised how vital it is they take security precautions in Afghanistan, as well as Pakistan, and remind them of the harm that could befall every mujahidin from the carelessness of a few." The al-Qaeda leader also nervously cautioned the "brothers" not to venture outside "except on a cloudy overcast day."

On August 22, 2011, nearly four months after bin Laden himself was taken out, Atiyah Abd al-Rahman ventured outside. If August 22 had been a cloudy overcast day, the sensors aboard the American unmanned aerial vehicle would not have found this man who was then described as "number two" within al-Qaeda. The solid-fuel rocket engine of an AGM-114 Hellfire missile roared to life and in an instant, al-Rahman had been vaporized by 20 pounds of high explosives.

Just a month later, on the morning of September 30, the notorious Yemeni-American terrorist archvillain Anwar al-Awlaki, was traveling through the monotonous gravel hills of the Marib desert in northern Yemen's al-Jawf province. In al-Awlaki's vehicle that day was Samir Khan, the editor of al-Qaeda's English-language internet journal *Inspire*. Like al-Awlaki, Khan had spent time in the United States learning the language and customs. The world had just marked the ten-year anniversary of the infamy of 9/11, and time for these two men was about to run out.

Indeed, they had American eyes on them that morning. At least one armed MQ-1B Predator was loitering high above, and at least one Hellfire was soon racing toward the dusty landscape. The Yemeni defense ministry later confirmed that there were no survivors.

When this author concluded his book *Birds of Prey: Predators, Reapers and America's Newest UAVs in Combat*, which was published in 2010, the battlefields across the Middle East and Southwest Asia,

According to documents from Osama bin Laden's own files, he was insisting as early as 2010 that his "brothers" should not venture outside their safe houses "except on a cloudy overcast day." (al-Qaeda photo)

the scenes of the bloody wars of the first decade of the 21st Century in Iraq and Afghanistan, seemed to have stabilized. These battlefields, over which unmanned combat air vehicles had first gone to war in 2001, had evolved into theaters of counterinsurgency rather than theaters of large battles. It was an environment in which the quiet approach of the drone, and the deadly precision of the drone strike, was an ideal tactic.

The Obama administration had come into office in 2009, eager to end the conventional wars that had nagged the previous administration, and hoping that the counterinsurgency would soon fade away, at least from the headlines of the Western media.

At the time, with the battlefields in their illusory state of stability, it seemed that the goal could be easily accomplished by deemphasizing the global terrorist threat and by terminating the use of the term "Global War on Terrorism" in official documents and press releases. Despite overwhelming evidence to the contrary, al-Qaeda was now *officially* described by phrases such as "on the run," "on its heels," or "decimated."

Hand in hand with its policy of linguistic de-emphasis, it did not take the new administration long to embrace the quiet precision

Anwar al-Awlaki was a self-styled imam and tech-savvy terrorist recruiter who emerged as America's leading terrorist target after Osama bin Laden was taken out in May 2011. On the morning of September 30, 2011, al-Awlaki, along with Samir Khan, was killed in Yemen by AGM-114 Hellfire air-to-ground missiles fired by an MQ-1B Predator. (Al-Qaeda photo)

Staff Sergeant Nelson Cherry inspects an MQ-9 Reaper with the 62nd Expeditionary Reconnaissance Squadron at Kandahar Airfield, Afghanistan, in 2014. (USAF photo by Staff Sergeant Evelyn Chavez)

of drone strikes as a substitute for conventional warfare. As widely reported, the number of missions increased to the point where more were being flown annually than had been flown during the entire Bush administration.

Mark Mazzetti and David Sanger wrote in the *New York Times* in February 2009, a month after the inauguration, that already "the Obama administration has expanded the covert war run by the Central Intelligence Agency inside Pakistan. . . . The strikes are another sign that President Obama is continuing, and in some cases extending, Bush administration policy in using American spy agencies against terrorism suspects in Pakistan."

Michael Boyle, an assistant professor of political science at La Salle University who served as a counterterrorism adviser for the Obama campaign, revealed in an August 2013 article in the *Guardian* that "once in office, Obama pivoted from his original counterterrorism positions and adopted an aggressive, but covert, policy of killing terrorist operatives abroad so that his domestic priorities could proceed unimpeded. Knowing that the American public is largely indifferent to the casualties caused in foreign lands, he gambled that a quiet, dirty war against al-Qaeda would allow him to refocus on his domestic priorities and end the wars in Iraq and Afghanistan."

Airmen of the 451st Expeditionary Aircraft Maintenance Squadron at Kandahar Airfield, Afghanistan, wrap up their work on an MQ-9 Reaper ahead of a 2013 strike mission. (USAF photo by Senior Airman Jack Sanders)

Captain Jason Ruiz of the 46th Expeditionary Reconnaissance Squadron does a preflight checklist on his MQ-1B Predator to prepare for a "push off" mission in 2010. In a push-off mission a unit at one remote battle location launches the aircraft and then releases the command to a unit back in the controllers at Creech AFB to fly the mission. (USAF photo by Senior Airman Matt Coleman-Foster)

The angry visage of Abu Yahya al-Libi. Born Mohammed Hassan Qaid in southwest Libya, he renamed himself after a 13th-Century Islamic ideologue. Captured in Afghanistan, he broke out of jail. He imagined himself one day ruling al-Qaeda until four Hellfire missiles slammed into a not-so-safe safe house in Mir Ali in North Waziristan in June 2012. (al-Qaeda photo)

Personnel from the 451st Expeditionary Aircraft Maintenance Squadron secure an MQ-9 Reaper in preparation for a mission on August 27, 2013, at Kandahar Airfield, Afghanistan. (USAF photo by Senior Airman Jack Sanders)

The "gamble" on a "quiet" war, and the refocus on domestic priorities helped carry the Obama administration through reelection in 2012, but it did not change the strategic situation. Even though Osama bin Laden had been killed in 2011, al-Qaeda was not decimated, nor had it even been contained. Al-Qaeda cells continued to metastasize throughout the region.

Interwoven throughout al-Qaeda networks are other sinister spider webs of jihadi terrorists, including the infamous Taliban. Once defeated in Afghanistan, it spread into Pakistan, and soon it was declared "resurgent" in Afghanistan. Also in Pakistan, there was the ominous Haqqani Network, the creation of Jalaluddin Haqqani and his son Sirajuddin Haqqani. Somalia, a failed state for decades, became the breeding ground for al-Qaeda affiliates and other terrorist groups, such as the vicious al-Shabaab group, as well as a proliferation of pirate gangs. From Mali to Niger to Algeria, there was the threat of the emerging al-Qaeda in the Islamic Maghreb. The Philippines had the al-Qaeda-affiliated Abu Sayyaf, while in Syria, the diabolical al-Nusra Front was looming. NextF came the once inconceivable rise of the Islamic State, which is discussed in Chapter 6.

Though the term was retired, it soon became evident that the Global War on Terrorism itself could not be ended simply by declaring it not to be a war.

Despite a half-year stand down in operations over Pakistan in early 2014, the drone strike campaign continued to be vigorously pursued. Boyle explained that politically, Obama was "shrewd enough to know that the Democrats have traditionally polled poorly

At Camp Lemmonier in Djibouti in January 2014, U.S. Navy personnel prepare to offload a pair of 34-foot patrol boats from a U.S. Air Force C-5 Galaxy cargo aircraft. Unmanned combat air vehicles arrive in the same way, but their arrival is usually not so well documented. (U.S. Navy photo by MC1 Eric Dietrich)

on national security relative to Republicans, and that a successful attack carries the risk of derailing his domestic priorities entirely. For Obama, and for many centrist Democrats, the answer is obvious: be more hawkish than the hawks and make it hard for anyone to attack you from the right."

As has been shown since the beginning of the century, piston-engine drones do provide an ideal tactical weapons platform for precision strikes against high-value targets in remote locations. At altitude, they are much quieter than jets. Indeed, their approach is barely audible. As they are slower than jets, they can orbit the target area, allowing their operators to carefully monitor the situation on the ground before and after the weapons release.

The signature weapons system that arms the drones is the 100-pound AGM-114 Hellfire missile, originally developed as a tank-buster. The blast radius of the 20-pound Hellfire warhead is roughly 20 yards in open terrain, significantly less than a general purpose bomb, and thus creating less collateral damage.

The MQ-1 Predators and MQ-9 Reapers that constitute the United States' unmanned combat air vehicle fleet are operated by both the U.S. Air Force and the Central Intelligence Agency, just as both entities once simultaneously and independently operated manned Lockheed U-2 spy planes, as well as unmanned reconnaissance drones of the Ryan Firebee/Lightning Bug family.

Both agencies operate out of Kandahar Airport in Afghanistan, flying missions in both Afghan and Pakistani air space, but the details are carefully managed by the Air Force and kept utterly secret by the CIA.

The U.S. Air Force Predators and Reapers are assigned to the 432nd Wing at Creech AFB, located about 35 miles northwest of Las Vegas. Though the aircraft are forward deployed to Afghanistan and elsewhere, the operators have mainly remained at Creech, operating aircraft that are half a world (and a 0.5- to 1.2-second time-delay) away. Likewise, British Royal Air Force Reaper controllers have also been also stationed at Creech.

An airman assigned to the 451st Expeditionary Aircraft Maintenance Squadron marshals an MQ-9 Reaper to the runway prior to launch March 20, 2015, at Kandahar Airfield, Afghanistan. (USAF photo by Staff Sergeant Whitney Amstutz)

The U.S. Air Force also has Predator and Reaper controllers elsewhere, including at Holloman AFB in New Mexico, while Air Force personnel operating RQ-4 Global Hawks are stationed at Beale AFB in California.

The CIA does not reveal its control locations, though their Special Operations Group is widely rumored to operate drones from CIA headquarters in Langley, Virginia, as well as from field locations, possibly including Kandahar. Many sources point to occasional, and even ongoing, operational cooperation between the CIA and the Air Force at the tactical level.

In the drone war against militants inside Pakistan, the American strikes occur mainly in the mountainous northwest, within the Waziristan region and in the lawless Federally Administered Tribal Areas along the Afghan border that are in fact *anything but* "federally administered." The gangs based here are a constant threat to Pakistani civil authority throughout the country and a constant vexation for Pakistan's military as well as for civil society throughout the rest of the country.

As this drone war continues, so too does a curious relationship between the American and Pakistani government. In spite of this lawlessness and aggravation rendered by the Taliban and others, a tradition arose during the Pervez Musharraf administration in the early days of the Global War on Terrorism that continues to this day: Pakistani leaders complain loudly in public about American drone strikes, calling them an affront to Pakistani sovereignty while quietly asking in private for *more* drone strikes!

Indeed, Pakistani officials routinely request specific targeted strikes to be conducted against particular Taliban or Haqqani Network leaders or assets that are of concern to them. The perfunctory complaints notwithstanding, the Pakistani government perceives a far greater threat to is sovereignty from organizations such as the Taliban or Haqqani Network who are, in the words of Mazzetti and Sanger of the *New York Times*, "seeking to topple the Pakistani gov-

ernment," and who continue to launch major mass-casualty attacks (specifically targeting civilians) inside Pakistan's major cities. For instance, Mazzetti and Sanger spoke of Pakistani military and intelligence officials complaining about "Washington's refusal to strike at Baitullah Mehsud" for months before he was finally targeted.

Since 2001, the U.S. Air Force (and reportedly the CIA as well) have also operated unmanned aerial vehicles from Camp Lemmonier in Djibouti. Located on the south side of the Djibouti-Ambouli International Airport the facility originated in colonial times as a French Foreign Legion base; it was turned over to the Djibouti government at the time of independence in 1977 and later abandoned. In early 2001, it was leased to the United States as a naval expeditionary base, and after September 11, it grew in both size and importance. It serves as the headquarters of the U.S. Combined Joint Task Force for the Horn of Africa (CJTF-HOA) and hosts U.S. Army and Air Force units, as well as those of the U.S. Navy and Marine Corps.

Lemmonier is a center for Special Operations forces operating throughout the region, from Somalia to Yemen and beyond, and is a home base for covert manned as well as unmanned reconnaissance aircraft operations. Reportedly it is a hub for other remote airfields from which UAV and UCAV operations are flown.

Djibouti-based Predators and Reapers continue to put pressure on the al-Qaeda in the Arabian Peninsula (AQAP) terrorists in Yemen. For example, on January 31, 2012, Abdul Monem al-Fahtani,

Hakimullah Mehsud was known as the "emir" of the Tehrik-i-Taliban of Pakistan, and commander of their Khyber, Kurram, and Orakzai components, until he was successfully targeted by an American unmanned combat air vehicle at Dande Darpakhel in North Waziristan on November 1, 2013. (Tehrik-i-Taliban)

Goodwill created by the Reaper Team forestalls the need for a Reaper strike. Staff Sergeant Elizabeth Rosato, member of the 755th Expeditionary Security Forces Squadron Reaper Team 1, meets with local Afghan school children near Bagram Airfield, Afghanistan, on March 11, 2013. The Reaper team conducts patrols "outside the wire" to counter improvised explosive devices and indirect fire attacks as well as to engage the support of local people in the ongoing effort to protect the base. (USAF photo by Senior Airman Chris Willis)

one of the perpetrators of the 2000 bombing attack on the USS *Cole*, was among 11 al-Qaeda terrorists killed near the city of Lawder in Abyan province. A few weeks later, a series of strikes across Yemen between March 9 and 14 killed more than two dozen AQAP militants. Among them were Abdulwahhab al-Homaiqani, an al-Qaeda leader who died at his hideout in Baydah Province. In turn, AQAP senior leader Mohammed Saeed al-Umda was killed near the border of Marib and al-Jawf provinces on April 22, and Fahd Mohammed Ahmed al-Quso was among those taken out on May 6 in southern Shabwa province.

These examples are part of a much bigger picture, but illustrate a capsule view of successful operations in a global war on terrorism by other names.

Beginning in 2011 at the time of the civil war in Libya, American Predators were also based at Naval Air Station Sigonella in Sicily for reconnaissance missions over Libya and the Mediterranean. The huge U.S. Navy base had been the hub of air operations for all branches of the United States armed forces throughout the Mediterranean since 1959. During the Cold War, the U.S. Navy flew anti-submarine patrols out of Sigonella, but fears of jihadi terrorist reprisals led the Italian government to prohibit the United States from flying *combat* missions with its unmanned aerial vehicles. Given that the base is on Italian soil, the United States deferred to the wishes of the landlord.

Relations between the parties chilled further when the U.S. Government turned down a 2011 request from General Claudio Debertolis, Italy's national armaments director, to arm the Predators and Reapers that his agency was buying from General Atomics Aeronautical Systems. In February 2016, after the Obama administration

had reluctantly allowed Italy to arm its Reapers, the Italians finally agreed to allow American Predator and Reaper armed strike missions into Libya. *Officially*, Italy agreed to permit only attacks that were launched to defend American special operations forces operating covertly in Libya.

In July 2015, meanwhile, Predator and Reaper operations began at Incirlik Air Base near Adana in southern Turkey. The United States had built the base, with its long runways, in 1951 as a reconnaissance and refueling base for missions along the southern border of the Soviet Union. It was used throughout the Cold War, though in 1974, Turkey threatened to close the base when the United States instituted an arms embargo after Turkey's invasion of Cyprus. Incirlik was a major U.S. Air Force transport and refueling hub during the first Gulf War and thereafter. However, Turkey prohibited its use as a base for combat operations during the second Gulf War, and this ban remained in place until 2015. As with Italy and Sigonella, Turkey had feared incurring the wrath of jihadists.

Wherever they are based, the Predators and Reapers have found themselves in the right places at the right times to chalk up some important success stories. On June 4, 2012, al-Qaeda second-in-command Abu Yahya al-Libi was among 16 killed at Mir Ali in North Waziristan. While he was the only one mentioned in the U.S. Defense Department press release, official Pakistani sources mentioned the higher tally. The Libyan-born al-Libi, previously known as Mohammed Hassan Qaid, had been associated with an organization called the Libyan Islamic Fighting Group, as well as with al-Qaeda. Captured earlier, he had been held at the detention facility at Bagram Air Base near Kabul, Afghanistan, when he was one of several high-ranking militants who escaped in a spectacular jail break on the night of July 10, 2005. His death was confirmed three months later by al-Qaeda boss Ayman al-Zawahiri in a video release.

The *New York Times* in 2008 quoted former CIA analyst Jarret Brachman as saying that al-Libi had "become the heir apparent to

A taciturn Afghan man suspiciously eyes members of the 755th Expeditionary Security Forces Squadron Reaper Team 1 as they patrol the perimeter of Bagram Airfield. (USAF photo by Senior Airman Chris Willis)

Jalal Baleedi, the notorious senior al-Qaeda leader in Yemen, was killed by a missile fired from an American unmanned combat air vehicle in February 2016. (al-Qaeda photo)

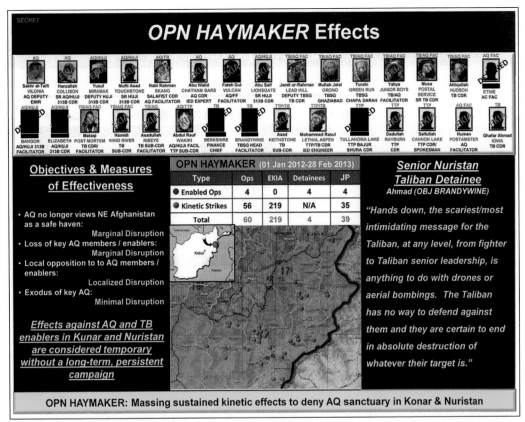

SECRET

OPN HAYMAKER Effects

AQ	AQ	AQ/HUJI	AQ/HUJI	AQ/TB	AQ	AQ	AQ/HUJI	TB/AQ FAC	TB/AQ FAC	TB/AQ FAC	TB/AQ FAC	TB/AQ FAC	AQ FAC	
Sakhr al-Taifi VILONIA AQ DEPUTY EMIR	Hanzallah COLLISON SR AQ/HUJI 313B CDR	Yusuf MIRAMAX DEPUTY HUJI 313B CDR	Mufti Asad TOUCHSTONE SR HUJI 313B CDR	Nabi Rahman SKANG CHATHAM BARS AQ FACILITATOR	Abu Walid VULCAN AQ CDR IED EXPERT	Fateh Gul LIONSGATE AQ/FF FACILITATOR	Abu Saif SR HUJI 313B CDR	Jamil ur-Rahman LEAD HILL DEPUTY TBSG TB CDR	Mullah Jalal ORONO TBSG GHAZIABAD	Turabi GREEN RUN TBSG CHAPA DARAH	Yahya JUNIOR BOYS TB/AQ FACILITATOR	Musa POSTAL SERVICE SR TB CDR	Attiquilah HUDSON TB CDR	ETNIE AC FAC

AQ/HUJI	AQ/HUJI		TB/AQ FAC	TB/AQ FAC	TB/AQ	AQ/TTP		TB	TTP/TB		TTP	TTP	TTP
BANGOR AQ/HUJI 313B FACILITATOR	ELIZABETH AQ/HUJI 313B CDR	Mataqi POST MORTEM TB CDR/ FACILITATOR	Hamidi WIND RIVER TB SUB-CDR	Asadullah RIBEYE TB SUB-CDR FACILITATOR	Abdul Rauf WAKIKI AQ/HUJI FACIL TTP SUB-CDR	BERKSHIRE FINANCE CHIEF	BRANDYWINE TBSG HEAD FACILITATOR	Asad KEITHSTONE TB	Mohammad Rasul LETHAL ASPEN TTP/TB CDR IED ENGINEER	TULLAHOMA LAKE TTP BAJUR SHURA CDR	Dadullah RAYBURN TTP CDR	Saifullah CANNON LAKE TTP CDR/ SPOKESMAN	Numan POSTAMSTER AQ FACILITATOR

AQ FAC	TB
Ghafar Ahmad IOWA TB CDR	

Objectives & Measures of Effectiveness

- AQ no longer views NE Afghanistan as a safe haven:
  Marginal Disruption
- Loss of key AQ members / enablers:
  Marginal Disruption
- Local opposition to to AQ members / enablers:
  Localized Disruption
- Exodus of key AQ:
  Minimal Disruption

Effects against AQ and TB enablers in Kunar and Nuristan are considered temporary without a long-term, persistent campaign

OPN HAYMAKER (01 Jan 2012-28 Feb 2013)

Type	Ops	EKIA	Detainees	JP
● Enabled Ops	4	0	4	4
● Kinetic Strikes	56	219	N/A	35
Total	60	219	4	39

Senior Nuristan Taliban Detainee
Ahmad (OBJ BRANDYWINE)

"Hands down, the scariest/most intimidating message for the Taliban, at any level, from fighter to Taliban senior leadership, is anything to do with drones or aerial bombings. The Taliban has no way to defend against them and they are certain to end in absolute destruction of whatever their target is."

OPN HAYMAKER: Massing sustained kinetic effects to deny AQ sanctuary in Konar & Nuristan

---

SECRET//REL FVEY

TF EAST LETHAL BURWYN KINETIC STRIKE STORY BOARD

040835Z NOV 2012, Dar-ye Pech District, Kunar Province (42SXD8362672203)

MISSION: TF East conducts a kinetic strike against Qari Munib (LETHAL BURWYN) in the Dar-ye Pech District, Kunar Province on 04 November 2012 in order to degrade the insurgent network in Kunar Province and enable the Battle Space Owners freedom of maneuver in RC-East.

SIGNIFICANCE: Qari Munib (LETHAL BURWYN) is a Taliban sub-commander operating in Dar-ye Pech District responsible for numerous attacks on ANSF and coalition forces. Qari Munib is associated with numerous Taliban district shadow governors, relays guidance, and provides BDA on attacks against Taliban officials in Pakistan.

SEQUENCE OF EVENTS

1. ~0230z GR76 reported SI at BDL compound for OBJ LETHAL BURWYN.
2. GR76 SI/IMINT correlated 5xMAMs left the compound and proceeded 150m SW of BDL compound. 5x MAMs remained static from 0320z-0740z at this location.
3. 0523z SKYRAIDER correlated SI activity on OBJ LETHAL BURWYN and established IMINT signature.
4. 0740z OBJ LETHAL BURWYN proceeded up ridgeline with 2xPAX and re-entered BDL compound. SKYRAIDER maintained IMINT lock on the compound.
5. 0819z OBJ LETHAL BURWYN departed BDL Compound, SKYRAIDER confirmed PID of IMINT signature.
6. 0835z SKYRAIDER engaged OBJ BURWYN resulting in 1xEKIA. TF East observed multiple PAX transport remains away from strike site.

RESULTS: JP—Pending EKIA, 1 x TOTAL EKIA

SKYRAIDER (MQ-9) correlated TI in open terrain

Watahpur — Shigal wa Sheltan

Dar-ye Pech

17 km

FOB FIAZ

SKYRAIDER (MQ-9) engages TI and confirms 1 x EKIA

NAI

BURWYN IMINT SIG.

N

This document is an alleged U.S. Defense Department standard update, circa November 2012, that described progress in an operation called "Haymaker" that was ongoing between January 2012 and February 2013. A "Senior Nuristan Taliban Detainee" named "Ahmad" is quoted as saying that "the scariest, most intimidating message for the Taliban, at any level, from fighter to Taliban senior leadership, is anything to do with drones." (Released by Wikileaks, this image is the work either of an anonymous U.S. government employee or an anonymous forger.)

Osama bin Laden in terms of taking over the entire global jihadist movement."

On September 24, 2012, as reported in the *Daily Times* of Pakistan and by Ismail Khan and Scott Shane in the *New York Times*, a drone strike against Mir Ali in North Waziristan claimed around a half-dozen militants. Among them was Abu Kasha al-Iraqi, the middle man between al-Qaeda's Shura Majlis and the Uzbek Islamic Jihad Group.

Success stories from the battlefront in the drone war continued to mount. On September 5, 2013, in the Ghulam Khan district of North Waziristan, Mullah Sangeen Zadran, deputy to Sirajuddin Haqqani of the Haqqani Network, along with Zubir al-Muzi, an al-Qaeda explosives expert from Egypt, were among those killed.

Nearly two months later, on November 1, five men in a vehicle racing through Dande Darpakhel came into the deadly sights of a U.S. Air Force UCAV. Among those who did not live to tell about it was Hakimullah Mehsud, the so-called "emir" of the Tehrik-i-Taliban (TTP), the "Pakistani Taliban," as well as the militant subchiefs, Abdullah Bahar Mehsud and Tariq

---

This alleged story board is a description of the killing of Taliban leader Qari Munib, code-named "Lethal Burwyn," in eastern Afghanistan in November 2012. (Released by Wikileaks, this image is the work either of an anonymous U.S. government employee or an anonymous forger.)

Mehsud. Hakimullah Mehsud also went by the names Jamshed Mehsud or Zulfiqar Mehsud. He had been the deputy to the infamous Baitullah Mehsud of the terrorist group Fedayeen al-Islam, who had been killed in a drone strike in August 2009.

In addition to al-Qaeda and the TTP, Hak imullah Mehsud had been associated with a long list of terrorist groups from the Afghan Taliban to various other Pakistani jihadist groups, such as Lashkar-e-Taiba, Lashkar-e-Jhangvi, and Jaish-e-Mohammed. The value of him as a high-value target can be reckoned by the $600,000 reward offered by the Pakistani government for information leading to his capture or killing. He was also wanted, dead or alive, by the United States, where the FBI had authorized a $5 million bounty.

Fast forward to 2016, as this book was being written, and American Predators and Reapers were still active. On the night of February 3–4, one of them took out a half-dozen militants of al-Qaeda in the Arabian Peninsula (AQAP) traveling through Shabwa Province, while a second drone destroyed another car in the coastal Abyan Province. Among the six who died in the latter strike was Jalal Baleedi (aka Hamza al-Marqashi), who was described by *Al Jazeera* as "one of al-Qaeda's senior commanders. . . . Originally from Yemen's mountainous Abyan province, Baleedi was identified in 2004 by the *Yemen Times* as being the field commander of AQAP in the southern governorates of Abyan, Shabwa, Lahj, Hadramout, and al-Beidha."

Al Jazeera went on to say that "recent reports suggested Baleedi pledged allegiance to and joined the Islamic State of Iraq and the Levant (ISIL) group with several other AQAP fighters, becoming the leader of ISIL in Yemen."

On May 21, 2016, three months after Baleedi was killed, the vehicle carrying high-value target Akhtar Mohammed Monsour through a broad valley near the Afghan-Pakistani border exploded in a cloud of fire and shrapnel that killed everyone aboard. A former cabinet minister in the pre-2001 Taliban government of Afghanistan, Monsour was the top Taliban leader, the so-called "Emir of the Faithful," who had succeeded the late and infamous Mullah Omar

An MQ-9 Reaper taxis across the ramp at Kandahar Airfield in Afghanistan. (USAF photo by Tech Sergeant Efren Lopez)

in 2013. U.S. Navy Captain Jeff Davis, a Pentagon spokesman, said that Monsour had been plotting actions that posed "specific imminent threats" to Americans in Afghanistan.

Taking out these terrorist leaders and terrorist motivators are just a few of many milestones (Barack Obama specifically called Monsour's death a "milestone") in the military history of armed unmanned aerial vehicles as weapons against specific high-value targets. By February 2016, when Jalal Baleedi went up in smoke, such strikes had become a routine part of 21st-Century warfare.

To focus a bit closer on combat operations, we turn now to the particulars of one specific strike, as viewed from the inside. While the details of unmanned combat air vehicle operations in Southwest Asia, especially in Afghanistan, retain high levels of security classifications, we refer to documentation released into the public domain through Wikileaks via the former CIA employee, later NSA contractor (and eventually an international fugitive) Edward Snowden. This example concerns the November 2012 attack on Taliban leader Qari Munib and information that was released by First Look Media through their online publication *Intercept* in October 2015.

According to this *alleged* inside information, the hit was part of the never-officially-revealed "Operation Haymaker." It was a joint Defense Department–CIA campaign against al-Qaeda militants in the mountains along the Afghan-Pakistan border, especially in Afghanistan's Kunar and Nuristan provinces, that took place between 2011 and 2013. Haymaker is said to remain classified because of its extensive use of local informants as human intelligence assets whose identity must be protected. As drone strikes are designed to target specific individuals, real-time human intelligence is considered mission critical.

For these operations, the Defense Department and the NSA are said to have used a system that was known as "Gilgamesh," which could locate and track specific cell phone GPS systems by mimicking a cell tower.

As described in the "leaked" documents, the targeting of Qari Munib, who was code-named "Lethal Burwyn" by the United States, came in response to a Central Command document titled *Request for Kinetic Strike Approval* that was dated October 30, 2012. He was targeted because he was said to "exercise command and control" over al-Qaeda units who had attacked both American and Afghan forces. A compound frequented by "Burwyn" was identified and placed under surveillance until the targeting authorization was issued.

With the strike approved, an MQ-9 Reaper known as *Skyraider* came overhead and began conducting real-time observation of the site. Several "military-age males," were observed walking to a nearby ridge then back toward the building. During this time, an image of resolution sufficiently high for a positive identification of Munib was obtained.

The missile achieved a direct hit. Reports that others from the nearby compound were able to gather around the crater are indicative of the narrow blast radius of a Hellfire warhead, which minimizes collateral damage.

On November 8, 2012, a Defense Department news release *did* confirm that Qari Munib had been killed, and that he had been "responsible for directing attacks against Afghan and coalition forces and coordinating the movement of weapons and ammunition for the attacks."

The collateral damage rate has been much less than it would have been in a conventional bombing campaign. The New America Foundation reported in its *Drone Wars Pakistan: Analysis* that between 2004 and 2013, the civilian and "unknown" death toll in 369 drone strikes was just 19.6 percent. The London-based Bureau of Investigative Journalism reported that as of February 22, 2016, there had been 423 American drone strikes in Pakistan since 2004, 88 percent of them since the Obama administration had come into office. The bureau's estimates of the percentage of civilian fatalities in these strikes ranged from 16.9 to 24 percent. The bureau's estimates of civilian fatality percentages for drone strikes from 2002 through April 2, 2016, in Yemen were between 12.5 percent and 13.4 percent. For Somalia between 2007 and April 11, 2016, the estimated percentages ranged from .01 percent to .03 percent.

Both of these reporting entities are among those who are critical of unmanned combat air vehicle operations, but the figures nevertheless show a high rate of effectiveness in limiting damage to civilians. This is despite the stubborn persistence of civilians to risk their own lives, as well as those of their own children, by continuing to seek the company of persons who are known to be targets of drone strikes.

Finally, one should certainly compare this data to the nearly 100 percent civilian casualty rate in terrorist attacks from New York in 2001 to Paris and San Bernardino in 2015, never mind civilian casualty rates in the unabated epidemic of suicide bombings and other attacks within Pakistan and Afghanistan and elsewhere since 2001.

"Combat operations in Southwest Asia have demonstrated the military utility of unmanned systems on today's battlefields and have resulted in the expeditious integration of unmanned technologies into the joint force structure," reads the official U.S. Department of Defense statement on the technical lessons learned on these distant battlefields. "However, the systems and technologies currently fielded to fulfill today's urgent operational needs must be further expanded and appropriately integrated into military department programs of record to achieve the levels of effectiveness, efficiency, affordability, commonality, interoperability, integration, and other key parameters needed to meet future operational requirements."

Perhaps the best endorsement of drone strikes comes from a Wikileaks document in which a "Senior Nuristan Taliban Detainee" named "Ahmad" is quoted as saying that "the scariest, most intimidating message for the Taliban, at any level, from fighter to Taliban senior leadership, is anything to do with drones or aerial bombings. The Taliban has no way to defend against them and they are certain to end in absolute destruction of whatever their target is."

Chapter 6

A LIMITED WAR AGAINST A WORLDWIDE CALIPHATE

It crept in like a serpent, largely unnoticed. Even as the United States government officially insisted that the resurgent al-Qaeda had been put "on the run," the strategic implications of the sinister rise of the Islamic State were largely ignored by governments and media around the world.

As late as 2013, the organization referred to by names such as Islamic State of Iraq and Syria (ISIS) or the Islamic State of Iraq and the Levant (ISL) (with "Levant" being a term for the eastern Mediterranean region centering on Syria, Lebanon, and Palestine) was little known. Even as the Islamic State had occupied and instituted its rule in areas of eastern Syria during the latter's civil war, analysts were only beginning to recognize the scope of the threat, and Western governments seemed to have been blindsided, despite its components having long been under scrutiny. Indeed, the Islamic State organization in Iraq had grown out of an organization that had been watched since 2004, and officially identified by the United States State Department as "al-Qaeda in Iraq."

On January 3, 2014, when the Iraqi government lost control of the major city of Fallujah, located only 40 miles west of Baghdad, many in the West *still* failed to grasp the significance of the Islamic State. Among those was President Barack Obama.

David Remnick of the *New Yorker*, who interviewed the president on January 7, 2014, wrote that "in the 2012 campaign, Obama spoke not only of killing Osama bin Laden; he also said that al-Qaeda had been 'decimated.' I pointed out that the flag of al-Qaeda [with which the Islamic State was affiliated from 2004 to 2014] is now flying in Fallujah, in Iraq, and among various rebel factions in Syria; al-Qaeda has asserted a presence in parts of Africa, too."

Calmly dismissing the importance of the Islamic State and of unfolding events in Fallujah, the president replied that "the analogy we use around here sometimes, and I think is accurate, is if a JV team puts on Lakers uniforms that doesn't make them Kobe Bryant."

"But that JV team just took over Fallujah," Remnick responded incredulously.

An optimistic commander in chief surrounded by worried senior military leaders. President Barack Obama talks with members of the Joint Chiefs of Staff following a meeting in the Situation Room of the White House on October 28, 2014. On the left with heads turned away are General Martin Dempsey, Chairman of the Joint Chiefs of Staff, and Deputy Secretary of Defense Robert Work. On the right are General Ray Odierno, Chief of Staff of the Army; Admiral James "Sandy" Winnefeld, Vice Chairman of the Joint Chiefs of Staff; and Admiral Jonathan Greenert, Chief of Naval Operations. (Official White House photo)

In the ensuing years, as the Islamic State spread its tentacles across the Middle East, and as the forces opposing it, especially by the Iraqi military, crumbled and collapsed, the president's ill-chosen analogy, and his administration's apparent failure to comprehend the strategic implications, became a lasting source of chagrin and embarrassment. More than nearly three years later, in the fall of 2016, as this book was going to press, the Iraqi government claimed to have won a long and bloody campaign to recapture Fallujah, but fighting was still ongoing in parts of the city.

The declaration of a worldwide Islamic caliphate, once considered implausible paranoia, came in June 2014. Led by the enigmatic Muslim cleric known as Abu Bakr al-Baghdadi (declared as the caliph of the caliphate), the Islamic State had started out as a gaggle of thugs and zealots, but had evolved into a full-fledged outlaw nation.

The Islamic State seized and controlled a contiguous "empire" of around 81,000 square miles in parts of Iraq and Syria that was roughly the size of Great Britain and more than twice the size of either Denmark or the Netherlands. The former Syrian city of al-Raqqah (aka Raqqa) became the capital of this new country. Mosul, once the second largest city in Iraq, became the largest city in the Islamic State. As this book was being written, Mosul had been under occupation for nearly three years and there was still no concrete plan for recapturing it.

For the roughly 3 million people within its borders, the Islamic State controlled all aspects of civil life from the police to the schools, ruling under a strict interpretation of sharia law, and working to eradicate populations of Christians, Kurds, Yazidis, and other minority groups. Meanwhile, millions are trying and dying to *escape*. Between the brutality of the Islamic State and the horrors of the Syrian civil war, floods of refugees are on the move. More than half a million have taken up residence in camps in Jordan, and 3 million went north to seek refuge in Turkey. Europe found itself with the worst refugee crisis in this century, and perhaps since the aftermath of World War II. Added to those from the Middle East were those try-ing to cross the Mediterranean from the chaos in Libya and points south.

Far from diminishing in size, the Islamic State continued to grow through its affiliate organizations, and through annexing non-contiguous territory in Afghanistan, Libya, Yemen, and elsewhere. With the Nigerian terrorist group Boko Haram having declared its allegiance to the caliphate in 2015, the Islamic State gained a presence in Cameroon, Chad, Niger, and Nigeria that doubled the global footprint of the worldwide caliphate while exacerbating the refugee crisis on the Mediterranean.

The United States did undertake a modest air campaign against the Islamic State with the initiation of Operation Inherent Resolve on June 15, 2014, five months after the fall of Fallujah and a week after the fall of Mosul. Operations were conducted by U.S. Navy carrier-based strike aircraft, as well as U.S. Air Force assets flying out of Kuwait and elsewhere. Despite these operations, widely criticized as too limited, the Islamic State remained generally secure within its borders.

Meanwhile, through its occupation of substantial Iraqi petro-chemical facilities, the Islamic State was earning millions of dollars in hard currency by selling oil on the black market. This was done with virtual impunity, in part because the United States prohibited Inherent Resolve air assets from attacking the transfer of petroleum products, assuming that oil truck drivers were civilians, and fearing environmental pollution in the aftermath of attacks that spilled oil or started fires. Though U.S. government spokespersons stated often that "degrading" the Islamic State was a high priority, the Obama administration remained reticent to "put boots on the ground" in the region after having made it a goal in their first term to withdraw from Iraq completely. Special Operations forces that *were* inserted "on the ground," were officially described as "advisors."

While the number of Inherent Resolve air strikes by American and allied forces was small, within this, there was now a role for the quiet efficiency of MQ-1 Predators and MQ-9 Reapers to take the war to the high-value targets within the Islamic State's rogue's gallery.

Take, for example, the case of Mohammed Emwazi, the savage sadist widely discussed in the Western media under the nickname "Jihadi John," a man with literal, not merely metaphorical, blood on his hands. Born in Iraq, Emwazi immigrated to the United

Abu Bakr al-Baghdadi was born Ibrahim Awad Ibrahim al-Badri near Samarra, Iraq, but pompously renamed himself after the father-in-law of Mohammed. He became the leader and mastermind of the Islamic State. After it was declared a world-wide caliphate in 2014, al-Baghdadi's henchman named him as its caliph. (Islamic State media)

Islamic State fighters on the march in their capital city of al-Raqqah, which was formerly part of Syria. (Islamic State media)

Kingdom with his family in 1994 when he was six years old. He attended school in Britain, learned to speak English with a British accent, and worked as a salesman for an information technology company in Kuwait. He apparently joined the al-Nusra Front in 2013, and within a year, he had become the most widely visible executioner in the Islamic State. They chose to use Emwazi in a series of video releases because he spoke English and because he undertook, with great enthusiasm, the executions of various people who had been kidnapped by the Islamic State. Beginning in 2014, the videos of Jihadi John and his bloody victims were broadcast worldwide, though his true identity remained a mystery because he always appeared on camera with his face covered. In February 2015, the *Washington Post* revealed that FBI and British MI5 investigators had finally confirmed that Jihadi John was really Emwazi.

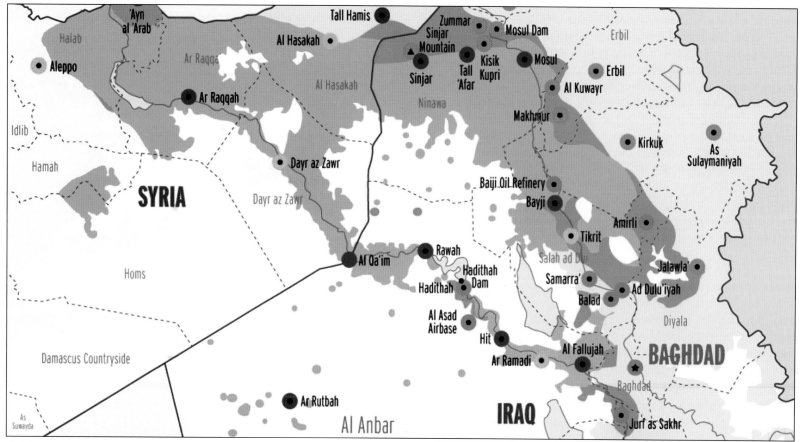

A 2015 U.S. Department of Defense map of the Islamic State. Secure Islamic State areas are in brown, while areas in which they are being challenged locally are in orange. Iran is in pale green on the right. (DOD)

Mohammed Emwazi was born in Kuwait, but grew up in west London. After graduating from college in England, he returned to Kuwait to work for an information technology company. He joined the Islamic State and became infamous as the English-speaking executioner nicknamed "Jihadi John." Islamic State video releases implicated him in more than two-dozen beheadings of Islamic State captives. On November 12, 2015, he was targeted and killed by MQ-9 Reapers belonging to the U.S. Air Force and Britain's Royal Air Force. (Islamic State media)

In the meantime, the United States and Britain began stepping up efforts to use unmanned combat air vehicles against the Islamic State. Among their missions, *"Get Jihadi John."*

Nine months later, these attempts finally bore fruit. A pair of American MQ-9 Reapers, accompanied by a single British Reaper, converged upon a car in which Emwazi was traveling. Pentagon Press Secretary Peter Cook told reporters that allied forces "conducted an air strike in Raqqa, Syria, on November 12, 2015, targeting Mohammed Emwazi, also known as 'Jihadi John.'" He described it as a "flawless . . . clean hit" in which Emwazi simply "evaporated."

In January 2016, the Islamic State online magazine *Dabiq* finally confirmed that Emwazi was dead. The publication noted that the "honorable brother" was killed "as the car he was in was targeted in a strike by an unmanned drone in the city of Raqqa, destroying the car and killing him instantly."

Staff Sergeant Trung Dinh, left, and Senior Airman Devin Milburn upload a GBU-12 Paveway II laser-guided bomb onto a U.S. Air Force MQ-9 Reaper. Dinh is a 432nd Aircraft Maintenance Squadron weapons load crew chief and Milburn is a 432nd Aircraft Maintenance Squadron support technician. (USAF photo by Airman 1st Class Christian Clausen)

An excellent side view of a Royal Air Force MQ-9 Reaper over Kandahar Airfield in Afghanistan. It is armed with four AGM-114 Hellfire missiles and a pair of 500-pound GBU-12 Paveway II laser-guided bombs. (Royal Air Force)

A U.S. Air Force 432nd Wing load crew member wiring a GBU-12 Paveway II laser-guided bomb onto an MQ-9 Reaper. (USAF)

International cooperation at Incirlik AB in Turkey. An unnamed Turkish Air Force Security Forces patrolman (left) and Staff Sergeant Ryan Schaefer (right) of the 39th Security Forces Squadron work as a team during a joint patrol at Incirlik. Beginning in July 2015, Turkey permitted Reaper operations against Islamic State targets by both the U.S. Air Force and the Royal Air Force from the base, which the Americans had built in 1951. (USAF photo by Senior Airman Ashley Wood

The strike that eliminated Jihadi John was facilitated by the use of Incirlik Air Base, the American-built facility in southern Turkey that had not been available for combat operations since 2003. Nervous about the potential fallout from its supporting the United States invasion of Iraq, Turkey had prohibited use of Incirlik for combat operations, a ban that remained in place until July 29, 2015, when Turkey finally gave a green light to U.S. Air Force and British Royal Air Force combat operations. Located 200 air miles northwest of al-Raqqah, Incirlik provided an ideal base for Reaper strikes against the heart of the Islamic State.

Among the others to be taken out after Incirlik operations began had been the notorious jihadi "black hat" hacker Junaid Hussain, who died in a drone strike at a gas station in al-Raqqah on August 25, 2015. Like Emwazi, he grew up in England and spoke perfect English. He even went by the name Abu Hussain al-Britani to celebrate his British roots. Indeed, before Emwazi was finally identified, it was believed that Hussain (who was already well known to Western intelligence services) might be Jihadi John. In 2011, while only 17 years old, Hussain has gone by the name "TriCk" as part of the Birmingham hacker collective TeaMp0isoN (Team Poison) who launched cyber attacks on such entities as Facebook, NASA, NATO, the United Nations, and former Prime Minister Tony Blair. For the latter, Hussain was arrested in 2012, but released in 2013, whereupon he moved to the Islamic State. Here, he became part of a network of Islamic hackers who called themselves the Cyber Caliphate. With them, he attacked the Twitter feeds of organizations ranging from the *International Business Times* to the U.S. Central Command. While in the Islamic State, Hussain reportedly married Sally Ann Jones, a British punk rock singer more than twice his age who had traveled to al-Raqqah to join the Cyber Caliphate.

A Royal Air Force MQ-9 Reaper on the ramp at Kandahar Airfield in Afghanistan. It is armed with four AGM-114 Hellfire missiles and a pair of 500-pound GBU-12 Paveway II laser-guided bombs. (Royal Air Force)

As grisly as they were, the atrocities of Mohammed Emwazi rated less concern from those who try to thwart them than those represented by the activities of the Cyber Caliphate because it extends the reach of the Islamic State for thousands of miles beyond its physical borders. The plan is, after all, for a *worldwide* caliphate.

Late in 2015, the fingerprints of the Cyber Caliphate were found on attacks that shocked the world. There were several attacks across Paris on November 13–14, 2015 (one day after Emwazi was killed), that left 130 dead and hundreds injured. These were followed on December 2 by the attack by Rizwan Farook and Tashfeen Malik in San Bernardino, California, where 14 were murdered and 22 were seriously wounded.

Though the White House continued its politically low-key response to the Paris and San Bernardino attacks, there was a perceptible increase in activity in the field where Inherent Resolve was being executed.

In a year-end summary, streamed live from Baghdad to the Pentagon, the Combined Joint Task Force spokesman for Inherent Resolve, U.S. Army Colonel Steve Warren, confirmed that 10 Islamic State leaders had been targeted and killed in drone strikes since San Bernardino. Using stronger language than had been heard for some time, he noted that "we are also striking at the head of this snake by hunting down and killing ISIL leaders."

Referencing a strike that had occurred on December 24, he noted that the target killed, Syria-based Charaffe al-Mouadan, had been "planning additional attacks against the West" and was directly linked to Abdelhamid Abaaoud, the leader of the cell responsible for the November terrorist attacks in Paris.

As the offensive against the Islamic State continued into 2016, Royal Air Force Reapers took out a pair of United Kingdom expatriate Islamic State fighters in an attack on al-Raqqah reported in the British media on January 12. Prime Minister David Cameron told the House of Commons that Reyaad Khan of Cardiff and Ruhul Amin of Aberdeen, who were well known to British security services, had been planning attacks in Britain.

When some indignant members of parliament complained that they had not been advised of the attack ahead of time, Cameron said that he acted out of urgency and a need for secrecy, adding that the actions were "necessary and proportionate, entirely lawful" and approved by Attorney General Jeremy Wright.

"We should be under no illusion," Cameron continued. "Their intention was the murder of British citizens. So on this occasion we ourselves took action."

One of the more notorious of the Islamic State snakes to whom Warren alluded was Tarkhan Tayumurazovich Batirashvili. Known for his fiery-red beard and his ruthless sadism, he was born in Georgia, the son of a Muslim Kistùan ethnic Chechen mother and an Orthodox Christian father. A veteran of the Russo-Georgian War of 2008, he later spent time in jail on weapons charges, but moved to the Middle East, where he was part of a series of anti-government jihadist foreign fighter groups active in the Syrian Civil War. In 2013, Batirashvili joined the Islamic State and began going by the name Abu Omar al-Shishani. By year's end, he had led the defeat of Syrian forces in several battles and was recognized as the Islamic State military commander and emir for northern Syria. Some reports identify him as the vicious jailer of Aleppo, in charge of foreign hostages.

During 2014, Batirashvili/al-Shishani earned places of distinction on both the Islamic State governing council and on the United States list of Specially Designated Global Terrorists, with a $5 million dollar price on his head.

A staff sergeant removes a wing access panel on an MQ-9 Reaper during a 100-hour inspection at Kandahar Airfield in Afghanistan. (USAF photo by Tech Sergeant Chad Chisholm)

ونسأل الله أن نكون ممن يعيد الخلافة الإسلامية ويفتح بيت المقدس

The vicious, red-bearded Chechen Tarkhan Tayumurazovich Batirashvili (left) immigrated to the Islamic State, changed his name to Abu Omar al-Shishani, and became a top Islamic State combat leader. He finally met his end in a March 14, 2016, drone strike. (Islamic State media)

In turn, there were numerous reports of his death, each refuted by his reappearance. At last, time seemed to have run out for the big man with the long red beard. In March 2016, CNN reported that it had learned from unnamed American sources that Batirashvili/al-Shishani was either killed or critically injured in a drone strike. The Pentagon finally confirmed the head had been lopped from this snake on March 14.

Such is the nature of the once and future conflict between the worldwide caliphate of the Islamic State and the West, especially the United States. The Islamic State holds its contiguous captured territory even as it expands the area under its influence by way of surrogates and affiliates in non-contiguous regions. The response consists of cautiously planned air attacks, carefully circumscribed to prevent civilian casualties, even as the Islamic State reaches into Europe and America to *deliberately* produce civilian casualties.

The drone strike has been proven to be one tactic that is both effective in striking at the head of the snake and striking fear into the *body of the snake* as well. However, the ability of the snake to replace its severed heads is well documented. Colonel Steve Warren admitted the frustration on March 18, 2016, when he said that "as we kill one, they'll simply promote somebody else. We'll kill them. They'll promote somebody else up and, in some cases, we'll kill them."

Against such a backdrop, many western commentators began speaking of the war against the Islamic State and jihadist terrorism as a "generational conflict," fatalistically characterizing it as having no end in sight. Indeed, as it was practiced during its first two years, Operation Inherent Resolve had made very slow progress toward the goal of "degrading" the Islamic State and scant progress toward its defeat.

In an interview with David Ignatius of the *Washington Post* that was published on May 10, 2016, U.S. Director of National

Marshaling an MQ-9 Reaper after it has returned from a mission at Kandahar Airfield, Afghanistan. (USAF photo by Tech Sergeant Chad Chisholm)

Intelligence James Clapper candidly concurred with Steve Warren and with the general pessimism about the state of the war against the Islamic State.

"We're killing a lot of their fighters," Clapper explained. "We will retake Mosul, but it will take a long time and be very messy. I don't see that happening in this administration [before 2017]. We'll be in a perpetual state of suppression for a long time. . . . I don't have an answer. The U.S. can't fix it."

Elaborating on the definition of "perpetual," Clapper used the word "decades."

Such a description reminds one of another war long ago, a war that also began with American "advisors" in harm's way. In his 1978 book *Air Power in Three Wars*, General William Momyer recalled a 1961 planning session with Secretary of Defense Robert McNamara. Momyer was then the director of operational requirements at U.S. Air Force headquarters. The topic was Vietnam.

"While the Army was sending the first of its Special Forces to Vietnam, we in the Air Force were activating our first special unit for guerrilla warfare since World War II," Momyer recalled. "Many senior airmen still questioned the wisdom of investing in such units, but Secretary McNamara stated that the Vietnamese conflict should be a 'laboratory for the development of organizations and procedures for the conduct of sub-limited war.'"

Like the Viet Cong and the North Vietnamese, the Islamic State does not conceive of such a thing as a "sub-limited war." Its lead-ership and its zealous fighters dream only of taking *total* war from the Middle East to the streets of Western cities and of establishing a *global* caliphate. With Western leaders speaking in terms of a conflict they call generational or *perpetual*, rather than of achieving victory, this 21st-Century sub-limited war will certainly be a long one, and perhaps also a lost one.

Whatever happens next in this evolving campaign, drones and drone strikes will remain an integral part of the story.

James Clapper (left), the Director of National Intelligence, walks with Lieutenant General Ronald Burgess (right), Director of the Defense Intelligence Agency. In May 2016, Clapper predicted a protracted war against the Islamic State, warning that "we'll be in a perpetual state of suppression for a long time." (Office of the Director of National Intelligence)

Colonel Steve Warren, the Operation Inherent Resolve spokesman, delivered a year-end press briefing via teleconference from Baghdad on December 29, 2015, in which he said that "in addition to our tactical operations, we are also striking at the head of this snake by hunting down and killing ISIL leaders." (DOD)

Chapter 7

SONS OF UCAV AND OTHER AMERICAN DRONES

The unmanned combat air vehicles in development in the United States during the second decade of the 21st Century run the gamut from high-performance jet attack aircraft to a spectrum of High Altitude Long Endurance (HALE) vehicles that may include the future of airborne interceptors of intercontinental ballistic missiles.

First, the jets. At the turn of the century, the Department of Defense launched the remarkable, forward-looking Unmanned Combat Air Vehicle (UCAV) demonstrator program, which seemed at the time to truly represent the immediate future of UAVs specifically designed and developed to work alongside the highest of high-performance warplanes.

The concept originated at the end of the 20th Century as an alternative to using manned aircraft to attack targets protected by heavy enemy air defenses. Both military tacticians and aerospace industry technicians were beginning to think conceptually of an unmanned aircraft that would, at some point in the future, not only laser-designate targets as Predators had in Kosovo, but conduct Suppression of Enemy Air Defenses (SEAD) missions on their own. Such missions, which targeted enemy radar systems, anti-aircraft artillery, and surface-to-air missile sites, were designed to prepare the way for a main strike force. Beginning during the Vietnam War, the aircraft flying these most deadly missions had been code-named "Wild Weasels," and the name continues to be used.

In the new doctrine that emerged at the turn of the century, military and industry planners defined the missions most suitable for unmanned, rather than manned, combat aircraft. As noted in the introduction, these were articulated in 2003 by Scott Meyers of General Dynamics Robotic Systems as "the dull, the dirty, and the dangerous." These include long, dull, repetitive reconnaissance missions; missions into a battlefield environment made dirty by chemical or biological weapons; or missions against targets that are very dangerous for human pilots.

The SEAD missions, especially the deadly Wild Weasel operations, were among the latter. As had been the experience of the U.S. Air Force in Operation Desert Storm in 1991, SEAD mission attack aircraft are exposed to high volumes of fire from anti-aircraft artillery and surface-to-air missiles, in which human crews risk their lives. In the UCAV future, only the airplanes would be at risk in SEAD missions. Military planners and airframe designers were moving beyond the notion of simply hanging weapons on reconnaissance drones.

The word "combat" was inserted into the acronym of a specific UAV project for the first time on March 9, 1998, when the U.S. Defense Advanced Research Projects Agency (DARPA) issued its document MDA972-98-R-0003, the Phase I request for proposals for an Unmanned Combat Air Vehicle Advanced Technology Demonstrator (UCAV ATD). As Major Rob Vanderberry of the Air Force's Air Combat Command put it, "These aircraft will allow Air Force leaders to breathe easier when making a combat decision. What UCAV lets us do is attack a target without the concern of losing a pilot, or having someone become a prisoner of war."

As this author described in great detail in *Birds of Prey*, the specific UCAV aircraft were the Boeing X-45A for the U.S. Air Force and

The Boeing X-45C, the son of UCAV and the father of the Phantom Ray, shares the sunset-washed ramp with two earlier warplanes from the former McDonnell facility in St. Louis, an F/A-18 Hornet and an F-15 Eagle. (DARPA)

the Northrop Grumman X-47A Pegasus for the U.S. Navy, which made their respective first flights in May 2002 and February 2003.

Initially, both the U.S. Air Force and U.S. Navy identified their aircraft as UCAVs, but later in 2003, the UCAV program was renamed as the Joint Unmanned Combat Air System (J-UCAS) program.

A milestone date in the J-UCAS program came on March 24, 2004, the first day that an unmanned aerial vehicle designed specifically for strike missions (an X-45A) released a 250-pound bomb over the Precision Impact Range Area in the Southern California desert near Edwards AFB. "What an historic day for aviation!" said George Muellner, the former Air Force general who was now the general manager of Boeing Air Force Systems. "Our team has shown the world that an autonomous unmanned combat aircraft can respond to human direction and successfully release a weapon from an internal bay."

The Air Force envisioned that an operational UCAS vehicle could be deployed with gravity bombs, as well as GBU-31 and GBU-32 Joint Direct Attack Munitions (JDAM) and other guided air-to-surface weapons tucked into the stealthy strike plane's internal bomb bay.

Plans were made for the initial prototype demonstrators to lead to more advanced demonstrators that were a step closer to larger and more capable operational aircraft. Boeing began work on the X-45C and Northrop Grumman on the X-47B. In 2006, however, the Pentagon's Quadrennial Defense Review recommended the cancellation of J-UCAS, or at least the "jointness" of it. The U.S. Air Force terminated the X-45C and traded it for a new strategic bomber program called Next Generation Long Range Strike (NGLRS). Meanwhile, the U.S. Navy moved forward with the X-47B under a new program known then as UCAV-N, and later as UCAS-D, with the "D" for Demonstrator.

Boeing later revived its X-45C aircraft as the company-financed Phantom Ray program; the X-47B entered flight test and is described in Chapter 16.

The X-45C was nearly completed at Boeing's Phantom Works advanced projects component in St. Louis when the U.S. Air Force decided to cancel its part in the J-UCAS program in 2006, so Boeing made the decision to carry on and finish it.

Dave Koopersmith, the vice president of Boeing Advanced Military Aircraft, a division of Phantom Works, summed it up when he said "Phantom Ray will pick up where the UCAS program left off in 2006 by further demonstrating Boeing's unmanned systems development capabilities in a fighter-size, state-of-the-art aerospace system. . . . We will incorporate the latest technologies into the superb X-45C airframe design."

On March 24, 2004, the Boeing X-45A became the first unmanned aerial vehicle explicitly designed for strike missions to drop a bomb. It was a 250-pound bomb released over the Precision Impact Range Area in the Southern California desert near Edwards AFB. (DARPA)

Both Boeing X-45A UCAV demonstrators on the ramp at the Dryden Flight Research Center on July 11, 2002, with the UCAV program's T-33 chase plane posed in the background. Air Vehicle 1 is color-coded in blue, its sister ship in red. (Bill Yenne photo)

A Northrop Grumman X-47B Joint Unmanned Combat Air System (J-UCAS) aircraft at Palmdale, California, in October 2010. (Northrop Grumman)

An eerie purple light glows from the intake in this moody image of an X-45C in its hangar. (DARPA)

When the first images of the Phantom Ray were revealed in May 2009, Graham Warwick of *Aviation Week* wrote, "If the [Phantom Ray] aircraft looks familiar, that's because it is; it's the X-45C that was completed, but never flown, when the [J-UCAS] program was canceled. . . . Unveiling of the Phantom Ray comes hard on the heels of U.S. Defense Secretary Robert Gates' April 7 announcement that the

[Next Generation Bomber] program is to be deferred and his comments that perhaps the next Air Force bomber could be unmanned. In effect, we are back to where we were before March 2006, when the J-UCAS program was planning to demonstrate technology for future unmanned strike/surveillance platforms."

The Phantom Ray made its debut flight on April 27, 2011, at Edwards AFB in California, the same location where the X-45A aircraft had been tested a decade earlier. The flight lasted 17 minutes, during which the Phantom Ray achieved an altitude of 7,500 feet and a speed in excess of 200 mph. After this little heralded coming out, the Phantom Ray receded into obscurity, at least as perceived by the general public.

Two years earlier, on April 4, 2009, the jet-propelled sibling of the Predator and Reaper made its first flight at the General Atomics Aeronautical Systems Gray Butte Flight Operations Facility, located only about 30 miles from Edwards.

Known as Predator C, or Avenger, the multi-mission UCAV was then described by the company as having been "designed and developed with the intent of making a UAS that was more survivable in higher threat environments and to provide the U.S. Air Force and other potential customers with an expanded quick-response armed reconnaissance capability."

It was noted that the aircraft would have "higher operational and transit speeds than current Predator-series aircraft, resulting in fast response and rapid repositioning for improved mission flexibility and survivability. Wide-area surveillance, armed reconnaissance, border surveillance, time-sensitive strike, and quick response capability missions for use against conventional and asymmetric threats (e.g., terrorists, pirates) are among its key missions."

For such missions, the Avenger could carry a mix of air-to-ground weapons (including gravity bombs and Hellfire missiles) similar to those that typically arm the Reaper. Like the other General Atomics aircraft, it is equipped with the company's Lynx Synthetic Aperture Radar (SAR) and various Electro-optical/Infrared (EO/IR) camera systems.

With a wingspan of 66 feet and a length of 41 feet, the Avenger is slightly larger than the Reaper and is capable of operations up to 60,000 feet, higher than either the Predator or Reaper and in the same class as the Northrop Grumman RQ-4 Global Hawk. Its endurance of 18 hours is similar to that of the Reaper, but about half that of the Global Hawk. Its top speed of 300 mph, however, is significantly greater. The Avenger is powered by a Pratt & Whitney PW545B turbofan engine, a member of the PW500 family that is used by the Cessna Citation business jet, among others.

The Avenger was designed to use the same General Atomics ground control station as existing Predator and Reaper drones, including the Advanced Cockpit Ground Control Station that was first used with the Avenger in November 2012. This system was developed to be compatible with the U.S. Air Force Unmanned Aircraft System Command and Control Initiative, which mandated interoperability within all U.S. Air Force and Defense Department unmanned aerial vehicle systems and operations.

In its early days, the Avenger was seen as an ideal candidate for major drone operators who were announcing plans for acquiring newer generation unmanned combat air vehicles, such as the

U.S. Air Force under its MQ-X program and Britain's Royal Air Force under its Scavenger (later Protector) program. Both of these services had been looking forward to an eventual successor to their Reaper UCAV fleets. However, MQ-X was canceled in February 2012 and the British decided to look instead into the extended range variant of the Reaper that General Atomics was planning.

In the meantime, in 2011, the U.S. Navy announced its Unmanned Carrier-Launched Airborne Surveillance and Strike (UCLASS) program, which is discussed at length in Chapter 17. For this, General Atomics proposed a carrier-compatible Avenger variant that would be known as Sea Avenger. The company developed a revised wing design that they described as using "proprietary wing technology that enables high-speed flight, while also supporting excellent low-speed handling qualities desired for aircraft carrier landings [and] fully autonomous launch and recovery from both USS *Nimitz* and USS *Ford* class carriers."

The second Avenger aircraft, known inside the company as "Tail 2," made is first flight on January 12, 2015, at Gray Butte, though the Avenger flight test program was being relocated to NAS China Lake where there was more uninterrupted airspace.

In addition to the potential of the Sea Avenger for the U.S. Navy, General Atomics has also had interest from foreign governments. In November 2015, *Bloomberg News* reported that the Indian Air Force wanted to acquire the Avenger because the idea of a high-performance aircraft that could operate against terrorists based throughout Pakistan without risking the life of an Indian pilot was appealing.

At the same time that Boeing was developing its fast and stealthy Phantom Ray, the company was also working on another unmanned aerial vehicle that was *neither*. The Phantom Eye is an advanced High Altitude Long Endurance (HALE) drone with a level of performance in both altitude and endurance that exceeds that

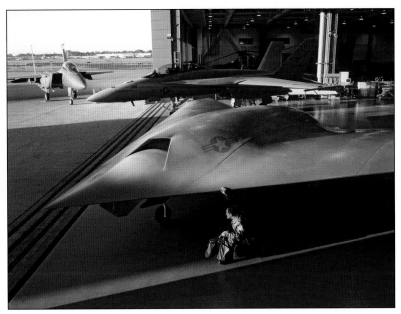

The Boeing X-45C shares an operational hangar with an F/A-18 Hornet, while an F-15 Eagle waits outside. (DARPA)

The Boeing Phantom Ray on the ramp at Edwards AFB in California in 2011. (NASA)

of America's signature HALE, the RQ-4 Global Hawk. It is said to be based on the Boeing Condor experimental vehicle, which demonstrated an endurance of more than 80 hours in 1989 while setting a UAV altitude record of 67,300 feet.

The Condor boasted a wingspan of 200 feet, while the Phantom Eye prototype has a 150-foot span, though the wing of an operational variant would be scaled up to around 225 feet. According to manufacturer specs, the Phantom Eye can operate at 65,000 feet and stay aloft for four days for missions involving "persistent intelligence and surveillance." Missions of up to 10 days are being discussed for a follow-on aircraft.

The Phantom Eye demonstrator aircraft was developed by Boeing's Phantom Works component in cooperation with Ball Aerospace, Aurora Flight Sciences, and MAHLE Powertrain of Germany. It is powered by a pair of 150-hp 2.3-liter automobile engines of the type originally developed by the Ford Motor Company for the Ford Fusion car, but which are turbocharged to operate in the thin upper atmosphere. In turn, Boeing tuned the engines to run on liquid hydrogen.

The Phantom Eye first flew on June 1, 2012, from NASA's Dryden Flight Research Center at Edwards AFB, but suffered damage on landing that delayed the second flight until February 25, 2013. In the

During its first flight on April 27, 2011, the Boeing Phantom Ray achieved an altitude of 7,500 feet and a speed in excess of 200 mph. (NASA)

Boeing's Phantom Eye prototype autonomous unmanned aircraft system lifts off its takeoff dolly from the bed of Rogers Dry Lake on its first flight on June 1, 2012, at NASA's Dryden (now Armstrong) Center at Edwards, California. (NASA)

With a host of windmills accenting the ridgeline in the background, the slow-flying Boeing Phantom Eye technology demonstrator floats over Edwards AFB on its second test flight on February 25, 2013. (NASA)

The Avenger is the unmanned jet strike aircraft developed by the same company that created the Predator and the Reaper, the world's most experienced unmanned combat air vehicles. (General Atomics)

As gaseous hydrogen vents from the top of the fuselage, ground crewmen secure Boeing's Phantom Eye technology demonstration aircraft following its landing on Rogers Dry Lake after its second test flight. (NASA)

course of its nine-mission, two-year test flight program, the aircraft demonstrated an endurance of 89 hours and reached 54,000 feet.

During that time, the U.S. Air Force considered a potential production series Phantom Eye for reconnaissance operations over broad areas, such as Afghanistan, while the U.S. Navy saw it as a possible communications relay platform or in a maritime surveillance role similar to that of MQ-4C Triton.

In May 2015, Phantom Works president Darryl Davis announced that Boeing was looking into equipping a future Phantom Eye derivative aircraft with solid-state lasers.

"I could hypothesize . . . the potential for a stratospheric UAS to

Frank Kendall, the Under Secretary of Defense for Acquisition, Technology and Logistics. Justifying the use of unmanned vehicles to target ICBMs, he said in 2014 that "if you're close enough to shoot at a rocket right after it launches from enemy territory, you're probably close enough for the enemy to shoot you." Kendall previously held the position of Director of Tactical Warfare Programs. (DOD)

carry a solid-state laser, doing sensing missions and maybe someday evolving to have the power output to be able to do some missile defense. . . . Those things are being studied by our team all the time. It all comes down to the pace at which solid-state lasers actually come to the marketplace. . . . There is a lot of interest from a lot of our customers, but there is an awful lot of technology maturation still to go on solid-state lasers."

Indeed, Boeing had the experience of the YAL-1A Airborne Laser Testbed, a 747-400 airframe armed with a Chemical Oxygen Iodine Laser (COIL) that was tested between 2007 and 2010. The YAL-1A/COIL system successfully intercepted missiles, albeit at enormous cost, and it was retired in 2012.

Of arming the Phantom Eye derivative, Davis referenced the lessons learned with the COIL, adding, "We don't want to be looking at chemical lasers, because they come with a logistics tail that becomes complex. A solid-state laser you can recharge and cool more often, whether it's in a persistent, stratospheric UAV or in a potential future fighter. As some of those payloads become more efficient and smaller in size with higher power outputs, we could very easily see, potentially in the next two decades, you could have that kind of a platform doing a sensing mission for sure, and potentially even some communications missions and then evolving someday into a stratospheric, persistent, directed-energy platform."

Three months later, in August 2015, at the Space & Missile Defense conference in Huntsville, Alabama, leading figures within the Defense Department were formally embracing the idea of a drone-based missile defense laser. Vice Admiral James Syring, the director of the Pentagon's Missile Defense Agency (MDA), told the conferees that in reviving the airborne laser concept, his agency would "pick which technologies we think have the most promise [and then fly] a low-power laser demonstrator. . . . The work that we're doing with the General Atomics Reaper and the work that we did with the Boeing Phantom Eye starts to show it can be done, in terms of these long-range sensing and tracking capabilities that we need . . . 65,000 feet is where we think we need to be. . . . If it had been easy we would have done it by now, but given the rapid progress in laser technology, it's not a huge reach."

The importance of an airborne laser, and why it is better than a ground-based missile defense system, is that it can strike an ICBM early in its flight, in its more vulnerable boost phase. At the Huntsville gathering in August 2015, Frank Kendall, the Under Secretary of Defense for Acquisition, Technology and Logistics (AT&L), made the case for a high-altitude drone, rather than a manned platform, such as the YAL-1A, explaining that "by closing in, you get a softer target: The booster, the rocket itself, is a lot softer than the reentry vehicles. But if you're close enough to shoot at a rocket right after it launches from enemy territory, you're probably close enough for the enemy to shoot you."

As with any unmanned platform, no crew would be close enough for the enemy to shoot them.

Chapter 8

THE UNITED STATES AND INTERNATIONAL COLLABORATIVE PROGRAMS

Through the years, international cooperation in military aircraft programs has always come with, and often at the expense of, a variety of compatibility issues. Often cited among potential advantages is a reduction in weapons acquisition costs by sharing economies of scale and avoiding duplication of development efforts. However, as a practical matter, complexities arising from divergent requirements typically offset economies of scale.

As will be seen in Chapter 9, the shortcomings of international UAV collaboration are typified by the long-delayed, convoluted, and trouble-plagued European Medium Altitude Long Endurance (MALE) aircraft that evolved from the Cassidian Talarion program.

Where there do seem to be actual advantages are in boosting operational effectiveness through interoperability with allies and partners, as well as accessing global technology to minimize any potential "capabilities gap." Of course, the biggest justification is political, as cooperation strengthens international alliances and relationships.

The United States has a long history of cooperative ventures and technology sharing, usually, though not always, with the United States as the lead partner. As viewed from within the U.S. Defense Department, international cooperation efforts include the cooperative research and development, as well as working with foreign partners in the evaluation and procurement of defense technology, systems, and equipment. A case in point is the 20th-Century acquisition from Israel Aircraft Industries of the RQ-2 Pioneer and the RQ-5 Hunter, as well as in the subsequent American production of the Pioneer.

Some relationships are consultative. In 1957, the United States, the United Kingdom, and Canada entered into the Tripartite Technical Cooperation Program (TTCP), a program aimed at familiarizing the partners with one another's national defense science and technology programs and to cooperate in a broad range of defense-related activities and projects. When Australia and New Zealand joined in 1965 and 1969, the program was renamed the Technical Cooperation Program in order to keep the same acronym. In the 21st Century, unmanned aerial vehicle technology is an important part of the TTCP.

Some relationships involve the sales of goods and services. Under the Direct Commercial Sales program, American companies sell directly to foreign governments under commercial export licenses issued by the Department of Commerce or the Department of State.

Since 1968, the Foreign Military Sales (FMS) program has been transferring defense equipment (much of it surplus) as well as services and training to nations and international organizations such as NATO. The transfers are either through sales or through U.S. government assistance grants and are made with State Department, and sometimes congressional, approval.

Such approvals are no routine matter. Indeed, more often than not a difficult and complex process is required for manufacturers to obtain export licenses for military hardware because of U.S. government export restrictions under various rules such as the Arms

The Predator XP is an unarmed variant of General Atomics' flagship Predator that has been created specifically to be licensed by the U.S. government for sale to surveillance-only aircraft customers in the Middle East, North Africa, and South America. (General Atomics)

Export Control Act of 1976, the Export Administration Act of 1979, or International Traffic in Arms Regulations (ITAR). The gatekeeper is the Defense Security Cooperation Agency (DSCA), which signs off on the transactions.

Exports are most rigidly restricted for defense technologies such as low-observable (stealth) and counter-low-observable technology, as well as communications security devices, data links and waveforms, geospatial intelligence, GPS, intelligence data, and night vision devices. Both the Defense Department and the State Department, as well as Congress, have also been very strict (while using separate and divergent criteria) about approvals for the sale of armed unmanned aerial vehicle technology.

To address the hurdles represented by ITAR, various companies have introduced products and product variants designed to meet the restrictions. For example, General Atomics Aeronautical Systems developed its Predator XP, an updated export variant of its basic RQ-1A Predator with a 55-foot wingspan and a proven endurance of more than 40 hours. First flown in 2014, it was specifically tailored to fit within ITAR and be easily licensed by the United States government to be marketed to a broad customer base, including countries in the Middle East, the Far East, North Africa, and Latin America.

The Predator XP is available with a new Maritime Wide Area Search (MWAS) mode, which provides the capability to complete a variety of maritime missions, including coastal surveillance, drug interdiction, long-range surveillance, small-target detection, and search-and-rescue operations. The aircraft also is equipped with an Automatic Identification System (AIS) for identifying vessels at sea.

Though it is specifically designed *not* to be armed, the Predator XP has a capability for a laser designator for target illumination for accompanying strike aircraft. It incorporates General Atomics' own Lynx synthetic aperture radar and Claw integrated sensor payload. General Atomics was also able to provide improved Intelligence, Surveillance, and Reconnaissance (ISR) capabilities. With the same dimensions as the RQ-1A, the Predator XP has an endurance of 35 hours and a service ceiling of 25,000 feet. The first flight of Predator XP, lasting 35 minutes, came on June 27, 2014, at the Castle Dome UAV facility within the U.S. Army Yuma Proving Ground in Arizona.

In the meantime, General Atomics is also exporting its MQ-9 Reaper, known within the company as Predator B, which was originally designed for offensive missions. This story provides a useful case study for the purpose of understanding the export process.

The United Kingdom was fast tracked, with General Atomics being granted an export license for the delivery of armed Reapers to the Royal Air Force with relative ease.

The RAF in turn formed its 1115 Flight at Creech AFB in the United States in 2005 to begin the training of its personnel to fly the MQ-1 Predator. In 2007, the RAF reactivated its 39 Squadron (which had flown light bombers during World War II) to operate American-made unmanned combat air vehicles. Flight 1115 became 39 Squadron's Flight A, and a newly formed Flight B was assigned

MQ-9 Reapers. A second Reaper unit, XIII Squadron, also a light bomber squadron in World War II, was reactivated in 2012.

By 2013, both UCAV squadrons were based at RAF Waddington in Lincolnshire, though their controllers were deployed to Creech and their aircraft to operational locations, including Afghanistan. In the skies over the latter, they were active under Operation Herrick, the code name for all British operations in that country through 2014. The Royal Air Force maintained 70 personnel based in Nevada, covering all trades from pilots to administration staff. Meanwhile, in Afghanistan, the 904 Expeditionary Air Wing at Kandahar Airfield was responsible for the support and operation of RAF assets, including both manned and unmanned aircraft.

Italy, already operating six MQ-1 Predators from General Atomics since 2004, was the next export customer to be approved for the Reaper/Predator B. While the RAF Reapers were armed, the Italian aircraft were not, in deference to the arms export restrictions. When permission to arm the Reapers was repeatedly requested by the governments of Prime Minister Silvio Berlusconi and his successor, Prime Minister Mario Monti, the Obama administration refused.

The seal of the Defense Security Cooperation Agency, the component of the U.S. Department of Defense that transfers defense equipment, training, and services to allies, as well as providing financial and technical assistance while promoting military-to-military contacts. (DOD)

Assigned to 28 Gruppo of the Italian Air Force (Aeronautica Militare), a veteran strike squadron, the Italian Reapers flew their debut operational reconnaissance sorties over Libya on August 10, 2011. As Luca Peruzzi reported in *FlightGlobal*, quoting the Italian Defense Ministry, "The aircraft took off from Amendola air base, near Foggia, Italy, to conduct an intelligence, surveillance, and reconnaissance mission, returning to the base about 12 hours later. . . . The Italian air force has, within the last month, achieved initial operational capability with the first two of six Predator Bs. Another two will follow by the end of the year, and the remainder will arrive by mid-2012."

A British Royal Air Force Reaper armed with a full complement of two GBU-12 laser-guided bombs and four AGM-114P Hellfire air-to-surface missiles is seen here operating over Afghanistan during Operation Herrick. (Photo by Tam McDonald, Ministry of Defence)

A Reaper assigned to 39 Squadron of the Royal Air Force in its shelter at Kandahar Air Field in Afghanistan. The RAF considers the Reaper's primary role to be to provide intelligence, surveillance, and reconnaissance, and this forms the vast majority of its missions. (Ministry of Defence)

A Royal Air Force pilot from 39 Squadron remotely controls a Reaper MQ-9 unmanned aerial vehicle during a training sortie over the West Coast of America from Creech AFB. Such aircraft were flown in Operation Herrick in Afghanistan from halfway around the world at Creech, while 39 Squadron's parent organization is at RAF Waddington in the UK. (Ministry of Defence)

In 2013, the French Air Force (Armée de l'Air) ordered the first two of an eventual dozen Reapers from General Atomics, which were delivered in January 2014, less than two months after the contract award. They were then promptly deployed to Namey in Niger to support French military operations in Mali against al-Qaeda in the Islamic Maghreb (AQIM). A third Reaper was delivered to France in May 2015, by which time the first two had amassed more than 4,000 hours of flight time.

Like the Italian Reapers, the French aircraft were unarmed, although there was considerable speculation in the defense media at the time that the French Reapers would soon be carrying ordnance. Indeed, in retrospect, it seems to the outsider looking at the transaction that it would have been improbable for France and Italy to buy an aircraft such as the Reaper *without* the assumption they would one day be allowed to arm them. Indeed, the continued American refusal to allow NATO allies to arm an aircraft that was clearly designed for the attack role was a continuing source of consternation in Italy and France.

"There was perplexity in Italy about the U.S. delay," retired General Leonardo "Dino" Tricarico, who had headed the Italian Air Force until 2006, told Tom Kington of *Defense News*. "It seemed impossible that a loyal ally could be ruled out, while the UK, with its lesser UAV capacity, could be given permission immediately. In Afghanistan we would have saved Italian lives if we had had armed drones."

Successive Italian prime ministers, including Enrico Letta and Matteo Renzi, lobbied the Americans for a green light to arm their

An RAF Reaper is pictured taxiing at Kandahar Airfield prior to a mission in the skies over Afghanistan. It is armed with two GBU-12 laser-guided bombs and four AGM-114P Hellfire air-to-surface missiles. (Ministry of Defence)

Reapers. They found an ally in Senator John Kerry, who became Secretary of State in 2013, giving the Italians a man on the inside of the Obama administration.

Nevertheless, a Presidential Policy Directive issued on January 15, 2014, by the Obama White House stated that "United States conventional arms transfer policy supports transfers that meet legitimate security requirements of our allies and partners in support of our national security and foreign policy interests. At the same time, the policy promotes restraint, both by the United States and other suppliers, in transfers of weapons systems that may be destabilizing or dangerous to international peace and security. . . . The United States will also continue vigorous support for current arms control and confidence-building

Royal Air Force Squadron Leader Adele Stratton with the 556th Test and Evaluation Squadron at Creech AFB stands beside an MQ-1 Predator. A systems operator, she was the first RAF UAV exchange officer at Creech. (USAF)

An MQ-9 Reaper of the Italian Air Force (Aeronautica Militare), seen here in 2013. Italy had been operating Predators since 2004, and received its first Reapers in 2011. (General Atomics)

efforts to constrain the demand for destabilizing weapons and related technology. The United States recognizes that such efforts bolster stability in a variety of ways, ultimately decreasing the demand for arms."

In fact, the "restraint" only served to *increase* "the demand for arms."

However, on November 3, 2015, two weeks ahead of the deadly attacks by Islamic State jihadists in Paris, the Defense Security Cooperation Agency finally approved the arming of Reapers that were exported to countries other than the United Kingdom.

"The Italian request to the Americans was also motivated by a sense of dignity in the [NATO] alliance," said Italian Defense Minister Roberta Pinotti. "We repeated it because we think we're old enough to decide for ourselves how to use [armed Reapers]. We do not need caregivers. Of course, we will perform a technical study and exercise parliamentary procedures should they become necessary."

In its press release, the DSCA wryly stated the obvious, noting that "Italy currently operates the MQ-9 system and will have no difficulty incorporating this added [offensive] capability into its air force."

The day after the announcement, the Italian newspaper *Corriere della Sera* cynically theorized that the American decision was "a bid to weaken European efforts to develop UAVs in-house, thus ending dependency on U.S. products."

When asked to comment, Dino Tricarico mused, making a reference to the stalled Future European MALE program, that "I wouldn't rule that out, but in any case the EU has been really late in developing its own drone."

"Italy may become the first country to benefit from a recently relaxed U.S. government unmanned air vehicle export restriction," wrote Beth Stevenson in *FlightGlobal*. "Worth some $130 million, Italy has requested 156 Lockheed Martin AGM-114R2 Hellfire II missiles, eight training missiles, 30 GBU-12 laser-guided bombs, 30 GBU-38 Joint Direct Attack Munitions (JDAMs), 30 GBU-49 laser-guided bombs, 30 GBU-54 laser JDAMs, plus installation kits, dummy missiles, and spares. The contractor for any future deal would be General Atomics. Rome cites the potential for increased contribution to NATO coalition operations, improved operational flexibility, and enhanced survivability for Italian forces as reasons for its request."

Among those coalition operations which Italy joined was Operation Sophia, a joint operation by the European Union Naval Force Mediterranean (EUNAVFOR Med) to which Italy assigned a Predator and a Reaper. Begun in April 2015, the objectives of Operation Sophia were the surveillance, assessment, and disruption of human smuggling and trafficking networks in the Mediterranean. As a coalition effort, it was based on Operation Atalanta, an ongoing counter-piracy operation by a naval force known as EUNAVFOR Somalia, that began in 2008 off the horn of Africa.

"It's a no-brainer for the Italian Air Force, which has been using drones for 11 years, to distinguish between a fishing boat and a craft

General Leonardo "Dino" Tricarico served as Chief of Staff of the Italian Air Force (Aeronautica Militare) after having served as Commander of the NATO 5th Allied Tactical Air Force. More recently, as a member of the Intelligence, Cultures and Strategic Analysis Foundation (ICSA), he was an outspoken critic of American refusal to allow arming of Italian Reapers, saying that "it seemed impossible that a loyal ally could be ruled out. . . . In Afghanistan we would have saved Italian lives if we had had armed drones." (Aeronautica Militare)

Italian Prime Minister Matteo Renzi (right) with President Barack Obama at the White House on April 17, 2015. He was the fourth prime minister of Italy to lobby for arming Italian Air Force Reapers. Despite the apparent cordiality seen here, it was another seven months before permission was finally granted. (Official White House photo)

used to smuggle migrants, thanks to intelligence capabilities that can guarantee a virtually perfect success rate," observed Dino Tricarico in an interview with the Italian news agency Adnkronos, when the issue was raised of whether or not the Reapers were too robust a weapon for chasing smugglers. "There is not yet a perception of the fundamental role that drones play in modern asymmetric conflicts. Military doctrines are certainly being re-written from scratch. Drones can easily carry out missions to combat criminal organizations that profit from [illegal] immigration."

In reporting the authorization for arming the Italian Reapers, Beth Stevenson reported in *FlightGlobal* that "the Spanish government is also progressing with its MQ-9 acquisition, which was authorized by DSCA on 6 October [2015]. . . . This includes four Block 5 Reapers, two ground control stations, and sensor and communication equipment. . . . Reaper was pitched against the Israel Aerospace Industries Heron TP for the Spanish requirement."

The formal communiqué came on February 17, 2016, with General Atomics announcing that the Spanish Ministry of Defense had awarded the company a contract for "the delivery of one Predator B [Remotely Piloted Aircraft] system for the Spanish armed forces to include four aircraft equipped with MTS-B Electro-optical/Infrared (EO/IR) sensors and GA-ASI's Block 20A Lynx Multi-mode Radar, two Block 30 Ground Control Stations (GCS), and Satellite Communications (SATCOM) and Line-of-Sight (LOS) data link capabilities by means of a Spanish–U.S. Foreign Military Sales (FMS) agreement."

As part of the deal, General Atomics teamed with Sener Aeronáutica, the aerospace component of Gruppo SENER, an engineering firm based in Getxbo in Spain's Basque region. Andrés Sendagorta, the company's vice president, commented that SENER "is delighted to make all its capabilities available to the Spanish armed forces in order to achieve the best integration of the new system in Spain," adding that "the MQ-9 is broadly considered to be the best system in its range to which SENER has been providing keen backing for years. Reaper will contribute significantly to strengthen our country's Defense and Security system and will provide increased protection to our forces."

It was an international collaborative program indeed.

An unarmed Italian Air Force (Aeronautica Militare) Reaper over the Italian countryside. (General Atomics)

The French Air Force (Armée de l'Air) received its first pair of Reapers in January 2014 and quickly deployed them to North Africa for operations against al-Qaeda in the Islamic Maghreb (AQIM). (General Atomics)

As the U.S. Defense Department points out in its *Unmanned Systems Integrated Roadmap*, the United States "has entered into bilateral and multilateral agreements with a variety of international partners for the joint development of defense technologies and systems. Under such agreements, DOD works with its foreign counterparts and shares existing technology, expertise, and resources to develop new technical information; develop new technology, defense systems, or platforms; or improve existing products. DOD has entered into several such international cooperative agreements with foreign partners to advance Unmanned Aerial Systems."

Frank Pace (left), president of Aircraft Systems at General Atomics, shakes the hand of Andrés Sendagorta, the vice president of SENER, to celebrate the cooperation between the two firms in the development of Reapers for the Spanish Air Force (Ejército del Aire). (General Atomics)

INSIDE THE EUROPEAN COLLABORATIVE PROGRAMS

In the latter half of the 20th Century, as Western Europe was gradually unifying itself economically (and even politically) through the Common Market and later through the European Union, its industrial entities were crossing borders to form cooperative ventures. In aviation, this included the Anglo-French cooperation on the technically sophisticated Concorde program.

On the military side, most leading-edge European manned aircraft programs have been multi-national cooperative ventures since the Panavia Tornado's development in the 1970s, succeeded by the Eurofighter Typhoon, which entered flight test two decades later. These programs brought together Germany and the United Kingdom, along with Italy and Spain. The idea had been to share costs, though adapting systems to the wants and needs of multiple parties can have the opposite effect and can introduce delays.

There were also merged companies formed under *international ownership*: Airbus Industrie, formed in 1967, brought together the leading aircraft firms in France, Germany, and the United Kingdom, with the eventual participation of Spain's Construcciones Aeronáuticas SA (CASA) and Fokker in the Netherlands.

This trend reached a milestone in July 2000 with a massive merger of European aerospace firms (including the Airbus participants). This formed a single business entity, the European Aeronautic Defence and Space Company (EADS), which was reorganized as Airbus Group NV in January 2014 with military programs falling within the Airbus Defence and Space component.

Given its sprawling network of resources, it was only natural that an entity such as EADS would decide to develop a sophisticated Medium Altitude Long Endurance (MALE) UAV that could be used for reconnaissance and patrol missions. Development of the aircraft would be through Cassidian, the former German aerospace firm that was central to European UAV programs. Though it became a component of EADS, and later of the Airbus Group, we use the Cassidian name when discussing its activities.

The EADS/Cassidian aircraft was named Talarion after the *talaria*, the winged sandals of the classical messenger god known as Hermes in Greek, or Mercury by the Romans. This is despite the fact that the UAV was intended to be slow and deliberate, not fleet footed.

The Talarion mockup, with a 90-foot wingspan (two thirds that of the Global Hawk) was displayed at the Paris Air Show in 2009, with France suggesting that it would order three dozen or more. The promised range of nearly 10,000 miles was a selling point, although

An artist conception of the European MALE 2020 aircraft on a maritime surveillance mission. A similarity with the earlier EADS/Cassidian Talarion vehicle is evident, though the MALE 2020 sports a T-shaped tail. (Airbus Defence and Space)

that was 30 percent less than that of the Global Hawk. While the Talarion was primarily a reconnaissance platform, it was noted by EADS that it could also be armed for "opportunity fire."

In addition to Cassidian, CASA was also involved, and Thales (formerly Thomson-CSF), the French electronics giant, developed the Advanced UAV Radar Architecture (AURA) systems. AURA included a Synthetic Aperture Radar (SAR) capability in both swath and spot modes and simultaneous Ground Moving Target Indication (GMTI) capability.

In 2011, Alenia of Italy joined the Talarion program. Alenia is one of several aviation components of the vast industrial conglomerate then known as Finmeccanica, whose holdings run the gamut from helicopters to electronics to satellites. (Finmeccanica, whose holdings once included the carmaker Alfa Romeo, renamed itself in

The EADS/Cassidian Talarion was unveiled in mockup form at the 2009 Paris Air Show, proudly hovering over the EADS Defence and Security exhibit. (Tangopaso, licensed under Creative Commons)

2016 as "Leonardo," after the 15th-Century inventor Leonardo da Vinci, whose inventions included various types of aerial vehicles.) Alenia, in various configurations, has been involved as a collaborator in numerous high-performance aircraft programs, including the Panavia Tornado and the Eurofighter Typhoon. Its previous UAV experience had included the Sky-X, a V-tailed aircraft that first flew in 2005, and the Sky-Y, a MALE with a 32-foot, 7-inch wingspan, which had its debut in 2007.

By the time the Talarion mockup was making the rounds, and Alenia was stepping in to add its expertise, the global economic recession had sent ripples through the aerospace world. Defense budgets withered and sales were not forthcoming, even from France, Germany, Spain, the United Kingdom, and major EADS partner countries. Indeed, Germany went elsewhere, committing to the acquisition of the Northrop Grumman RQ-4 Global Hawk, while the United Kingdom acquired the General Atomics MQ-9 Reaper unmanned combat air vehicle for its Royal Air Force.

Finally, Cassidian decided in March 2012 to suspend work on the Talarion program.

"Cassidian said several times during the last few months that we will only continue to invest in the Talarion program if we would get a firm commitment from our potential customers," noted a company statement. "Unfortunately, we did not get this commitment so far. Therefore we decided to ramp down the program.

"Talarion died. The program is finished," observed Dr. Thomas "Tom" Enders, the executive chairman of EADS, on July 27, 2012. "We have invested our own funds for this project. To go further, we need a serious commitment of [European countries], we have not had it. Therefore the program is dead [but] technologies we have developed are alive and we have acquired experience."

The Talarion mockup was marked with a composite European insignia representing Germany, Spain, and France, the nations of industrial partners involved in the program, Cassidian, CASA, and Thales, respectively. Turkey was also interested and Italy was involved later. (Airbus Defence and Space)

An Italian Alenia Sky-X aircraft as photographed at the Paris Air Show. (Duch.seb, licensed under Creative Commons)

The Talarion vehicle parked on a runway, unmarked with insignia. (Airbus Defence and Space)

This, in turn, left EADS, and indeed all of Europe, without a viable indigenous MALE program, a fact that became a controversial and much-discussed topic in the European aviation media, where the reliance of Europe on American or Israeli MALE UAVs was loudly decried.

"Drones have indeed become unavoidable in modern conflicts," wrote Véronique Guillermard of the Paris daily *LeFigaro*. "However, Europe has missed the turn leaving the United States and Israel [to] dominate this market."

In 2013, France's Defense Minister, Jean-Yves Le Drian, announced that his country would meet its needs through the purchase of a dozen Reapers from General Atomics Aeronautical Systems under the assumption perhaps that they would one day be armed.

Reacting to France's decision to buy American, Alain Ruello of France's *Les Echos* called it a humiliation for EADS, but added that "it is because concerned industrialists and their respective States have been unable to build an autonomous European industrial sector, after 20 years of procrastination and a lot of money spent."

However, the suspension of the Talarion project and the media commotion did not mark the end, or even an interruption, of official interest in a European MALE UAV. In November 2013 at a meeting of defense ministers in Brussels, seven European countries, France, Germany, Greece, Spain, Italy, Netherlands, and Poland, formed what Jean-Pierre Stroobants and Nathalie Guibert of *Le Monde* called a "users of drones club."

"Already holders, or future holders of drones, these States are committed to developing, by 2020, a European MALE," wrote Stroobants and Guibert. "The countries concerned, through the European Defence Agency (EDA), promise to share experiences and to 'identify opportunities for cooperation' in various fields: training, logistics, maintenance, development. . . . The purpose of the 'club' is not to miss out on a crucial element by the respective armed forces, and the industrial implications are significant. This is to avoid a definitive dependency of Europeans in a market dominated by the United States and Israel."

Stroobants and Guibert pointed out that by that time, European countries were "several years frozen by a lack of political will and the generalized reduction of defense budgets. Ministers do not want to open the meeting empty-handed."

Dr. Thomas "Tom" Enders, then the executive chairman of EADS, announced the end of the effort toward the first pan-European MALE in July 2012 with the words "Talarion died. The program is finished." Enders later became CEO of Airbus. (Airbus Group)

With Talarion languishing, EADS teamed with IAI of Israel to undertake an "interim" MALE program called Système Intérmaire de Drone MALE (SIDM). The result, based on the IAI Heron, was the Harfang (Snowy Owl). It is seen here displayed at the Paris Air Show. (Calips, licensed under Creative Commons)

Also mentioned was that another group (Austria, Belgium, the Czech Republic, and the United Kingdom) had also declared their readiness to invest in the project and to examine its technological implications, without yet committing to a potential joint production effort with the "club."

Meanwhile, Le Drian promoted his own idea of a "club Reaper," suggesting that those countries acquiring or planning to acquire that unmanned combat air vehicle could join forces to customize their Reapers with indigenous avionics.

Out of the "users of drones club" idea, and the obvious need to move beyond Talarion in pursuit of a new MALE program, there came a high-level meeting of corporate leaders at Le Bourget Airport, north of Paris, on October 18, 2013. In attendance were Bernhard Gerwert, Eric Trappier, and Giuseppe Giordo, the respective CEOs of EADS, Dassault, and Alenia, who sat down to define the parameters of a renewed effort.

A French Air Force (Armée de l'Air) Harfang UAV on the ramp at Bagram Airfield in Afghanistan. France deployed Harfangs to both Afghanistan and North Africa. (USAF photo by Senior Airman Felicia Juenke)

"What emerged from the meeting of the 18th?" asked Alain Ruello at *Les Echos* a few days later. "In big lines, three manufacturers leave project Talarion and its most glaring defects, for a new program with more efficient sensors, and with the possibility of arming. Its development would cost a billion euros. The allocation was as follows: the airframe from EADS, the systems from Dassault, that other equipment from Alenia. The identity of the leader has not been disclosed at the meeting. . . . Gerwert, Trappier, and Giordo linked their commitment to the non-negotiable condition that one of the three potentially interested countries (Germany, France, or Italy) would assume the role of sole contractor to avoid the vexations of most European armaments projects."

Initially, the new vehicle was identified as the Future European MALE, which yielded the obvious, though awkward, acronym FEMALE. However, as Ruello pointed out, the executives "quickly changed their minds, fearing that the acronym was not worth them receiving a few taunts. . . . They have retreated to a more classic 'MALE 2020.'"

However, at the time, the three firms planned to deliver the aircraft in 2022, not in 2020. Whereas the Talarion was always described as having a reconnaissance mission as its primary role, the idea of arming the MALE 2020 was a prominent part of the official narrative, probably to allow it to compete with the Reaper.

Frédéric Lert of France's *Aerobuzz* had the best name for the program, describing the unavailing quest for a European MALE as the "Arlesiana" of European military aviation, a reference to Francesco Cilea's opera, *L'Arlesiana*, in which the hero is consumed for three acts with his continuing obsession with a woman from Arles (an

The Watchkeeper WK450 reconnaissance UAV was developed jointly by Thales UK and Elbit Systems of Israel and based on the Elbit 450 UAV. (Ministry of Defence)

Arlesiana), who never even appears before the curtain finally comes down.

"Is the era of domination by Israeli and American drones over?" asked Lert in June 2015. "The Paris Air Show gave a remarkable collection of projects all more beautiful than others. . . . Last month, Berlin, Paris, and Rome launched a study of definition in order to prepare the phase of development of a European MALE drone. Transposed into the corporate world, it is somewhat the equivalent of a meeting to prepare for the next meeting."

In the meantime, EADS had already moved forward on an international collaborative effort with Israel Aerospace Industries (IAI) to develop an "interim" MALE under a program called Système Intérmaire de Drone MALE (SIDM), which was to provide the French Air Force (Armée de l'Air) a long-endurance reconnaissance capability. The new aircraft, named Harfang (Snowy Owl), was based on the IAI Heron to which it bears a strong similarity, with a twin-boom configuration and a Rotax 914 engine driving a pusher prop.

Three Harfangs were operationally deployed to Afghanistan in February 2009 as part of France's NATO commitment, where they helped to provide security for Bagram Airfield outside Kabul. The Harfang fleet also supported French operations over Libya in 2011 and over Mali in 2013. By January 2014, as France was planning to replace its Harfangs with American Reapers, Arie Egozi of *Flight-Global* reported that Morocco had expressed an interest in surplus Harfangs, adding that "it is not clear what payloads will be carried."

Another international UAV program involving an aircraft of Israeli origin adapted for a European service is the Watchkeeper WK450. A reconnaissance aircraft similar in size and mission to the Harfang, the Watchkeeper is a variation on the Elbit 450, which is discussed in Chapter 11. The WK450 was developed by a team

Perplexed by the death of Talarion, Jean-Yves Le Drian (left), France's Minister of Defense, decided that France would meet its long-endurance UAV requirements through acquisition of American Reapers. He even suggested a "Club Reaper" under which users of that aircraft would pool resources. He is seen here at the National Assembly in 2014 with Environment and Energy Minister Marie-Ségolène Royal. (Voice of America)

Drone Strike! UCAVs and Unmanned Aerial Warfare in the 21st Century

involving Elbit, but led by Thales UK, the British subsidiary of the French company, and is manufactured by a Thales-Elbit–controlled entity known as UAV Tactical Systems that is based at Leicester in the UK.

The Thales-Elbit collaboration won the British Ministry of Defence Watchkeeper contract in 2005, having prevailed in a four-way competition that included industrial teams led by BAE Systems, Lockheed Martin, and Northrop Grumman. The plan was for the acquisition of 54 aircraft to be operated by the British Army's Royal Artillery, which had previously operated the Hermes 450. Early development and flight testing took place in Israel, with the first flight over the United Kingdom coming in 2010.

The Watchkeeper operationally evaluated over the Salisbury Plain in England, flying from the Ministry of Defence aircraft test facility at Boscombe Down in Wiltshire, as well as in operations from Aberporth on the west coast of Wales. The aircraft became operational in March 2014 with the Royal Artillery's 47th Regiment, which is based in Wiltshire.

In turn, an undisclosed number were deployed to Afghanistan as a force protection measure, though this was not officially revealed until September 2014. It was here that Watchkeepers served as airborne spotters for air strikes by Royal Air Force MQ-9 Reapers.

Shortages of trained controllers for the Watchkeeper fleet have been reported. Jack Searle of the Bureau of Investigative Journalism wrote in December 2015 that only 36 of the 54 aircraft ordered a decade earlier had been delivered, and the Royal Artillery had fewer than a dozen qualified controllers to fly them. With this in mind, 16 trainees and an undisclosed number of WK450s arrived on Ascension Island, a British Overseas Territory in the equatorial Atlantic, in January 2016 for a crash course of flight training. Ascension was picked for its good flying weather, which contrasts to the mid-winter rain and sleet of England and Wales.

"I think you'll be staggered by how few pilots we've got," Major Tom Luker, the second-in-command of the 47th Regiment, stated publicly in December 2015, adding that the Ministry of Defence "is really under pressure to have some form of operational output from Watchkeeper, essentially because, as taxpayers, we've been waiting for this capability for several years . . . in 2016 we've got to increase both the tempo and momentum of training. . . . As we enter the famous UK winter we are expecting to have a combination of relatively high winds, potentially excessively rainy or snowy conditions that will affect the runway, but also a low freezing layer. Now all of these affect the current build standard of Watchkeeper. So what we've needed is somewhere that is relatively warm and relatively benign particularly over the winter months, somewhere where we can have relatively easy access to airspace, ideally from a military airbase. There are some closer places than Ascension but for a variety

A Watchkeeper WK450 during flight trials at Parc Aberporth in West Wales. (Ministry of Defence)

The second EADS/Cassidian Barracuda unmanned combat air vehicle in its hangar in Germany. (Airbus Defence and Space)

Coincidentally, it was Cassidian, the lead EADS subsidiary in the Talarion program, that also took the lead among EADS constituents in the Barracuda program. First revealed in the aviation enthusiast press in 2006, it was also reported in the German news magazine *Der Spiegel*. Described as a technology demonstrator for a reconnaissance aircraft that was primarily intended as a reconnaissance platform, it is widely reported to possess an offensive attack capability.

The aircraft was built and initially tested at the former facilities of EADS predecessor Deutsche Aerospace (before that, of Messerschmitt) at Manching, near Munich. In April 2006, flight testing of the sleek aircraft marked with Luftwaffe serial number 99+80, and with both German and Spanish flags on the tail, moved to a remote facility in Spain.

"With the first flight of our technology demonstrator for unmanned high-performance military systems we have thrust the door wide open to one of the most promising future global markets in our branch," said Dr. Stefan Zoller, the Cassidian boss. "We now have an additional, more powerful test platform at our disposal for the further development of our core technological competencies in this extremely important field."

Meanwhile, Dr. Rolf Wirtz, the head of UAV Mission Avionics at Cassidian, described the Barracuda in detail, noting that the experimental aircraft was powered by a Pratt & Whitney Canada turbofan engine. He described it as being about 25 feet long, with a wingspan of more than 23 feet and a maximum takeoff weight of about 6,600 pounds.

When the demonstrator was lost in a landing crash at San Javier AB in Spain, reportedly due to a software glitch, EADS suggested

of reasons, not least diplomatic, Ascension Island has been hit on as the location."

While a European MALE to compete with the Reaper or Global Hawk remains, year after year, as an unseen *Arlesiana*, various consortia of European aerospace firms continue to flirt with the idea of a flying wing stealth drone inspired by the X-45 or X-47. These include the Barracuda, a joint German-Spanish project, and the Neuron (also spelled nEUROn), which is a French-led program with Swedish and Italian participation. Like the European MALE, they date back to the first decade of the 21st Century, but unlike the *Arlesiana*, they have actually resulted in flying demonstrators.

An EADS/Cassidian Barracuda unmanned combat air vehicle banks into a turn during a test flight over Labrador. (Airbus Defence and Space)

the program be abandoned. Two years later, however, it was back on track. A summer season flight test program for a second Barracuda aircraft (serial 99+81) took place in 2009, 2010, and 2012 over Newfoundland and Labrador with the Barracuda based at Canadian Forces Base Goose Bay in Labrador.

Cassidian further elaborated on the Barracuda demonstrator by stating that it was "designed as a technology test bed with a modular structure and a flexible configuration, enabling a wide variety of systems and flight profiles to be tested and a wide range of mission requirements to be demonstrated. The avionics system was developed as an open and modular structure that allows a large number of sensors and data link solutions to be integrated with the demonstrator. Electro-optical and infrared sensors, laser target designators, an Emitter Locator System (ELS) consisting of detectors for picking up radio-magnetic signals, and advanced Synthetic Aperture Radar (SAR) systems that operate on the multi-sensor principle can all be accommodated in the Barracuda's payload bay."

In July 2012, Cassidian announced that the aircraft had completed five test flights in the context of the research and development program known as Agile UAV in a Network Centric Environment (Agile UAV-NCE).

These flights "involved the Barracuda technology demonstrator flying in combination with another unmanned aerial vehicle, which was simulated by a converted Learjet. The two aircraft flew missions where they each had different role profiles that were autonomously coordinated and synchronized with one another. Carried out by Cassidian's Barracuda project team, the test flights delivered vital information regarding flight with several networked UAS and the autonomous distribution of roles between unmanned aerial vehicles in complex mission scenarios. The role distribution was predefined in each case. Coordination between the two UAS was largely automated. However, the missions could be adapted by uploading new mission data while the aircraft were in the mission zone. This was accomplished via the new network-centric data link."

Zoller, still the man in charge, said proudly that with the "latest" flights by the technology demonstrator "we have made another great leap forward in our developments for the world's most promising future markets in our industry."

As with the Talarion, the promising future for the program did not reveal itself in the near term. Today, a Barracuda in Luftwaffe markings that carries the serial number 99+82 is prominently

A Dassault Neuron experimental unmanned combat air vehicle is dramatically displayed at the Paris Air Show in 2013. (Aerolegende, licensed under Creative Commons)

displayed in the lobby of the former Cassidian, now Airbus Defence and Space, headquarters building in Manching.

France's Neuron (aka nEUROn), meanwhile, dates back to the Logique de Développement d'UCAV (LOGIDUC) program that was initiated by Dassault Aviation in 1999. It should be noted that Dassault has long been the leading producer of high-performance combat aircraft in France, going back to the mid-20th Century and its extensive Mirage series, and continuing up through today's Rafale. Over the span of six decades, Dassault had delivered more than 8,000 military and civilian aircraft to customers in 90 countries.

Dassault's company-financed LOGIDUC project included the AVE-D Petit Duc, said to be the first stealth UAV in Europe, which first flew in July 2000. Subsequent, larger variants were the AVE-C Moyen Duc of 2001, and the Grand Duc, a full-size variant of the Moyen Duc that was renamed Neuron in 2003.

Beginning that year, a number of other European aerospace firms joined Dassault in the program, beginning with Thales, in a deal that was announced personally by France's Defense Minister, Michèle Alliot-Marie, and which was intended to "realize a new unmanned military technology that covers all future activity in combat and strategic reconnaissance aeronautics."

In turn, the Swedish aerospace firm Saab joined the Neuron program in 2005, having earlier developed its own swept wing, high-performance UAV, known as SHARC (for Swedish Highly Advanced Research Configuration). The SHARC demonstrator had flown and demonstrated capabilities such as autonomous takeoffs and landings, and, according to Saab, "autonomous decisions."

Under chief project manager Thierry Prunier, Dassault remained in the lead as the 50-percent-control prime contractor for Neuron,

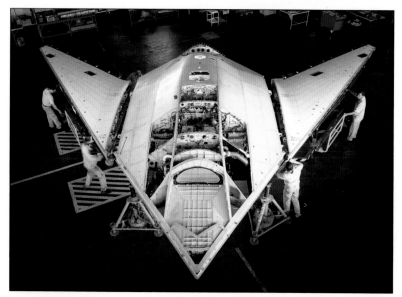

The mating of the wings and fuselage of the Neuron demonstrator at the flight test base of Dassault Aviation in Istres, France. (Dassault Aviation)

responsible for overall architecture and design, flight control systems, and final assembly, while Thales provided data-link and command interface. Saab took responsibility for avionics, while Italy's Alenia Aeronautica joined the program in 2005 to handle the electrical systems, the weapons firing system, and the integrated weapons bay.

Other subcontractors include EADS CASA in Spain for the wing and ground control station, Hellenic Aerospace in Greece for the rear fuselage, and Rüstungs Unternehmen Aktiengesellschaft (RUAG) in Switzerland.

Beginning in 2006, the French government funded half of the estimated $480 million to take the Neuron through flight testing; Saab and the Swedish government put up 18 percent; the Spanish government chipped in about 10 percent. This would theoretically be recouped in international sales of Neurons with an estimated unit cost of $29 million.

The long-awaited first flight of the Neuron took place from the French Air Force Istres-Le Tubé Air Base near Marseilles on December 1, 2012, nine years after Dassault and Thales initiated the program. This marked the first flight of a European stealth aircraft and the first flight of a European unmanned combat air vehicle.

With this, there began a flight test program that lasted for nearly three years. In March 2015, Dassault announced that the Neuron demonstrator had reached the 100-flight milestone, and reported that during those, flown out of Istres, the demonstrator "and associated equipment demonstrated exemplary availability and reliability."

The first phase of the program had evaluated the flight envelope, and had tested the electro-optical sensor and datalink performance. A second phase was devoted to stealth evaluation, including infrared and electromagnetic signature/detection confrontations against operational systems.

It was announced that the demonstrator was then disassembled, crated, and shipped to the Italian air base at Decimomannu on Sardinia, a major NATO training base. From here, the program continued with flight tests on the Salto di Quirra missile and weapons test range near Perdasdefogu. These were managed by Alenia, the Italian partner in the Neuron program.

As noted by ground observers, the vehicle seen operating out of Decimomannu had decals of the flags of participating countries on its landing gear. Normally, such things appear on vertical tail surfaces of multi-national demonstrator aircraft, but the Neuron has no vertical tail surfaces. Likewise, the "tail number" appeared on the gear door. The final digits in this number, which was XAV-5A-003, suggested to analysts that the aircraft flown in Sardinia was the third of several, not a lone prototype.

In August 2015, Alenia announced that the Italian test phase had concluded, reporting that "the 12 highly sensitive sorties have allowed [us] to verify the characteristics of Neuron's combat capability, its low-radar cross section and low infrared signature, during missions flown at different altitudes and flight profiles and against both ground-based and air radar 'threats,' using in this latter case a Eurofighter Typhoon. During the deployment in Italy, the Neuron confirmed its already ascertained excellent performance and high-operational reliability."

Beth Stevenson of *FlightGlobal* reported that "the UCAV demonstrator will now move to Sweden, where Saab will be the industrial lead during the testing at Vidsel air base, where low observability trials will take place, as well as weapon delivery testing from the aircraft's weapons bay."

The European aircraft most often compared to the Neuron is the Taranis from BAE Systems (British Aerospace until 1999), a stealthy flying wing aircraft similar in appearance to the X-47 and the Neuron. Named for the Celtic god of thunder, the Taranis has been seen as central to the British drive toward an indigenous unmanned combat air vehicle. The path leading to the Taranis goes back to the early part of the 21st Century and the Future Offensive Air System (FOAS) study. This British Ministry of Defence (MOD) project sought a successor to the Tornado GR4 and went so far as to question the future of manned combat aircraft in an unmanned combat air vehicle environment.

FOAS was canceled in June 2005 after the United Kingdom joined the American J-UCAS program, but when J-UCAS was terminated a year later, the United Kingdom embraced the idea of an indigenous replacement. The MOD initiated its Deep and Persistent Offensive Capability (DPOC) project, which was itself canceled in 2010. In the meantime, the Taranis program was first announced in December 2005, placing it on a timeline similar to that of the Neuron.

However, while Dassault sought international partners for Neuron, BAE Systems partnered only with British firms, such as Rolls Royce, which supplied an Adour moderate bypass turbofan engine for the aircraft. Also coming aboard were London-based Smiths Aerospace (part of General Electric Aviation Systems after 2007) and Farnborough-based QinetiQ.

The latter company, an aerospace research firm with broad expertise, is perhaps best known in the UAV world for its Zephyr family, which consists of a number of unmanned High Altitude Long Endurance (HALE) solar-powered vehicles. Among these, the Zephyr 7 set the world's official endurance record for an unrefueled, unmanned aerial vehicle in a July 2010 flight that lasted 336 hours, 22 minutes, and 8 seconds. Using solar cells and rechargeable batteries, the Zephyr's successor vehicle, the Mercator, will be designed to remain airborne for months, if not indefinitely.

BAE Systems, meanwhile, also had a pedigree in unmanned aerial vehicles that included its Corax (Raven) flying wing and its High Endurance Rapid Technology Insertion (HERTI) vehicle, both of which flew in the early years of the 20th Century. Indeed, the HERTI flew reconnaissance missions over Afghanistan at the same time that American Predators were first active in that air space.

In unveiling the Taranis, BAE Systems officially noted that the program would "make use of at least ten years of research and development into low observables, systems integration, control infrastructure, and full autonomy. It follows the completion of risk-reduction activities to ensure the mix of technologies, materials and systems used are robust enough for the 'next logical step.'"

Not predicted at the time was that it took the better part of *another* 10 years just to get the Taranis off the ground. As was the case with the Neuron at roughly the same time, it was a slow road. Work on the airframe of the Taranis prototype began at Warton in Lancashire in 2008, but it was not rolled out for ground testing until 2010. The optimistic schedule for a debut flight in 2011 slipped for 2 years.

A sudden announcement on October 25, 2013, that the Taranis had already made its first flight and was already in flight test came as a big surprise. Having said that much, the MOD said no more. In February 2014, BAE Systems revealed that the first two flights had taken place at the Woomera Test Range in South Australia on August 10 and 17, 2013. The report was that the Taranis had "surpassed expectations."

It was announced at the time that the plan was for the Taranis to be operational "post 2030," nearly two decades after its debut. Given such a leisurely timeline, it was only natural to anticipate that there would be some twists and turns along the way; and there were, even before the first flights.

As the Neuron demonstrator (or demonstrators) was in flight test, discussions were already ongoing that would potentially fold Neuron technology into an international warplane whose operational career was even further in the future. In a March 2012 article for *Aerospace Daily & Defense Report*, Amy Svitak noted that France and the United Kingdom "have agreed on five primary mission sets, including suppression and destruction of enemy air defenses (SEAD/

A high-angle view of a Dassault Neuron unmanned combat air vehicle on the runway. (Dassault Aviation)

In addition to BAE Systems and Dassault, major firms to be involved in FCAS included Thales for electronics and Rolls Royce for engines, as well as Italy's Selex ES, the electronics subsidiary of Finmeccanica, and France's Safran Group, known for electronics, aircraft engines, and the Sperwer UAV discussed in Chapter 10.

In summarizing the FCAS program and justifying it as an international venture, Bernard Gray, the MOD's Chief of Defence Materiel, told the media in November 2014 that "by working together and drawing on a common vision we will see military, technological and financial benefit and sustain skills to fulfill our mutual needs and aspirations in the combat air sector."

As the same time, Laurent Collet-Billon, who headed the French Directorate General of Armaments, betrayed a more cautious perception of Anglo-French cooperation against a backdrop of centuries of rivalry and mistrust between the two countries. Indeed, he cautiously stressed the importance of French national pride when he said, "the technological excellence of [the French]

A Dassault family portrait of a Neuron leading a formation that includes the company's popular Falcon business jet (top) and the Rafale multi-role fighter jet. (Dassault Aviation)

DEAD), airfield attack, strategic strike, air interdiction in a contested environment, and armed reconnaissance. Secondary missions could include anti-ship, close air support, and defensive counter-air measures."

She added that "both nations are targeting a per-aircraft cost that will be lower than that of Dassault's Rafale combat jet and Britain's Eurofighter Typhoon, though achieving such cost objectives likely requires that the jointly developed system be based on a single, common variant."

The program, now a joint international program known as Future Combat Air System (FCAS), a successor in the minds of the British to FOAS and DPOC, combined Taranis and Neuron technology into a system that could challenge the future of manned warplanes.

On November 5, 2014, the British MOD formally announced that "the British and French defense procurement agencies have awarded contracts to three industry groups for the two-year feasibility phase of the joint [FCAS] program. . . . A UCAS capability would, by the 2030s, be able to undertake sustained surveillance, mark targets, gather intelligence, deter adversaries, and carry out strikes in hostile territory."

defense aerospace industry must be maintained over the long term. It is a matter of sovereignty and operational superiority. This requires an ambitious investment strategy open to partnerships. The Franco-British cooperation on the unmanned combat air vehicle Future Combat Air System meets this demand and paves the way for the future of the European combat air sector."

On the downhill slope of the second decade of the 21st Century, the principal multi-national European high-performance drone programs were those that had been born in the middle of the first decade, none of which had proceeded beyond flight test, and one of which, the European MALE 2020, had yet to make its first flight.

This takes us back to the original rationale for multi-national programs, the idea that the sharing of technology and expertise will enhance the final product and reduce both development time and overall bottom-line costs. At face value, the logic inherent in this premise is unquestionable, though as a practical matter, reality rarely aligns with the ideal, and progress moves at a glacial pace.

The quality of the end product *may* be compromised by the disparate needs, demands, and special requirements of various parties involved in the programs, but there seems little doubt that the schedule *is* compromised.

Taranis taxiing at BAE Systems in Warton, Lancashire, prior to its maiden flight in August 2013. The aircraft is named for the Celtic god of thunder. (Ray Troll, BAE Systems)

The Taranis vehicle during ground testing at the BAE Systems military aircraft factory in Warton, Lancashire. (BAE Systems)

Chapter 10

EUROPEAN NON-COLLABORATIVE PROGRAMS

Even as multi-national cooperative ventures were becoming the signature programs within the European unmanned aerial industry, two programs stand out that follow the old model of single-nation aircraft projects. One, from France, is described as the "best-selling tactical UAV system in Europe." The other is an Italian MALE unmanned reconnaissance/strike aircraft that has evolved on a much faster track than the long-delayed multi-national "Future European MALE" discussed in Chapter 9.

While major French efforts, such as Neuron, have been built on a foundation of collaboration between multi-national businesses, the Sperwer (Dutch for Sparrowhawk) vehicle comes from a merged company involving two major French firms, though neither has a lineage as a maker of airframes.

The Sperwer originated in 2002, developed by Société d'Applications Générales de l'Electricité et de la Mécanique (SAGEM). This firm was an electrical products company dating back to 1925 that perfected telex machine technology while France was under German occupation during World War II, and which later developed Inertial Navigation Systems (INS) for France's first ballistic missiles. By the 21st Century, SAGEM was best known for its extensive line of civilian cell phones.

In 2005, SAGEM merged with the leading French jet engine manufacturer, Société National d'Etudes et Construction de Moteurs d'Avion (SNECMA) to form the Safran (Rudder Blade) Group, though both components retain their original identity.

The Sperwer is a tactical drone with a wingspan of 13 feet 9 inches, a service ceiling of 16,000 feet, and an endurance of around 6 hours. It was deployed by the French Army's 61st Régiment d'Artillerie at Chaumont as an artillery spotter, where it is known as the Système de Drone Tactique Intérimaire (SDTI), or Intermediate Tactical Drone System.

A CU-161 Sperwer unmanned aerial vehicle flies off the catapult ramp on an operational flight at Camp Julien, near Kabul in Afghanistan. (Lieutenant-Colonel Dana G. Clarke, Royal Canadian Air Force)

The Sperwer has also been used in a reconnaissance role by the Canadian armed forces as the CU-161, and by the Swedish Air Force as the UAV01 Owl. Other users include the Royal Netherlands Air Force, Greece's Hellenic Army, and the United States Air National Guard. Canada, France, and the Netherlands all used the aircraft over Afghanistan.

In its marketing literature, SAGEM notes that the "best-selling tactical UAV system in Europe, Sperwer has become a NATO reference." The phrase "best-selling" is defined by the delivery of 25 full systems, including ground control stations and 140 individual aircraft within Sperwer's first decade in production. They are principally manufactured by SAGEM in Montluçon in central France, about 175 miles south of Paris, although the prime contractor for the Canadian Sperwer was Oerlikon Contraves of Switzerland (now a component of Germany's Rheinmetall Air Defense AG).

Though the first-generation Sperwer was largely withdrawn from front line service by 2010, SAGEM has since marketed the improved and "multi-mission capable" Sperwer B (originally called Sperwer Mk.II) aircraft, which has the capability of functioning as an unmanned *combat* air vehicle. The payload capacity of the new aircraft has doubled over that of the original to 220 pounds and it has twice the endurance (up to 12 hours of sustained flight) with armament such as the Rafael Spike-LR anti-tank missile and the Bonus munition from Nexter. Other systems include the SAGEM Euroflir 350+ optronics pod with electro-optical/infrared sensors, electronic and communications intelligence (ELINT/COMINT), and synthetic aperture radar (SAR) such as the Selex Picosar.

"Drawing on SAGEM's state-of-the-art technologies and on users' operational feedback," the company has declared, the second-generation aircraft "is a modernized version of the Sperwer system combining extended autonomy, high-performance image chain, and reduced footprint. Combat-proven, it is being used daily on missions in international theaters. Operational from unprepared areas, close to military units, Sperwer Mk.II provides highly accurate observation, threat detection, and target designation to land forces as well as fire coordination for artillery."

The Sperwer B boasts a reduced operational footprint for easier deployment, with a full system transportable via a C-130 aircraft, or "integrated on light all-terrain vehicles," from which it can be catapult launched and recovered by parachute and airbags during day or night. The MC2555LLR catapult launcher is provided by Robonic Ltd. of Tampere, Finland.

In June 2012, the French Direction Générale de l'Armanent (DGA) awarded a contract for five Sperwer B vehicles for the 61st Régiment d'Artillerie, which has in recent years been deployed overseas to both Afghanistan and Chad.

A *Sperwer vehicle belonging to France's 61st Artillery Regiment takes center stage on the Avenue des Champs Élysées in Paris during the 2014 Bastille Day parade. (Pierre-Yves Beaudouin, licensed under Creative Commons)*

A *French Army Sperwer at Eurocorps Quartier Aubert de Vincelles in Strasbourg during the Rapid Reaction Corps Brigadex exercise in April 2014. (Claude Truong-Ngoc, licensed under Creative Commons)*

Meanwhile, Sagem has also developed its Patroller, a light surveillance UAV based on the airframe of the German Stemme ASP S15 powered glider, which uses the same ground control station as the Sperwer. After a first flight in June 2009, the Patroller entered a long and leisurely flight test program culminating in "official tests" at Istres Air Base in southern France. During these, the Patroller demonstrated the performance of its new-generation electro-optical system for long-range observation, and the simultaneous and real-time operation of optical and radar imaging. Meanwhile, the test program also established performance parameters, including an endurance of more than 20 hours and a service ceiling of 20,000 feet.

In September 2015 Safran signed what they described as an "exclusive commercial and industrial collaboration agreement concerning the Patroller" with the Egyptian aircraft manufacturing component of the state-owned Arab Organization for Industrialization. The contract called for final assembly of Patroller aircraft in Egypt.

A CU-161 Sperwer unmanned aerial vehicle rests on its launcher in front of the long-abandoned Tajbeg Palace, nine miles southwest of central Kabul, Afghanistan. (Corporal John Bradley, Royal Canadian Air Force)

On April 5, 2016, French Minister of Defense Jean-Yves Le Drian and Vincent Imbert, the deputy director of the Direction Générale de l'Armament (DGA), formally announced the selection of the Patroller as the French Army's newest Système de Drone Tactique (SDT), or Tactical Drone System. The plan was for the Patroller to replace the Sperwer in service with the 61st Régiment d'Artillerie. Having signed for Safran, CEO Philippe Petitcolin commented that "the selection of the Patroller confirms French industry's leading position in the European surveillance drone market. Our teams are ready to meet this challenge, and they will be worthy of the trust placed in us by the country."

The comment was an obvious reference to the long-languishing Future European MALE unmanned aerial vehicle program.

In Italy, meanwhile, Alberto Galassi, the CEO of Piaggio Aero, took a jab at the lingering Future European MALE when he touted his own company's entry into that field. He happily called Piaggio's Hammerhead drone "the first European-developed state-of-the-art MALE UAS, capable of performing at the highest technological

A side view illustration of the Piaggio P-1HH Hammerhead Medium Altitude Long Endurance (MALE) UAV. (Piaggio Aerospace)

level aerial, land, coastal, maritime, offshore, COMINT/ELINT, and electronic warfare missions."

Indeed, the program that led to the first flight of the demonstrator had taken just three years, while the pan-European project had gone on for more than a decade without a first flight.

The Hammerhead program began in 2011, while Piaggio itself had originated in 1884 building railroad locomotives and rolling stock. The company turned to military aircraft before World War II, and rolled out their legendary Vespa motorscooter in 1946. The company reentered the aircraft market in 1948 and split into two parts, motorcycles and aircraft, in 1966. The Piaggio P180 Avanti, a twin-turboprop, canard-configuration, executive transport, was introduced in 1990. Having evolved through a long series of variants, it is still in production. This aircraft, in turn, formed the basis for the Piaggio P-1HH MALE UAV, which was named "Hammerhead" because of the appearance of the canards on the forward fuselage.

The Hammerhead program was financed by Tawazun Holding in the United Arab Emirates, an investment and arms manufacturing company in the United Arab Emirates, which was seeking to bankroll the development of a maritime patrol drone. The company had also looked at the Bombardier Q400 and Saab 340 turboprop as candidates for its patrol drone before deciding to go with Piaggio in 2012. Tawazun, which is discussed in more detail in Chapter 13, provided the financing through its Abu Dhabi Autonomous Systems Investments (ADASI) division.

Selex ES, the electronics subsidiary of Finmeccanica, developed the Hammerhead's surveillance systems, while also contributing to

In November 2013, Alberto Galassi, the chief executive officer and director of Piaggio, described the company's P-1HH Hammerhead as "the first European-developed state-of-the-art MALE UAS, capable of performing at the highest technological level." It was an obvious dig at the long-languishing "Future European MALE" program. (Piaggio Aerospace)

its avionics and mission system, and its sensor suite, featuring Sea-Spray 7300E radar, customized data link solutions, and the skyIS-TAR mission management system. As noted by Piaggio, skyISTAR is "ideally designed for patrolling and ISR missions, and responding to diverse threats that range from terrorist attacks to illegal immigration, protection of Exclusive Economic Zones, infrastructures, and critical sites. Sensor fusion, data management and exploitation features of skyISTAR enable highly effective border control, wide area surveillance, targeted surveillance, environmental, and disaster control missions."

If Tawazun had provided the impetus for producing an unmanned variant of the P180, the incentive for *arming* the aircraft came from the continued refusal of the United States government to allow Italy to arm is Predators and Reapers. This inconvenient fact was underscored by Italy's National Armaments Director, General Claudio Debertolis, in an interview with *Aviation Week* that came in May 2013, just one month before the Hammerhead was publicly unveiled at the Paris Air Show.

The first unmanned flight of the Hammerhead Technology Demonstrator took place over the Mediterranean Sea on November 14, 2013, from the Italian Air Force Base at Trapani in western Sicily. It was announced that the Hammerhead had a service ceiling of 45,000 feet, a mission payload of 2,000 pounds, and an endurance of 16 hours. It was powered by two Pratt & Whitney Canada PT6A-66B turboprop engines driving Hartzell low noise, contra-rotating, five-blade scimitar propellers.

Piaggio described the avionics package as including a Vehicle Control & Management System (VCMS) to command aerodynamic control surfaces and manage onboard equipment and a Mission Management System (MMS) based on the Selex ES skyISTAR for the mission specific equipment. The VCMS is operated from the ground control station by way of an airborne datalink system and a triple redundant flight control computer. The Automatic Take-Off and Landing (ATOL) system has dual redundant external sensors.

A mockup of the P-1HH Hammerhead Medium Altitude Long Endurance (MALE) UAV was shown at the Piaggio Aerospace display at the Paris Air Show in June 2013. (Julian Herzog, licensed under Creative Commons)

The Piaggio P-1HH MALE UAV, seen here in an artist conception, is called "Hammerhead" because of the appearance of the canards on the forward fuselage. (Piaggio Aerospace)

As with most UAVs, the Hammerhead is marketed as an unmanned aerial *system*, which in this case involves two aircraft and a ground control station. The initial acquisition by the Italian Air Force was of three such systems. In March 2016, the United Arab Emirates, as expected, became the first export customer for the P.1HH with an order for four systems and a total of eight aircraft.

In marketing the Hammerhead, Piaggio had plenty of positive features to acclaim, but there are two weaknesses with which the program is plagued, one technical and the other political.

Technically, it has been pointed out that basing the drone on a manned aircraft with a large fuselage volume came with considerable size and weight penalties when compared to an aircraft that was not originally designed to have people aboard. In its March 10, 2016, issue, *Defense Industry Daily* observed that "the Hammerhead gives buyers extra speed, and sometimes extra payload and range, in exchange for less endurance and the possibility of higher operating costs. The P180 Avanti II may offer remarkable efficiency for its aircraft class, but a twin-engine passenger aircraft conversion isn't likely to match thinner and slower single-engine, never-manned designs."

Meanwhile, it is industry politics that have made it hard to market the aircraft in Europe, where insiders of the EADS consortium dominate the market. *Defense Industry Daily* has also commented on how political intrigues were responsible for the failure to resurrect the Future European MALE UAV project, at the same time it is exactly that same political milieu that mitigates against an outsider such as Piaggio.

The publication notes that Hammerhead's "clear positioning as a qualified candidate won't require a lot of development investment, Europe doesn't look especially promising. European programs prefer to hand out favors to large, established firms, even if it means re-inventing the wheel; recall the Tiger attack helicopter program and corresponding rejection of Agusta Westland's similar and ready-to-buy A129. Selex ES has ties to Italy's Finmeccanica, but those ties would have to eclipse Alenia's UAV partnership with EADS, and Italy won't be in the driver's seat of a European UAV partnership. European success would be a pleasant surprise, but it would be a surprise."

When it comes to arming the Hammerhead, potential customers were long at odds with the American export restrictions that kept Italy's Reapers unarmed from 2011 to 2015. As *Defense Industry Daily* explains, "Piaggio's use of Pratt & Whitney turboprops gives the United States enough leverage to block sales using its ITAR weapons export laws."

The discussion continued, noting that "as a surveillance-only UAV, Piaggio will need to depend on customers who are acceptable to the United States, and whose need to cover large areas with fewer assets eclipses the value of longer orbits. That's a limiting definition. If Piaggio does develop weapon options that don't require American approval, they'll open an important sales window, but other countries are also working to close that gap. Piaggio's long-term advantage would be the Hammerhead's swifter reaction time for close air support, which is nonetheless a tradeoff for shorter ongoing coverage."

One might hasten to add that a MALE in the hand is more attractive that one not yet in flight test, but time will tell.

Chapter 11

UNMANNED AERIAL COMBAT, THE MIDDLE EAST STANDOFF

Shaping up as the future Middle East flashpoint is the potential conflict between Israel and Iran. Perhaps it could be said that a drone war between Israel and Iran has been ongoing, given that Palestinian groups such as Lebanon-based Hezbollah and Gaza-based Hamas have been operating small, Iranian-supplied UAVs (albeit mainly small reconnaissance drones) over Israel since the early years of the 21st Century.

Both countries are actively developing unmanned combat air vehicles as well as reconnaissance drones that possess the inherent capability to be armed for combat, though the Israel Defense Forces specifically do *not* comment on the arming of their unmanned aerial vehicles. This has led to the assumption that it is being done more widely than reported or suggested.

Conversely, Iran is highly assertive in pointing out the combat potential of its vehicles. Indeed, there is scarcely a piece of hardware in the Iranian military arsenal that is *not* described as a potential contributor to the "inevitable" annihilation of the State of Israel.

The two leading producers of tactical UAVs in Israel are Elbit Systems and Israel Aerospace Industries (IAI), with the latter being by far the largest aviation company in the country.

Elbit Systems was born in 1966 as a component within Electronic Industries and is active in a wide range of defense electronics, communications, and computing activities. Elbit began developing UAVs at the end of the 20th Century and has since produced its Skylark series of miniature tactical UAVs and its Hermes series of longer-endurance drones. The parasol-winged Hermes 450 has a wingspan of 34 feet 5 inches and an endurance of 20 hours in its basic configuration or 30 hours in the 450ER variant. It is nominally described as a reconnaissance UAV, but is known to have a secondary air-to-ground attack capability using underwing-mounted missiles.

Based at Palmahim AFB south of Tel Aviv, the Hermes 450 has seen extensive service with the Israeli Air Force in the 2006 Lebanon War, various actions inside Gaza, and in the Israeli Defense Forces attacks on Port Sudan (in the country of the same name) that took place in January and February 2009 and which required the drones to make an 1,800-mile round trip. The targets of the attacks were a substantial number of Fajir-3 artillery rockets, manufactured in Iran and being delivered by the Iranian Republican Guards Corps via ship into Sudan, from which they were to be smuggled into Gaza for use against Israel. The Israeli government neither confirmed nor denied

Israel Aerospace Industries unveiled members of its Loitering Munitions Family at the Singapore Air Show in February 2016. The family includes the Harpy, an autonomous anti-radiation vehicle for SEAD/DEAD missions, and the Harop, an electro-optical/infrared-guided, "man-in-the-loop" aircraft, designed to locate, track, and destroy high-value static and mobile targets. (Israel Aerospace Industries)

Elbit Systems is headquartered in the Matam industrial park on the south side of Haifa, Israel, near the largest and oldest dedicated high-tech park in Israel. Adjacent to the Israel Electric Corporation tower are the offices of Intel, as well as Elbit.(Zvi Roger, Haifa Municipality Publicity and Advertising Division, licensed under Creative Commons)

that it had been involved in the strikes. Other attacks attributed to Israel have taken place over the years since 2011.

In 2014, the Revolutionary Guards reported shooting down a Hermes 450 near the Iranian nuclear facility at Natanz, 150 miles south of Tehran and nearly 1,000 miles from Israel. Given that this, like the Sudan missions, is five times the advertised range of the aircraft, a launch from a third country may be indicated.

The Hermes 450 has also been widely exported to such countries as Azerbaijan, Botswana, Brazil, Columbia, Croatia, Cyprus, Georgia, Macedonia, Mexico, and Singapore. The United States procured the Hermes 450 for tactical evaluation, and for use by U.S. Customs and Border Protection for border patrol.

The United Kingdom acquired a substantial number of Hermes 450s and used them extensively over Afghanistan. The aircraft was also later used as the basis for the WK450 Watchkeeper reconnaissance drone that was developed by Thales for the British Army and first deployed to Afghanistan in 2014.

In September 2015, Thales teamed with the Polish firm WB Electronics to develop a version of the WK450 for Poland's armed forces that would be armed with the FreeFall Lockheed Martin Fury, the glide bomb version of the Thales Lightweight Multi-role Missile. The Fury is seen as a simpler and more economical alternative to the larger AGM-114 Hellfire. Being a non-American system, it also falls outside American arms export restrictions.

The Elbit Systems Hermes 450 is a multi-payload unmanned aerial vehicle designed for long-endurance tactical missions. Seen here is a Hermes 450 operated by U.S. Customs and Border Protection. (Gerald L. Nino, USCBP)

U.S. Customs and Border Protection is one of more than a dozen military and law enforcement organizations around the world that operate the Elbit Hermes 450. (Gerald L. Nino, USCBP)

Making its first flight in December 2009, and flying its first operational mission in July 2014 was Elbit's Medium Altitude Long Endurance (MALE) UAV. It was designated as Hermes 900, but is also known as Kochav (Star). A V-tailed aircraft with a wingspan of 49 feet 3 inches, it is powered by a Rotax 914 engine driving a pusher prop. This is the same basic powerplant as the IAI Heron and the General Atomics MQ-9 Predator.

In July 2014, Elbit Kochavs were pulled out of flight testing for operational missions over Gaza during Operation Protective Edge, but then returned to test status. The Hermes 900 did not *officially* enter service until November 2015.

Elbit has also inked agreements to export the Hermes 900 to the armed forces of Brazil, Chile, Columbia, and Switzerland, as well as to the Mexican Federal Police.

Israel Aerospace Industries was established in 1953 as the Bedek Aviation Company and became involved in a wide range of projects, notably the maintenance and modification of imported warplanes. IAI was an early innovator in the development of lightweight battlefield surveillance drones during the 1970s, first with its Scout UAV, and soon thereafter with the Pioneer, which served with the U.S. Army, U.S. Navy, and U.S. Marine Corps under the RQ-2 designation. The IAI Hunter was acquired by the United States armed forces under the designation BQM-155 (later RQ-5). Indeed, the twin-boom, pusher-prop IAI drones were widely marketed (and widely copied) throughout the world before and since the turn of the century.

Under its MALAT component, IAI's Military Aircraft Group has continued to develop leading-edge unmanned aerial vehicles in the 21st Century. Beginning in April 2014 the MALAT Division was divided into three sections, a MALAT proper to oversee the overall unmanned aerial system business organization, MALAT Technologies to concentrate on engineering and production of the UAVs themselves, and RAKIA to handle "special" programs.

In the 21st Century, MALAT's portfolio includes the Bird Eye family of small unmanned aerial vehicles, and the Mosquito and Ghost micro UAVs, though its primary tactical unmanned aerial vehicle business centers around the Heron (Machatz), a MALE UAV. The twin-boom, pusher-prop layout of the Heron is clearly derived from that of the Pioneer and Hunter.

A full-scale mockup of an Elbit Hermes 900 UAV, also known as Kochav (Star), on display in Israel. (Tal Inbar)

An Israel Aerospace Industries Heron (Machatz) belonging to the Royal Australian Air Force on display in 2014 at the Centenary of Military Aviation Air Show at RAAF Base Williams in Point Cook, Victoria (Hpeterswald, licensed under Creative Commons)

A UAV's eye view of the building in northern Gaza used as the intelligence operation facility of the Palestinian Authority until taken over by Hamas as an operations center. It was also used for detaining and interrogating Fatah operatives and those suspected of cooperating with Israel. (Israel Defense Forces, licensed under Creative Commons)

First flown in 1994, the Heron has the capability of providing data via six sensors simultaneously. Among its other features are satellite communication for extended range; two simultaneous Automatic Takeoff and Landing (ATOL) systems; fully redundant, state-of-the-art avionics; and retractable landing gear.

The Heron has been widely used by the Israel Defense Forces to fly reconnaissance missions over adjacent territories, including ongoing routine surveillance of the Gaza Strip, and to support IDF ground forces in operations against Palestinian militants. In the case of the latter, the 21st Century has seen a much closer link between UAV operators and the supported ground units. During Operation Cast Lead, the 2008–2009 Israeli incursion into Gaza, Heron UAV squadrons were attached to brigades, where controllers operated within the brigade command post within earshot of brigade commanders, providing much improved tactical awareness and reaction times.

Early in the 21st Century, IAI received international orders for the Heron from India, Singapore, and Turkey. In 2008 and 2009, Canada and Australia, respectively, entered into lease agreements to operate Herons as part of their operations in Afghanistan. In 2010, the German Luftwaffe leased three, plus two ground stations, as a first step toward wider acquisitions.

Since 2010, the Azerbaijani Air Force has obtained five Herons, the Ecuadorian Navy two, and the Royal Moroccan Air Force took

Seen here in flight is a Super Heron unmanned aerial vehicle from the MALAT component of Israel Aerospace Industries. Unveiled in 2014, it has an endurance of at least 45 hours. (Israel Aerospace Industries)

delivery of three. The federal police forces of both Brazil and Mexico have also received Herons, and they have been evaluated by the U.S. Navy.

First flown secretly in around 2004, but not officially unveiled until 2010, the IAI Heron TP, also known as Eitan (Steadfast), is an advanced Heron variant with what IAI describes as "an extended performance envelope." Officially revealed features include simultaneous and flexible operation of payloads; ATOL systems; and triple, fully redundant, state-of-the-art avionics. Also noted are all-weather capability and a capability of operating above commercial airline traffic, meaning a service ceiling above 45,000 feet.

It is also described as a "multi-purpose MALE UAV system [with a] large internal volume for a variety of payloads," which tends to support the widely held supposition that the Eitan has an offensive weapons capability. Indeed, Eitans were almost certainly utilized in the 2009 strikes at Port Sudan.

Eitans were also operational during Operation Protective Edge, also known as Operation Resolute Cliff, the IDF action against Hamas rocket sites in Gaza during July and August of 2014. So too were other IDF drones, both in direct attacks and in acquiring targets for other aircraft.

While Israeli, like American, drones are routinely blamed for killing civilians, the Ramallah-based organization Defence for Children International Palestine specifically blamed an armed Eitan for the August 24, 2014, death of Rawya Joudeh and four of her children. The allegations were tempered somewhat when the IDF released a Hamas training manual on urban warfare, which said in part that "the process of hiding ammunition inside buildings is intended for ambushes in residential areas and to move the campaign from open areas into built up and closed areas . . . residents of the area should be used to bring in the equipment."

In June 2015, IAI announced the completion of flight tests that would result in an expansion of the Eitan/Heron TP capabilities by integrating it with the M-19HD high-definition electro-optical payload system. The M-19HD is described as a "multi-spectral, multi-sensor observation and targeting payload (which can simultaneously incorporate up to seven sensors) [enabling] continuous day/night surveillance under all weather conditions and provides outstanding acquisition ranges due to its powerful sensors, high stabilization, and unique image processing capabilities."

Said Avi Elisha, the general manager of IAI's Tamam Division, "We are proud to integrate the M-19HD payload on IAI's flagship UAS, the Heron TP. We strongly believe that its high-performance and unique image processing features can confer significant advantages on supplying Heron TP customers in their operational activities."

The M-19HD was described as having been designed to "withstand severe environmental conditions . . . in demanding high-end applications on various platforms such as high/medium-altitude long-endurance unmanned aerial vehicles (HALE/MALE UAVs), fixed-wing aircraft, combat helicopters, aerostats, and maritime vessels."

A Super Heron on display at a 2015 air show at Rishon LeZion, Israel's fourth largest city. (LLHZ2805 licensed under Creative Commons)

The most recent member of the IAI MALAT Heron family is the Super Heron, which was officially unveiled at the Singapore Air Show in February 2014. While earlier Herons are powered by 100-hp gasoline engines, the Super Heron is equipped with a 200-hp "heavy fuel" diesel engine made by Tucson, Arizona-based HFE International.

Described as a MALE system, the Super Heron specifically has a ceiling of 30,000 feet and an endurance of 45 hours, with a top speed of 170 mph. The company notes that it possesses provisions for a large SATCOM antenna and "large and heavy payloads [with] multiple hard points for various payloads (fuel tanks, Sigint, radar and more)."

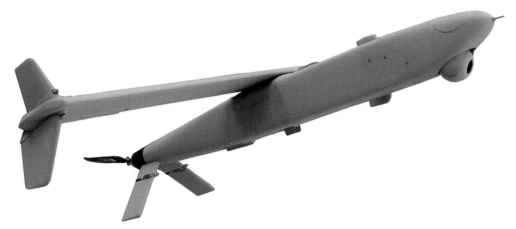

The Green Dragon tactical loitering munition provides "significant situational awareness and firepower in a compact envelope." It is powered by a silent electric motor and is operated from a small tablet-sized control panel. (Israel Aerospace Industries)

Subsystems upgrades noted by MALAT include advanced avionics, triple redundancy, advanced computerized systems, and advanced communications systems, including SATCOM for beyond-line-of-sight communications. Multiple operational configurations are available for intelligence, maritime patrol, and persistent surveillance.

IAI MALAT also produces the much smaller Panther family of tilt-rotor, vertical takeoff, and landing unmanned aerial vehicles, which the company describes as a "solution to a wide variety of tasks when pin-point automatic takeoff and landing is a requirement." First unveiled in 2010, the 143-pound Panther is complemented by the 26-pound Mini-Panther, which has a two-hour endurance. Powered by electric motors, both vehicles are capable of extremely quiet operations, and both are controllable by a command center that fits in two backpacks.

Introduced in October 2015, the Front Engine, or "FE," Panther has a hybrid power plant in which the electric power is supported by an internal combustion engine. Nevertheless, the FE Panther weighs scarcely more than the electric Panther.

The Panther family aircraft are marketed for such missions as covert special operations, silent observation and stakeout, convoy escort and protection, and border and coastal surveillance, as well as Intelligence, Surveillance, Target Acquisition, and Reconnaissance (ISTAR) missions.

Meanwhile, through its Elta Systems subsidiary, IAI is also developing drone detection, identification, and flight disruption technology. First unveiled at the Seoul International Aerospace and Defence Exhibition (ADEX) in October 2015, the Drone Guard system addresses the difficulty involved in detecting small, low-visibility UAVs with low radar cross sections. The system uses ELM-2026–series three-dimensional radar and electro-optical sensors, as well as

Joseph Weiss became CEO and president of IAI in 2012, having previously served as general manager of its Missiles and Space Group. (Israel Aerospace Industries)

The IAI M-19HD EO (high-definition electro-optical) payload system is a multi-spectral, multi-sensor observation and targeting payload that can simultaneously incorporate up to seven sensors. (Israel Aerospace Industries)

dedicated electronic attack jamming to disrupt UAVs in flight. The radar, from the short range ELM-2026D to the 20-km-range ELM-2026BF, uses what Elta describes as "special drone detection and tracking algorithms, as well as adapting them with [electro-optical] sensors for visual identification of the target."

Elta also notes that it had "developed advanced adaptive jamming systems which can be used in concert with its detection and identification sensors, or as a continuously operated stand-alone system. The jamming disrupts the drone's flight and can either cause it to return to its point-of-origin ('Return Home' function) or to shut down and make a crash landing."

Said Nissim Hadas, Elta's president, "We believe that in the near future every critical asset and public site will require these safety measures for protection against hostile drones." The implication is that in the new world of hostile Micro UAVs, one cannot be without a system such as Drone Guard.

Also outside the MALAT division, IAI's MBT Missiles Division produces unmanned vehicles that it calls "loitering munitions," though they are generically labeled with many other names and nicknames. They are sometimes referred to as unmanned combat air vehicles or as lethal unmanned aerial systems. They are also and more accurately called "suicide drones," as they are essentially piston-engined cruise missiles with an operational profile from which they will not return. The primary mission is Suppression of Enemy Air Defenses (SEAD) and attacking enemy radar installations by crashing into them.

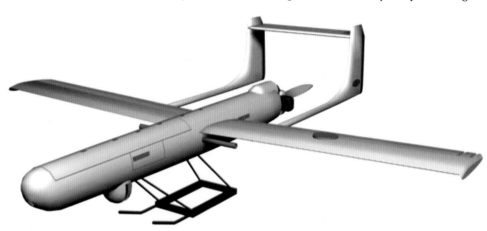

The Mohajer-2 (Migrant) from Qods (Ghods) Aviation Industry was a strategic reconnaissance UAV pressed into service during the Iran-Iraq War as Iran's first UCAV. A variant may still be in production in Venezuela. (Illustration by Aspahbod, licensed under Creative Commons)

The term "loitering" comes into play because, unlike familiar cruise missiles that fly and strike, these aircraft can *fly around* once they reach a target area, searching for a specific target whose precise location may not have been known at the time of launch.

The concept is not new. The first of this family was the Harpy, which dated back into the late 20th Century. In turn, the Harpy was part of a joint IAI/Raytheon Systems program known as the Combat Uninhabited Target Locate and Strike System (CUTLASS) that was first displayed in the 1999 Paris Air Show. The proposed CUTLASS aircraft combined the airframe of a Harpy with the advanced sensors made by Raytheon.

As reported by Sandra Erwin in the June 2001 issue of *National Defense Magazine*, CUTLASS was "designed to loiter, seek and destroy ground targets, but unlike unmanned combat aircraft, it is expendable and does not return to base after a strike mission. Because it loiters, it can be confused with an unmanned air vehicle (UAV), but it is essentially a cruise missile."

The CUTLASS program was company-funded with the hope of selling it to the U.S. Navy, but this did not happen. A few years later, in 2004, the Harpy became the center of an underreported squabble between Israel and the United States over IAI's sale of the aircraft to China. When the Chinese asked for system upgrades, the United States tried to block the transaction, fearing that the Harpy posed a threat to Taiwan. The Americans used the rationale that the Harpy contained American technology and subsystems, which was denied by Israel. In addition to Israel and China, the Harpy is also reported to be in service with Chile, India, South Korea, and Turkey.

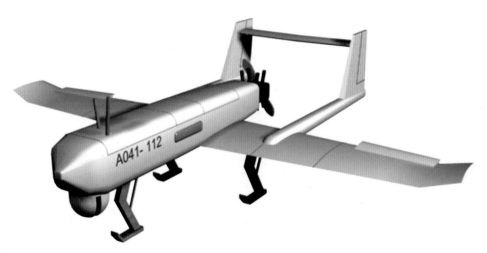

The Mohajer-4 is a 21st-Century unmanned reconnaissance and strike aircraft from Qods (Ghods) Aviation Industry. (Illustration by Aspahbod, licensed under Creative Commons)

IAI describes the Harpy as an "autonomous weapon, launched from a ground vehicle behind the battle zone [which] detects, attacks, and destroys enemy radar emitters, hitting them with high-hit accuracy. Harpy effectively suppresses hostile SAM and radar sites for long durations, loitering above enemy territory for hours."

In turn, IAI's MBT developed an improved loitering munition, known as Harpy 2, or Harop, which was first mentioned in 2005. A major difference between the two is that while the Harpy is a "fire and forget" vehicle, Harop is electro-optical/infrared-guided, with a "man in the loop" that is designed to locate and track, as well as to destroy both static and mobile targets.

According to *Defense Update Magazine*, because of the Harpy, IAI/MBT was invited in 2005 to join a project spearheaded by Matra BAE Dynamics Alenia (MBDA), a sprawling consortium of Europe's leading missile companies that formed in 2001 through a massive merger of Aerospatiale-Matra Missiles of France (formerly part of EADS), British Matra BAE Dynamics (formerly of BAE Systems), and Alenia Marconi Systems of Italy. The project was to submit a proposal, which MBDA called "White Hawk," to the British Ministry of Defence (MOD) for its Loitering Munition Capability Demonstration (LMCD) program. According to *Defense Update*, the White Hawk "was not selected for the program, as the MOD insisted on an 'all British' team."

In the meantime, the online publication *DefenceTalk.com*, quoting Defence & Aerospace Publishing Services Switzerland (DAPSS), reported in 2004 that the Turkish Air Force had ordered 48 Harops

directly from IAI, adding that "more than 100 autonomous Harpy-1s are already in service with the TAF. . . . The autonomous Harpy-1 can attack only the source of detected RF signals and stops attacking once the transmitter is turned off. In addition to RF-homing, the Harop can also be directed by its operator to attack a target detected by its optronics payload, or can be re-directed to another search area."

Having previously exported the Harop to Turkey, Azerbaijan, and India, IAI publicized a series of flight demonstrations for other, unnamed, potential customers during the spring of 2015. As the company noted, "during the exercises, the missile loitered for several hours until the target was selected. Then, with maximum precision it dived directly on to it."

IAI, in describing the aircraft, noted that the "Harop, with a warhead of [33 pounds], can be used in a range of battle scenarios, including low and high-intensity conflict, urban warfare, and counterterror operations. Harop is launched from transportable launchers and navigates toward the target area, where it can loiter and search for targets for up to 6 hours. Once a target, whether stationary or moving, is detected, it is attacked and destroyed. The attack can be performed from any direction and at any attack angle, from flat to vertical."

In February 2016, IAI chose the Singapore Air Show to unveil additional members of its family of loitering munitions, which are known generally as Harpy NG (New Generation). They were designed to counter an opposing newer generation of air defense radar threats that evolved in the second decade of the 20th Century.

Iran's Mohajer-4 is loosely based on the forgotten McDonnell Douglas Sky Owl, which was in turn based on the British R4E Sky-Eye multi-mission UAV. (Author's collection)

The Iranian Karrar (Striker) is a turbojet-powered, high-speed unmanned combat air vehicle. (Illustration by Aspahbod, licensed under Creative Commons)

These threats are met through, among other things, the extension of the radar frequency bands that are covered.

Boaz Levi, the general manager of IAI's Systems, Missiles & Space Group, said at the show that the new vehicles were "intended to refresh, update, and complement our already successful family . . . with a special emphasis on solving operational problems in urban areas."

Specific Harpy NG vehicles include a Harop repackaged with a new anti-radar seeker, which is said to provide better flying characteristics, "including longer loiter time, extended range, higher altitude as well as commonality in maintenance and training."

An all-new vehicle is the Green Dragon, a low-cost, all-electric tactical loitering munition. Like other IAI loitering munitions, it is carried in and launched from a sealed canister. In this case, up to 16 such canisters can be carried in a small truck, and operated by someone with a tablet-sized control panel. As the company describes it, the Green Dragon is designed to "provide small ground units and special operations units with significant situational awareness and firepower in a compact envelope."

It is further noted that the Green Dragon operator "has a built-in 'abort and go around' capability to prevent unnecessary collateral damage or mistaken targeting."

Our discussion of the Harop system provides a useful transition point to our discussions of Iranian unmanned aerial vehicles, given that Harop's loitering capability makes it an ideal weapon to be used for hunting ballistic missile launchers in a hostile, concentrated air defense environment, which would certainly be on the mission plan during a war between Israel and Iran.

In Iran, the main center of aircraft production is the state-owned Iran Aviation Industries Organization (IAIO), which operates the Iran Aircraft Manufacturing Industrial Company (HESA), a factory complex in Shahinshahr, near Isfahan, that was originally built in the 1970s by Bell Helicopter Textron to produce Bell 214 helicopters. Another developer of Iranian UAVs is the Shahed Aviation Industries Research Center, although final assembly of its advanced Shahed 129 UAV is done at HESA. Malek Ashtar University in Tehran, meanwhile, is a center of UAV research and engineering.

One of the earliest operational Iranian military UAVs was the first of the Mohajer (Migrant) strategic reconnaissance series, which were generally around 10 feet in length and weighed less than 200 pounds, depending upon model. Like many other drones rooted in the 20th Century, it was powered by a small piston engine driving a pusher prop.

The original Mohajer came into service during the Iran-Iraq War of the 1980s in response to a requirement by the Iran Revolutionary Guards Corps for an observation platform to look behind Iraqi lines. The first Mohajer prototypes were developed and produced by university engineers, and four of them were completed and pressed into service in 1981.

The Mohajer was later mass produced by Qods (Ghods) Aviation Industry, a manufacturing entity formed in 1985 and otherwise known for its Ababil (Swallow) and Saeghe (Thunderbolt) pusher prop target drones. Qods is now a division of IAIO. The Mohajer aircraft served through the end of the Iran-Iraq War in 1988. According to GlobalSecurity.org, some Mohajers were armed with rocket-propelled grenades to attack Iraqi positions, which made them the first armed UCAVs to be used in combat.

In turn, a longer-range second-generation vehicle equipped with an autopilot for operations beyond the range of the radio controller was introduced under the name "Mohajer-2." Thereafter, the original vehicle was retroactively redesignated as Mohajer-1. An even longer-range aircraft known as Mohajer-3, or Hodhod (Hooded Bird) was in service by the turn of the century. Because the earlier aircraft had probably been armed at some point, it can be extrapolated that this capability has been built into subsequent variants. Operationally, the Mohajer aircraft were used to conduct surveillance flights over Afghanistan during that country's civil war in the 1990s.

The fourth and substantially redesigned variant, the Mohajer-4, was reportedly first flown in 2002 and is capable of operations up to 7 hours in duration at altitudes up to 15,000 feet. Whereas the earlier aircraft had cylindrical fuselages, the more box-like Mohajer-4 resembles the British R4E SkyEye multi-mission UAV that first flew in 1973, with a major difference being that the SkyEye's wings were slightly swept and the Mohajer's are straight with upturned tips. A derivative of the SkyEye was later adapted by McDonnell Douglas as a prototype vehicle known as Sky Owl.

In November 2004, the London-based Arab language daily *Asharq Al-Awsat* reported that a Mohajer-4 operated by Hezbollah flew into Israeli airspace from Lebanon at an altitude of about 1,000 feet, overflew the city of Nahariya, and crashed into the Mediterranean without being intercepted. Other such incidents may have occurred, or may yet ensue. The drones have also been used for surveillance missions across the Middle East. Indeed, one was downed on May 16, 2015, after entering Turkish airspace. The much smaller Qods Ababil drones have also been reported overflying Middle East battlefields.

The Mohajer-4, including subvariants such as the Hodhod A/100 and Shahin, remains in production along with some earlier variants, including the Mohajer-2N, introduced in 2014, which has a six-hour endurance. Referring to satellite imagery and other sources, Emili Blasco of Spanish-based *Diario ABC* reported in 2012 that a Mohajer-2 production line had been established in Venezuela.

Another Iranian UAV in generally the same class as the Mohajer is the H-110 Sarir (Throne), which was first revealed publicly in April 2013. It has the overall appearance of being a reverse-engineered copy of the IAI Hunter, complete with the twin booms, twin tail, and twin engines driving both a pusher and tractor propeller. Though it is identified as a reconnaissance vehicle, various Iranian media reports and obvious underwing pylons indicate that it is intended to function as an unmanned combat air vehicle.

Iran's best known, and certainly its fastest, unmanned combat air vehicle is the long-range Karrar (Striker) vehicle. The turbojet-powered vehicle appears to be based on, or at least inspired by, Beechcraft/Raytheon MQM-107 Streaker target drones, which were sold to Iran before the Iranian Revolution of 1979. The tail, however, appears to have been copied directly from the South African Denel Dynamics Skua, also a high-speed target drone.

"The Iranian aircraft shows typical U.S. design features," Denel Dynamics CEO Jan Wessels told the South African publication *Engineering News*. "The wings are underneath the fuselage and the engine is on top; on the Skua, the wings are above the fuselage and the engine is underneath. [But] the tailplane on the Karrar looks as if it was cut-and-paste from our design. We've got absolutely no aerospace and defense dealings with Iran, in strict adherence to South African arms export laws. But the Iranians could easily have photographed Skuas at the various international air shows we exhibit at."

With a length of approximately 13 feet, it is 5 feet shorter than a Streaker, while its top speed of around 560 mph is equivalent to that of the Streaker.

Like a guided missile, or the above-mentioned target drones, the Karrar is launched from a zero-length launcher without a runway and is recovered (if not expended) by parachute. Unlike

The Shahed 129 (Eyewitness), seen here in the markings of Iran's Islamic Revolutionary Space and Air Force (IRSAF), is an unmanned combat aerial vehicle that bears a strong resemblance to the American Reaper or the Turkish Anka. With an endurance of 24 hours, it is the longest-range Iranian unmanned aerial vehicle. (Armed Forces of the Islamic Republic of Iran)

a missile, however, the Karrar is designed to carry external ordnance. With four wing pylons and another under the fuselage, it can carry a bomb load of up to 1,000 pounds, or up to five Kowsar or Sadid anti-ship missiles. High on the potential target list are the U.S. Navy ships operating in the Persian Gulf and the Strait of Hormuz.

The Karrar was unveiled on August 23, 2010, just one day after the activation of the nuclear reactor in Bushehr, with Iranian President Mahmoud Ahmadinejad in attendance.

"This jet is a messenger of honor and human generosity and a savior of mankind, before being a messenger of death for enemies of mankind," Ahmadinejad told a crowd at Malek Ashtar University in Tehran. "The jet, as well as being an ambassador of death for the enemies of humanity, has a main message of peace and friendship. [Its purpose is to] keep the enemy paralyzed in its bases . . . until the enemies of humanity lose hope of ever attacking the Iranian nation. . . . If there is an ignorant person or an egoist or a tyrant who just wanted to make an aggression, then our Defense Ministry should reach a point where it could cut off the hand of the aggressor before it decided to make an aggression. We should reach a point when Iran would serve as a defense umbrella for all freedom-loving nations in the face of world aggressors. We don't want to attack anywhere (Iran will never decide to attack anywhere), but our revolution cannot sit idle in the face of tyranny."

Whereas the emphasis with the Karrar UCAV is on speed, that of the Shahed 129 multi-role UAV is on endurance. An advanced aircraft, it is Iran's first Medium Altitude Long Endurance (MALE) UAV and is capable of 24-hour missions. Piston-engined and driven by a pusher propeller, it is in the same size and weight class and comparable to the American Predator and Reaper and the Israeli Heron. It is estimated to be 26 feet long, with a wingspan of 52 feet, compared to 27 feet and 48.7 feet, respectively, for the Predator. It has a V-tail similar to that of the slightly larger MQ-9 Reaper.

The name, which means "Eyewitness," suggests that the Shahed 129 is primarily a reconnaissance vehicle, though it also carries as many as four underwing-mounted Sadid-1 anti-ship and ground attack missiles.

The Shahed 129 program was ongoing by 2007, and the official debut came in July 2012, when it took part in the Great Prophet war games. Operationally, the Shahed 129 is used over Iran's border areas, and in a maritime role to patrol the Persian Gulf and the Sea of Oman. They have also been widely reported over Syria both on apparent reconnaissance missions and attacking ground targets.

A more advanced MALE drone from IAIO is the Fotros, which was officially unveiled in November 2013. It is named for a fallen angel who, according to Shia mythology, was redeemed by Shiite leader Hussein ibn'Ali, the son of Fatimah Zahra, the daughter of Mohammed.

The Fotros, which is considered to be Iran's largest UAV, bears a strong resemblance to the IAI Super Heron and has an operational endurance of up to 30 hours, depending on payload. This is greater than the Shahed 129 or Predator, but half again less than the Heron. The mission profile for the Fotros was similar to that of the Shahed 129.

IAIO is also developing a jet-powered stealth UCAV known as "Sofreh Mahi," a term that is translated alternately as "Eagle Ray" or "Flat Fish." In any case, it does resemble a ray, which literally *is* a flat fish. In 2010, at the time of its official unveiling, Iran's *Mashregh News* quoted General Aziz Nasirzadeh, the deputy commander of the Iranian Army Air Force, as saying that it had made a "successful flight," passing "all radar-evading" tests, and that the Sofreh Mahi had been designed for both reconnaissance and bombing missions. To date, only mockups have been shown publicly.

Another Iranian UAV that has attracted a great deal of attention is the reverse-engineered copy of a Lockheed Martin RQ-170 Sentinel that made a forced landing in Iran in December 2011. It is discussed in more detail in Chapter 15.

Israel and Iran stand as the two most ambitious and most technologically capable developers of unmanned aerial vehicle technology in the Middle East. They are also more than mere rivals, given Iran's ongoing threats of Israel's destruction. The standoff between the two remains asymmetrical, given that only Israel is a nuclear power, although Iran has made substantial progress toward nuclear weapons, and may well continue.

From 2006 to 2015, the international community imposed sanctions on Iran in an effort to curtail its weapons program and dismantle its nuclear enrichment centrifuges. However, these sanctions were mainly removed by the signing of the Joint Comprehensive Plan of Action (JCPOA) in July 2015.

The plan provided Iran with a strategic windfall, lifting sanctions, permitting Iran to recover approximately $100 billion of frozen assets, and generously allowing Iran to continue its nuclear activities, albeit at a reduced level. Instead of being compelled to dismantle its nuclear program as the West had originally demanded, JCPOA permitted Iran to retain 6,104 of its installed centrifuges. Iran agreed to install no further centrifuges and limit its stockpiles of enriched uranium until 2025, with the understanding that after 2030 there would be no restrictions on the Iranian nuclear weapons program.

JCPOA stipulated inspection allowances of potential Iranian nuclear weapons facilities by the International Atomic Energy Agency (IAEA), but the IAEA is required to give substantial advance notice. Restrictions were placed on ballistic missile development through 2023, as well, but these were largely ignored by Iran, with missile tests beginning within weeks of the JCPOA signing.

In considering Iran's strategic intentions, one must return to the day when Mahmoud Ahmadinejad referred to the Karrar UCAV as the "ambassador of death," and told his audience and the world that "the scope of Iran's reaction will include the entire earth. We also tell you (the West) that all options are on the table."

UNMANNED AERIAL COMBAT, THE SOUTH ASIA STANDOFF

In looking at potential major conflicts in Asia, few loom more fearsome and more imminent than that between longtime antagonists India and Pakistan, who fought a series of major conventional wars between 1947 and 1971, and who both possess nuclear arsenals, India since 1974 and Pakistan since 1998. While in the Middle East, Israel has nuclear weapons and Iran will probably have them in a relatively few years, India and Pakistan both *already* have them.

Each country, meanwhile, has been actively developing military unmanned aerial vehicles for reconnaissance, as well as for active combat, though the latter would probably not involve the delivery of nuclear weapons.

In India, the center of military aircraft development is at the state-owned Hindustan Aeronautics Limited of Bangalore. Dating back to 1940, the originally private company was managed in its early years by the American entrepreneur William Douglas Pawley, who had earlier come to China as a sales rep for Curtiss-Wright. He had set up the Central Aircraft Manufacturing Company (CAMCO), a joint venture with Chinese interests to build Curtiss warplanes inside China, and he later played a role in the formation of the famous Flying Tigers. At Hindustan, he pursued a business model similar to that of CAMCO, but the Indian government incrementally gained full control of the company.

In the world of unmanned aerial vehicles, meanwhile, Hindustan's activities are limited to a joint venture with Israel Aerospace Industries (IAI) in the development of the Naval Rotary Unmanned Aerial Vehicle (NRUAV). The autonomous NRUAV aircraft is adapted from the Chetan, a variant of the Chetak, which itself is a variant of the Aerospatiale Alouette helicopter that is license-built by Hindustan.

Also Indian state-owned is the Defence Research and Development Organisation (DRDO) in New Delhi. Seen as the center of UAV development in India, DRDO dates to 1958, having evolved out of the Ministry of Defence Technical Development Establishment. In turn, much of DRDO's UAV work is concentrated within its subsidiary, the Aeronautical Development Establishment (ADE), which is based in Bangalore, near Hindustan.

One of DRDO's earliest unmanned aircraft programs was the Lakshya, a target drone similar to the Beechcraft/Raytheon MQM-107 Streaker, which had its first flight in 1985, though it did not complete its flight test program and enter service until 2000. A completely different sort of UAV was the Nishant, a piston-engine, pusher prop, rail-launched reconnaissance drone similar to the IAI Hunter that made its debut around 1995.

DRDO has also produced small expendable target drones, including the Abhyas and the Ulka, the latter being rocket-propelled

The Lakshya (Target) originated in India with the Aeronautical Development Establishment (ADE) as a remotely piloted high-speed target drone, but evolved into a reconnaissance and target acquisition vehicle. (Kaushal Mehta, licensed under Creative Commons)

and capable of speeds up to Mach 1.4. Micro unmanned aerial vehicles developed by DRDO for tactical surveillance include the backpack-size Imperial Eagle and the Netra, which entered service in 2012.

India followed the lead of Iran in adapting its MQM-107–derived target drone for use as a non-expendable unmanned aerial vehicle. Just as the Iranians reworked their Streakers as Karrar attack drones, the Indians are doing the same with their Lakshya vehicles. With this in mind, Lakshyas were extensively tested on multiple missions at the Chandipur test range as early as 2002. Upgraded with Hindustan PTAE-7 turbojets, they were conducting low-level operations

Indian Prime Minister Narendra Modi (in pale blue vest) making a visit to the Israel Aerospace Industries pavilion at the Aero India Exhibition in Bangalore in February 2015. India is a longtime operator of IAI UAVs. (Israel Aerospace Industries)

A reconnaissance variant of the Lakshya vehicle conducted its first pre-programmed test flight in January 2012, operating as low as 40 feet. (Defence Research and Development Organisation)

during 2010 that were officially described by DRDO as being in the vehicle's target drone role, having been designed to "simulate the trajectory of low-level cruise missiles."

In 2012, flights were being made down to an altitude of 50 feet with the Lakshya now being touted as a high-speed battlefield reconnaissance and target acquisition aircraft.

During the second decade of the 21st Century, India is among many other counties in the development of a Medium Altitude Long Endurance (MALE) UAV that has both a reconnaissance and a combat role. Developed by DRDO, the Rustom (Warrior) UAV evolved out of the Light Canard Research Aircraft (LCRA) program that was

The Defence Research and Development Organisation (DRDO), India's military research and development agency, is headquartered in New Delhi. (Ashish Bhatnagar, licensed under Creative Commons)

The DRDO Rustom-1 prototype on display. It is said to have been based on the Light Canard Research Aircraft developed by a team led by the late Professor Rustom Damania. (Kaushal Mehta, licensed under Creative Commons)

conducted in the late 20th Century by the National Aerospace Laboratory and the Indian Institute of Science in Bangalore. The aircraft name is a double (or triple) entendre, as LCRA was headed by Professor Rustom Damania, who was named for the Persian leader Rostom Farrokhzad, who battled Muslim invaders in the 7th Century. Damania was inspired by his having handmade an aircraft from a 1970s-era Rutan Long-EZ homebuilt airplane kit, so the original LCRA aircraft bore a strong resemblance to Burt Rutan's earlier designs. The current aircraft is more than twice as large as the early version, with a wingspan of 67 feet 7 inches. Known as Rostam H in its reconnaissance role, and as Rostam II in its UCAV role, it is intended to replace the IAI Heron in service with India's armed forces. Powered by a pair of wing-mounted NPO Saturn 36MT turboprops, it has an endurance of more than 24 hours.

In 2012, DRDO and ADA announced that they were developing a stealthy, jet-propelled unmanned combat air vehicle known as the Autonomous Unmanned Research Aircraft (AURA), that was similar in appearance to the American X-45 and X-47B vehicles. The Aeronautical Development Agency described AURA as a "self-defending high-speed reconnaissance UAV with weapon firing capability," and suggested that it carry precision-guided munitions in internal weapons bays. A service ceiling of 30,000 feet was also mentioned.

Little additional information was forthcoming until 2015, when Defence Minister Manohar Parrikar told the Rajya Sabha, the upper house of India's parliament, that AURA would be powered by a non-afterburning variant of DRDO's GTRE GTX-35VS Kaveri turbofan engine.

When it comes to their nuclear forces and the bulk of their respective conventional military might, India and Pakistan are clearly one another's major potential antagonist. However, Pakistan is unique among major military powers in that its military activities are directed *internally* as much as they are toward India. While India looms large, India's *potential* wartime foe Pakistan is already at war, fighting a serious and exasperating campaign against the militant groups such as the Taliban and the Haqqani Network that operate with virtual impunity in Waziristan and Pakistan's northwestern tribal areas. As has been demonstrated since the beginning of the 21st Century with American attacks in that same area, unmanned combat air vehicles are often the ideal aerial weapon in counterinsurgency operations.

Flying from bases in Afghanistan, as well as from secret locations within Pakistan itself, the United States has long been striking the identical militant targets that have so vexed the Pakistani armed forces. As noted in Chapter 5, Pakistan has complained loudly (and perfunctorily) in public about the insult that such raids deal to its sovereignty, while privately imploring the Americans to give them access to American drones so that they can do the same thing!

American reticence to export drone technology to Pakistan has resulted in Pakistani industry being on track to become one of the world's leading developers of unmanned aerial vehicle technology.

Drone Strike! UCAVs and Unmanned Aerial Warfare in the 21st Century

In Pakistan, the equivalent of India's DRDO with respect to UAVs and UCAVs is the Islamabad-based National Engineering and Scientific Commission (NESCOM), a civilian-controlled scientific and engineering organization operating in partnership with the Pakistan Air Force since 2001. Technically, it is a subsidiary of the Strategic Plans Division of the Ministry of Defence.

Another state-owned entity is the Pakistan Aeronautical Complex in Kamra, near Islamabad. Founded by the Pakistan Air Force in 1971, it is primarily involved in manufacturing and heavy maintenance of larger manned aircraft, but it does build target drones and a license-built version of the Italian Selex Falco reconnaissance UAV, one of the recent UAVs that bear a resemblance to early Rutan homebuilt kits.

A Rustom-1 on display in January 2016. (Udayblr, licensed under Creative Commons)

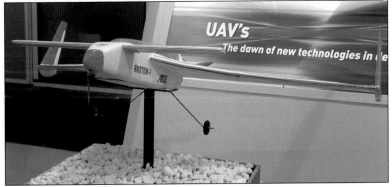

A model of a Rustom-1 UAV at the Internationale Luft und Raumfahrtausstellung (International Air Show) in Berlin in 2012. (Bin im Garten, licensed under Creative Commons)

A DRDO Nishant UAV on the vehicle from which it is launched. It is used for reconnaissance, surveillance, and target designation, among other roles. It is rail-launched from a hydro-pneumatic launcher and can be recovered by a parachute. (Kaushal Mehta, licensed under Creative Commons)

A sizable number of unrelated entities, both private and state-owned, are active in the development of indigenous Pakistani UAVs. Both Integrated Dynamics of Karachi and Surveillance and Target Unmanned Aircraft (SATUMA) in Islamabad are known for developing and building an extensive portfolio of smaller reconnaissance UAVs and target drones.

SATUMA products range from the Stingray MAV to the Flamingo and Jasoos medium-range tactical reconnaissance UAVs. Small, shorter-endurance surveillance UAVs from Integrated Dynamics include the Border Eagle and the Desert Hawk, which can operate with either an electric or internal combustion engine. Integrated Dynamics also produces target drones, including the rocket-propelled Firefly and the turbojet-powered Tornado.

Global Industrial Defence Solutions (GIDS) of Rawalpindi is a consortium of several aerospace firms, including the Advanced Engi-neering Research Organisation (AERO), that develops indigenous aircraft and systems and actively market foreign aircraft and defense systems in Pakistan. GIDS and its components have been develop-ing reconnaissance UAVs with combat air vehicle capability inde-pendently and in cooperation with NESCOM. Among these are the Uqab, Shahpar, and Burraq.

Built by GIDS and first flown in March 2008, the Uqab is a twin-boom, pusher prop aircraft with a 16.25-foot wingspan that evolved from the SATUMA Jasoos. It is primarily designed for both the Pakistan Navy and Pakistan Army as a reconnaissance and artillery spotter vehicle, but it can be armed. It first entered ser-vice with the navy at Mehran Naval Base in July 2011. GIDS has announced interest in potential export sales for the Uqab from Bahrain, Egypt, Indonesia, Turkmenistan, and the United Arab Emirates.

Models of the Rustom-1 and the Nishant on display at the Internationale Luft und Raumfahrtausstellung (International Air Show) in Berlin in 2012. (Bin im Garten, licensed under Creative Commons)

A model of the DRDO Rustom-H HALE UAV on display in Aero India 2009 in Bangalore. (Licensed under Creative Commons)

The Shahpar and Burraq, which entered service with the Pakistan Air Force and Pakistan Army in 2012 and 2013, respectively, are both single-engine aircraft with a pusher prop configuration and a canard foreplane. The Shahpar is another tactical reconnaissance UAV that has a secondary role as an unmanned combat air vehicle, but the Burraq made its debut with Hellfire-sized missiles (probably mockups) mounted on its underwing pylons, indicating that its primary role was that of a UCAV.

A November 2013 press release from the Inter Service Public Relations (ISPR) media branch of the Pakistan armed forces noted that the two aircraft represented the beginning of a fleet of "indigenously developed Strategic Unmanned Aerial Vehicles (UAVs)." The company is swift to point out that with the exception of its Austrian-built Rotax 912 powerplant, the Shahpar is entirely built in Pakistan of Pakistani components. These include an autonomous GPS-based tracking and control system and the Zumr-I multi-sensor turret.

As Usman Ansari at *Pakistan Defence Forum* reported in November 2013, the Shahpar vehicle was identified at the time of

The insignia of the National Engineering and Scientific Commission (NESCOM), a center of UAV and UCAV development in Pakistan. Based in Islamabad, it is a civilian-controlled scientific and engineering organization that is a subsidiary of the Strategic Plans Division of the Ministry of Defence. (NESCOM)

An armed Pakistan Air Force Burraq unmanned combat aerial vehicle taking off. Built by the National Engineering and Scientific Commission (NESCOM), it bears a strong resemblance to the Chinese CH-3 attack drone, which in turn resembles the Rutan Long-EZ home-built kit aircraft of the 1970s. (Chang Hsiao-liang)

its unveiling as "an autonomous UAV with an endurance of 7 hours and which could relay data in real time out to a range of 250 km. Observers have said the Burraq appears to be a Pakistani variant or development of the Chinese Rainbow CH-3 UCAV, but little else is known beyond speculation based on the CH-3's specifications. Former Pakistan Air Force pilot Kaiser Tufail said additional information will be difficult to obtain for now because sources will be 'wary about leaking what is considered confidential stuff.'"

Usman Shabbir of the Pakistan Military Consortium told Ansari that "Shahpar can carry about a 50-kg payload and has around 8 hours endurance. Burraq, based on CH-3 specs, would carry around a 100-kilogram payload and 12 hours endurance."

Lieutenant General Asim Bajwa of the ISPR revealed in 2015 that the Barraq had its combat debut on September 7 of that year when it was used to attack "a terrorist compound" in the Shawal Valley of northwest Pakistan. "Three high-profile targets" were eliminated.

It is no secret that the catalyst for the Burraq was the desire by the Pakistani armed forces to be able to attack the Taliban and the Haqqani Network, and the American refusal to sell them such aircraft as the Predator and Reaper. Therefore, the machine that emerged is designed to parallel the operating envelope of the American Predator.

Politically, the ongoing rivalry with the Americans is nearly as big a conflict for the government of Pakistan as its war with the Islamic insurgents who have pledged to destroy it.

A line of Shahpar unmanned aerial vehicles at the Global Industrial Defence Solutions facility in Rawalpindi, Pakistan. (GIDS)

Chapter 13

NATIONAL PROGRAMS

As we have seen, the respective arms races between Israel and Iran and between India and Pakistan have resulted in extensive UAV and UCAV development that is ancillary to a wider program of weapons development and deployment. With European UCAV development focusing on cooperative ventures, relatively few other countries have a national UCAV development program. The United States, the world leader in the field, has been discussed, and China, America's rival in this as in many other endeavors, is the subject of Chapter 14. Other countries with indigenous UCAV programs include Austria, Russia, Turkey, South Africa, and the United Arab Emirates.

In Austria, the Schiebel S-100 Camcopter, an unmanned rotary-wing aircraft, was developed early in the 21st Century by a company that started out making small electronic components for appliances in the 1950s. The program evolved from one that originated with the development of a stabilized camera platform for aerial photography and motion picture filming.

The S-100 can be operated manually using daylight or infrared cameras, or programmed to fly an autonomous mission profile using a triple-redundant flight computer. As Schiebel points out, in both scenarios the S-100 is automatically stabilized via redundant Inertial Navigation Systems (INS), and navigation is accomplished using redundant Global Positioning System (GPS) receivers. It has two fuselage payload bays, hardpoints on each side, and an internal auxiliary electronics and avionics bay.

The armed variant of the Camcopter carries side-mounted Thales Martlet Lightweight Multi-role Missiles (LMM), 40-pound, 4-foot weapons originally developed for the UK Ministry of Defence to arm Agusta Westland AW159 Wildcat helicopters.

The first S-100 customer was the army of the United Arab Emirates, which bought 40 aircraft. The German navy became the first maritime force to acquire the aircraft, buying them for use aboard K130 *Braunschweig* Class corvettes. The Chinese bought 18 S-100s in 2010, and in 2014, they became the principal unmanned reconnaissance aircraft used aboard the ships of the Italian navy (Marina Militare). They were sold to Libya before the 2011 revolution, and Russia plans to deploy the license-built Gorizont variant aboard its naval vessels. Other governments acquiring an aggregate total of more than 100 Camcopters include those of Brazil, Canada, Egypt, India, Jordan, South Africa, and the United States.

Russia has a long history of high-speed, turbojet-powered reconnaissance drones going back to the days of the Soviet Union. Beginning in the 1960s, the Tupolev design bureau produced a series of

A Schiebel S-100 Camcopter operating in the Langkawi archipelago off the northwestern coast of Malaysia in 2013. This aircraft is equipped with an L-3 Wescam MX-10 electro-optical/infrared tactical surveillance system that features a fully stabilized camera, thermal imager, and laser illuminator. The pylons on the side are where air-to-surface missiles can be attached. (Schiebel)

An unmanned Schiebel S-100 Camcopter of the United Arab Emirates Air Force flying over Abu Dhabi during the International Defense Exhibition (IDEX) in February 2013. (Schiebel)

A Schiebel S-100 Camcopter equipped with an Israeli Tamam POP 300 modular electro-optical surveillance and observation system flying over Malta with the Ministry of Aviation Supply (MOAS). (Schiebel)

such vehicles, including the Tu-123 that evolved out of the Tu-121 cruise missile program. The Tu-141 reconnaissance drone, similar in configuration and mission to the American Ryan Firebee family, was operational from the mid-1970s through the end of the Cold War, and it is still used by Ukraine.

Since 2006, the Zala Aero Group, headquartered in Izhevsk in the western Urals 600 miles east of Moscow, has been delivering small reconnaissance drones to the Internal Affairs Ministry. These include aircraft roughly the size and shape of the Boeing-Insitu ScanEagle and smaller vehicles, including mini-helicopter UAVs and quadcoptors on the scale of those operated by hobbyists.

In 2007, the former Mikoyan-Gurevich design bureau, now called Russian Aircraft Corporation MiG, rolled out a mockup of its Skat (Manta Ray) vehicle. The company, famous for more than half a century of Soviet and Russian MiG jet fighters, had produced a stealthy flying wing UCAV similar in appearance to the Northrop Grumman X-47B, the BAE Systems Taranis, and the Dassault Neuron. With a 38-foot wingspan, it was a little more than half the size of the X-47B and slightly smaller than the Neuron.

It was said that a production version would be powered by an RD-5000B turbofan engine, a derivative of the Klimov RD-33D that was designed for the MiG-29 fighter. Armament, like that of the comparable UCAVs, would consist of precision-guided munitions that would be accommodated in a pair of internal weapons bays.

For five years, little more was said about the Skat. Then, in June 2013, the Russian news agency RIA Novosti reported that MiG was going to develop an unmanned combat air vehicle based on the Skat configuration for the Russian defense ministry. Sergei Korotkov, MiG's director general, announced that "we signed a R&D contract for UCAVs on 15 May. The contract requirements include a mockup for a future UCAV for the defense ministry. We are already ahead on

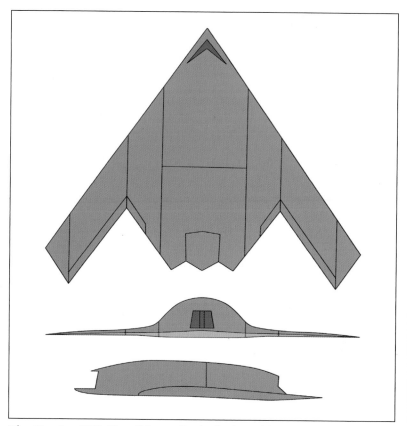

The Russian MiG Skat (Manta Ray), designed by Mikoyan, is an unmanned combat air vehicle developed for the Russian Defense Ministry. A stealthy aircraft, it carries its Mach 3.5 Kh-31 air-to-surface missiles in an internal weapons bay so as to not interrupt the smooth surface contours. (Illustration based on a drawing by Allocer, licensed under Creative Commons)

this, based on our Skat program." Again, as in 2007, little further information followed the 2013 announcement.

Turkey is an example of a country that, unlike nearby Iran and Israel, remained on the sidelines of major global conflicts throughout most of the latter 20th Century and into the 21st. However, this changed dramatically with the multi-sided Syrian Civil War, which began during the naively named "Arab Spring" of 2011. In the ensuing years, Turkey has had a major and vicious conflict raging along 450 miles of its southern border.

The largest aerospace company in the country is Turkish Aerospace Industries, founded in 1984, which maintains a 1.6-million-square-foot factory within a 6-square-mile complex in Ankara. The company's principal business involves the assembly and maintenance of foreign aircraft that serve with the Turkish armed forces, including American F-16 fighters, Spanish CASA CN-235 patrol aircraft, Italian SIAI-Marchetti SF.260 trainers, and Eurocopter Cougar helicopters. Turkish Aerospace also designs and manufactures tactical aircraft based on foreign designs, including the T129 attack helicopter based on the Italian Agusta Mangusta.

By the second decade of the 21st Century, Turkish Aerospace had emerged as an important center of UAV and UCAV design and development. Many of these are smaller surveillance drones, such as the Baykus (Owl) and the Gözcü (Observer), both of which have served with the Turkish armed forces on the southern border. First flown in 2007 and described as an Intelligence, Surveillance, Target Acquisition, and Reconnaissance (ISTAR) UAV, the rotary-engine Gözcü has a 12-foot 4-inch wingspan, a payload capacity of 18 pounds, and a service ceiling of 12,000 feet.

On December 30, 2010, Turkish Aerospace marked the debut flight of its Anka, a Medium Altitude Long Endurance (MALE) unmanned aerial vehicle designed with both ISTAR and UCAV missions in mind. Unencumbered with ordnance in a reconnaissance role, the Anka has an endurance of 24 hours. The Anka is named for the Zümrüd-ü Anka, a phoenix-like bird from Turkish mythology. With a pusher prop configuration and a V-tail, it is similar in appearance to the General Atomics MQ-9 Reaper. The Anka is roughly two-thirds the size of that American aircraft, being 26.2 feet long with a wingspan of 56.7 feet. During flight test, the Anka reached an altitude of 26,000 feet, comparable to the ceiling of the Reaper.

The Anka is equipped with an electro-optical/forward-looking infrared laser range finder, a laser designator and spotter camera, and synthetic aperture radar with a ground moving target indicator. Turkish Aerospace itself developed all of the airborne and ground based flight control software, though the payload hardware and software was developed by such Turkish firms as Aselsan and Milsoft, and the ground control system is by Savronik, headquartered in Eskishehir in western Turkey. The Anka is manufactured in Ankara, with components supplied by subcontractors elsewhere, including the Pakistan Aeronautical Complex in Kamra.

The powerplant is a 4-cylinder Thielert Centurion engine, which originated in Germany and is based on a Mercedes Benz OM668 engine. As an illustration of the inescapably international nature of the aerospace business, Thielert was sold in 2013 to Continental Engines of the United States, which itself is now a part of the state-owned Aviation Industry Corporation of China (AVIC).

A Turkish Aerospace Industries Anka Medium Altitude Long Endurance (MALE) UAV on display at the 2014 Farnborough Air Show (MilborneOne, licensed under Creative Commons)

The Turkish Aerospace Industries Anka bears a strong resemblance to the American General Atomics MQ-9 Reaper, though it is somewhat smaller. Both are designed to operate in a strike configuration. (Turkish Aerospace Industries)

As with unmanned aerial vehicles in American service, the Turkish Air Force groups its drones into "systems," consisting of multiple aircraft (in this case three) controlled by a single control center. When the Anka entered service in January 2013, the plan was to acquire 10 systems, including 30 aircraft.

In May 2013, Turkish Aerospace rolled out the Anka +A, the armed UCAV variant. Powered by turbocharged engines, the production model of this vehicle had a gross weight of 4 tons, compared to 1.5 tons for the Anka A used for ISTAR missions. Armament included Turkish-made Roketsan Cirit 70mm laser-guided air-to-ground missiles. Six feet long and weighing 33 pounds, the Cirit is about the same length, but a third the weight of an American AGM-114 Hellfire missile, standard armament for Predators and Reapers. Like the Hellfire, the Cirit can accommodate a range of warheads, from high explosive to incendiary to anti-armor.

By 2016, the Turkish Ministry of Defense had confirmed the Anka A to be flying operational reconnaissance missions, though operational Anka +A attack missions had not yet been officially disclosed.

The penultimate builder of Turkish tactical drones is Baykar Makina. A family-owned engineering firm started in Istanbul in 1984, they originally specialized in precision motors and pumps for the automotive industry; today, Baykar is active in fields from biomedical to aviation. The latter includes command and control interface systems, electromechanical servo actuators, electric power units, flight control systems for various classes of fixed-wing and rotary-wing unmanned aerial vehicles, mission computer systems, and automated takeoff and landing systems.

The company's promotional literature draws attention to ongoing relationships with technical institutions such as Adana-based Cucurova University, and Yildiz Technical University in Istanbul, where Baykar was involved in the "Three Redundant Development of Tactical Class Flight Control System Software Components" project.

Entering the field of complete UAV systems in the first decade of the 21st Century, Baykar delivered Turkey's first indigenous mini-UAV to the Turkish armed forces in 2007. Over the ensuing decade, the company delivered more than 75 Bayraktar Mini UAVs, grouped into 19 systems. With a 2012 sale to the Qatar armed forces, the Bayraktar Mini UAV became the first Turkish UAV to be exported.

In 2009, Baykar rolled out its Bayraktar TB2 tactical MALE UAV, developed in cooperation with the Istanbul-based Kale Group in the space of just two years, much more expeditiously than many comparable MALE UAVs, notably the multi-national European MALE program that languished for a decade.

The Bayraktar Block A aircraft made its first autonomous flight on June 8, 2009, at Kesan Airport, about 125 miles west of Istanbul near the Greek border. Flying out of Sinop on the Black Sea north of Ankara, the aircraft made its first night flight four months later. The development of the Bayraktar Block B production variant began in January 2012, leading to a first flight at Kesan on April 29, 2014.

The Bayraktar TB2 is officially characterized by the Turkish Defense Ministry as a "Tactical UAV Class" to avoid the political discomfort of it being seen as a rival to the larger Anka from government-owned Turkish Aerospace, which is also a pusher prop MALE UAV. By comparison, the Bayraktar has a wingspan of 39.3 feet, compared to 56.7 feet for the Anka, and has a maximum takeoff weight of 1,433 pounds, only 40 percent the weight of the Anka. In addition to size, obvious differences in appearance include the Anka having a Reaper-like V-tail, while the Bayraktar has a twin-boom layout supporting an A-frame (or inverted V) tail.

While the Anka is powered by a Thielert Centurion, Baykar chose the Rotax 912 piston engine (the same engine that powers the Pakistani Shahpar and a cousin to the American Predator's Rotax 914) to power the Bayraktar TB2.

Both the Anka and Bayraktar are rated for an autonomous flight endurance of 24 hours, but in 2014, the latter became the first to demonstrate this. In June of that year, the Bayraktar also set a Turkish

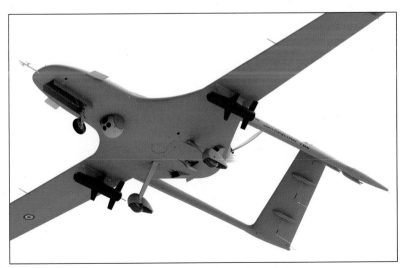

A bottom view of an armed Bayraktar TB2 tactical unmanned combat air vehicle. A Medium Altitude Long Endurance (MALE) class system, it was originally developed for tactical reconnaissance and surveillance missions. (Baykar Makina)

UAV altitude record by operating with a full payload at 27,030 feet.

While the Turkish armed forces deploy the Anka in systems of three vehicles and a ground station, the Bayraktar TB2 system is twice that size, consisting of six and two, respectively, plus three ground data terminals and two remote video terminals. Containing redundant command and control systems, the ground control station supports a staff of three: the pilot, the payload operator, and the mission commander.

The aircraft itself is equipped with redundant rotary and linear servo actuators supported with triple alternators powered by lithium ion batteries. The avionics sustain autonomous operations, including autonomous emergency landings at alternate airfields. Operations are monitored through a tail-mounted, heated camera, while payload and telemetry data are recorded to an onboard data recorder.

While the Bayraktar TB2 was initially deployed as a reconnaissance aircraft, there had always been a plan for it to be adapted for offensive weapons delivery. As such, the aircraft was first tested as an unmanned combat air vehicle in December 2015, successfully firing Roketsan MAM-L smart munitions and Roketsan Mizrak-U 160mm guided air-to-surface missiles.

The latter weapon was developed in the second decade of the 21st Century under the program known as Uzun Menzilli Tanksavar Sistemi (UMTAS) in Turkish, or Long Range Anti-tank Missile (LRAT) in English. Designed principally to arm attack helicopters, the Mizrak-U is 5.7 feet long, roughly comparable to the Roketsan Cirit or the American Hellfire, and weighs 82.7 pounds, compared to around 100 pounds (depending upon configuration) for the Hellfire. While the Hellfire is radar guided, the Mizrak-U uses either laser or homing infrared guidance.

In South Africa, Denel Dynamics (Kentron until 2004) is a leading producer of missiles, target drones, and other munitions, and more recently of unmanned aerial vehicles. It is part of the Denel conglomerate whose aviation component conducts maintenance and modification work on a broad range of international aircraft, and which is the originator of the Rooivalk attack helicopter.

Denel Dynamics is located in the Irene district of Centurion (formerly Verwoerdburg), a city midway between Pretoria and Johannesburg. Centurion is home to both AFB Swartkop and AFB Waterkloof, the latter being the principal base of the South African Air Force.

Denel's military unmanned systems follow two distinctive tracks. On one side are high-speed target drones characterized by the Skua, and on the other are light reconnaissance UAVs illustrated by the Seeker.

The Skua is a Mach .86 jet-propelled target drone designed for zero-length launches from land or from ships or sea. Being 19.5 feet long with a wingspan of 11.6 feet, it is comparable in purpose and appearance to, and slightly larger than, the American Beechcraft/Raytheon MQM-107 Streaker. When Iran developed its Karrar (Striker) unmanned combat air vehicle, basing it on the MQM-107, it made the tail of the aircraft a direct copy of that of the Denel Skua.

The Seeker family of drones are small, twin-boomed, piston-engined, pusher prop UAVs similar in appearance to the familiar IAI Hunter and Pioneer configuration. The family dates back to 1986 and their operational use during the long border war fought by the South African Defence Force against Angolan rebels and Cuban expeditionary forces. They provided reconnaissance and artillery spotting services, and achieved unanticipated success in compelling the enemy to expend their limited supply of surface-to-air missiles in order to protect mobile missile sites.

The original Seeker I was withdrawn from military service in 1994 but remained in non-military government service with such agencies as the Department of Environmental Affairs and Tourism. The Seeker II variant was designed for military export, finding customers in the air forces of Algeria and the United Arab Emirates. The Seeker II evolved into the Seeker 200 tactical Unmanned Aerial System marketed by Denel with state-of-the-art avionics, Automatic Take-off and Landing (ATOL) capability, and an electro-optical multi-sensor payload.

The Seeker 400 incorporates numerous improvements over earlier variants, including real-time day and night reconnaissance and electronic intelligence capabilities, an 18,000-foot service ceiling, and an endurance of 16 hours with a 200-pound payload. The Seeker 400 is also designed to be an unmanned combat air vehicle capable of firing laser-guided missiles from a stand-off distance of 6 miles.

Working with the Seeker 400, Denel's unmanned Tracking and Communications Unit (TCU) facilitates dual payload operation and transmission of high-definition imagery and can be located 650 feet from the manned control center, providing a measure of safety in an environment where there is a threat of an air strike.

Denel also produces the Hungwe, a scaled down, catapult-launched, skid-landed surveillance UAV that is advertised as being useful in border patrol, anti-piracy, and search-and-rescue operations. It is also optimized for a mission largely unique to Africa: surveillance of wild animal parks.

In April 2004, Denel was also one of the first companies outside the United States to undertake development of a large-scale MALE UAV. Named "Bateleur," after the eagle of that name, the project was company-funded, with limited interest having been expressed by the South African Air Force. A full-scale mockup was displayed five months later in September 2004 at an air show held at AFB Waterkloof. The aircraft had a wingspan of 49 feet 3 inches, making it roughly a third the size of the Northrop Grumman RQ-4 Global Hawk MALE reconnaissance UAV. Endurance parameters in the 18–24-hour range and a payload capacity of 1,000 pounds were mentioned.

According to the South African journal *Engineering News*, "The original conception for the Bateleur included use of existing and proven systems and subsystems from Denel's Seeker II tactical UAV and Skua high-speed target drone, as well as commercial off-the-shelf equipment, in order to keep development costs down. For example, the idea was that the Bateleur would use the same ground control station as the Seeker II."

At the time, it seemed like an aircraft such as the Bateleur had a promising future, not only in South African service, but in the export market where a MALE UAV with a lesser price tag than a Global Hawk would have been an attractive investment.

Maryke Lynn of *Ad Astra* magazine noted that "an overseas partner is currently contributing to the development funding while a number of overseas parties have already expressed their interest in the development. These are being actively followed up and the local client, the [South African Navy and South African Air Force], are being targeted in terms of their imminent Maritime and coastal Patrol Aircraft (MPA) requirement. An experienced five-man team from Denel Aviation has temporarily relocated to the Aerospace Systems Irene premises and are currently forming an integral and essential part of the [Bateleur] design and development team. Denel Aviation will be responsible for the design and manufacture of the airframe production tooling and the aim is to embark on a first test flight program during the first half of 2007 with initial operational capability possibly being achieved during 2010."

Emphasizing the maritime role of the Bateleur, she went on to point out that "drug and other contraband smuggling across our long coastline is rife and piracy in busy sea lanes is on a worldwide

The mass delivery of Bayraktar TB2 unmanned aircraft in June 2015. They were handed over to the Turkish 4th Mechanized Infantry Brigade at Kesan Airport. (Baykar Makina)

The first combat-capable Bayraktar TB2 vehicle was delivered in December 2015, armed with Roketsan UMTAS anti-tank missiles. (Baykar Makina)

increase. [UAVs] will soon form part of a credible deterrent to illegal operators and as such be an essential link in the protection of [South Africa's] coastline and borders as well as playing a significant role in fulfilling national intelligence requirements."

In July 2008, *Engineering News* reported that a deal involving a Bateleur acquisition by Brazil was imminent. The magazine cited as its source Brazilian Air Force Colonel Nelson Silveira, the Brazilian project officer on the joint South African–Brazilian program that was developing Denel's A-Darter infrared homing air-to-air missile.

Silveira revealed that "a memorandum of understanding on cooperation on UAVs was signed between the two countries a year ago. An initial South African proposal regarding the Bateleur was made to the commander of the Brazilian Air Force in mid-May. The Brazilians are expecting to receive a full proposal, including time frames and cost estimates, from South Africa in the near future. This joint UAV project would be modeled on the current joint A-Darter project, which is proving highly successful."

However, no first flight for the Bateleur came in 2007 as once hoped, nor indeed in 2010. The interest by the air forces of South Africa and Brazil faded, and the Bateleur disappeared from the Denel website.

Since the turn of the 21st Century, the United Arab Emirates have emerged as a major player in the global arms market, first as a base for venture capitalist investment firms and later as a home to actual manufacturers. The latter include makers of systems from electronics to firearms and, more recently, of UAVs and UCAVs. The latter business is seen as being a potentially very lucrative one of the UAE for several reasons. First, the reluctance of the United States to allow international sales of armed drone technology, and second, the difficulty that European manufacturers have had in completing complex unmanned programs, as witnessed by the troubled European MALE program discussed in Chapter 9.

This has opened the way for a business opportunity for UAE firms. As Gareth Jennings, an analyst at IHS Jane's told Marietta Cauchi of the *Wall Street Journal* in November 2013, "Most of Europe has a dearth of viable working MALE UAVs to offer the export or even its own domestic market. It seems to be a field in which the Middle East feels it can gain a foothold in the export market."

The Roketsan UMTAS (Uzun Menzilli Tanksavar Sistemi), or Mizrak-U, is a long-range air-to-surface anti-tank missile. It is seen here mounted on a Turkish-built T129 attack helicopter at the 2014 Farnborough Air Show. (MilborneOne, licensed under Creative Commons)

A good cutaway drawing of the Bayraktar TB2 Medium Altitude Long Endurance (MALE) unmanned combat air vehicle. (Baykar Makina)

An overview of the avionics systems developed by Baykar Makina for its tactical UAVs. (Baykar Makina)

The following labels appear with the avionics systems above:

Flight Control Computer — Power Distribution System — Mission Control Computer — Actively Balanced Lithium Battery System

INS System — Pitot-Statik Data Unit — Magnetometer Unit — Sensor Board

GPS Receiver — Inertial Measurement Unit — Control Surface Linear Servo Actuator — Control Surface Rotary Actuator

Dual Redundant Servo Actuator — Landing Gear Linear Actuator — Landing Gear Rotary Actuator — Brake System Linear Actuator

Rotary Actuator — Data Recorder — Ruggedized Camera — Heated Pitot Static Sensor

An important example of a UAE firm filling the void is Tawazun Holding of Abu Dhabi, the company that financed development of Italy's Piaggio Hammerhead MALE reconnaissance and armed combat drone. Not exactly a household name, Tawazun is a strategic investment firm "focused on the long-term development of Abu Dhabi's industrial manufacturing and technology capabilities and knowledge-transfer with a specific focus on the defense sector."

The aim of Tawazun is to make Abu Dhabi "the Middle Eastern expert hub for strategic manufacturing." Formed in 2007, the company develops ventures through industrial partnerships, strategic investments, and putting together complex multi-party deals. Tawazun also manufactures locally in the UAE. Its Abu Dhabi Autonomous Systems Investments (ADASI) division, through which the Hammerhead financing was funneled, also manufactures the Al Sabr rotary-wing surveillance drone that is a spinoff of Austria's Schiebel S-100 rotary-wing drone.

In addition to ADASI, Tawazun owns Caracal International, the region's leading manufacturer of firearms, sniper rifles, and other light weapons.

Across Abu Dhabi, only 11 miles south and west of Tawazun's downtown headquarters in the Mussafah district, is a sprawling industrial park that is home to Adcom Systems, which began operations in 1989. A consortium of more than a dozen smaller firms with expertise ranging from radar to missile technology, Adcom specializes in both target drones and surveillance UAVs with its Yabhon family of aircraft, some of which are being adapted as unmanned combat air vehicles.

In an interview with Ayesha al-Khoori published in the February 19, 2013, issue of the English-language Abu Dhabi daily *The National*, the company's strategic plans were discussed by Adcom's Ali al-Dhaheri, the CEO of Adcom Systems and the man credited with designing the company's aircraft.

"Our manufacturing industries are advanced," he explained. "Israel and the United States are the only countries who can manufacture similar drones. Being able to create drones like them means we are also advanced in this field. . . . The drones' purpose is to aid in disasters, civil use, border control, traffic control, and city control. We are peaceful people but the drones can also be used in military services and war zones, hence the addition of the missiles. The aircraft is built to certified standards from the United States, so the quality, according to aviation, is very high and is used for long-term aircraft use."

Most of the aircraft in Adcom's Yabhon-H and Yabhon-R series are canard-configuration reconnaissance UAVs with piston engines driving pusher props. The smallest is the Yabhon-H, with double delta wings with laminar airfoils spanning 10.76 feet. The Yabhon-R and Yabhon-R2 MALE long-range reconnaissance UAVs have wingspans of 21.3 feet and 27.89 feet, respectively, and endurance ratings of 27 and 30 hours. The smaller Yabhon-RX, with a wingspan of 19 feet, has a twin-boom configuration, an endurance of just 6 hours, and is rail-launched for search-and-rescue or border control missions. Adcom's Smart Eye 1 tactical surveillance drone also has a shorter endurance of 6 hours; its configuration features a double pair of wings, both spanning 14.4 feet.

Adcom has also developed two larger, longer-endurance MALE drones designed for, as the company describes them, "strategic missions," including border surveillance, communications relay, special operations, and "intelligence preparation of the battlefield."

These aircraft are the (unnumbered) Smart Eye, which has a twin-boom configuration like the Yabhon-RX, and the United 40, which has a double-wing configuration like that of the Smart Eye 1. The United 40 was so-named because it was developed in 2011, the 40th anniversary of the formation of the United Arab Emirates. Adcom credits the ultra-long endurance of 120 hours of both aircraft to glider-like, high-aspect ratio wings that span 68.9 feet in the case of the Smart Eye and 65.61 feet for the United 40. The two

A Denel Dynamics Seeker 400 UAV flies over Cape Town Stadium in June 2013. The venue was built for the 2010 FIFA World Cup and represents modern structures as observed in high-altitude surveillance today. (DanieB52, licensed under Creative Commons)

A Denel Dynamics Skua target drone on display at Africa Aerospace and Defence 2012, an exposition held at AFB Waterkloof, Pretoria, South Africa. (Darren Olivier, licensed under Creative Commons)

The Yabhon-R is a United Arab Emirates UAV designed for short takeoff and landing using semi-prepared short runways. It can land on wheels or by emergency parachute system. (Adcom Systems)

The Smart Eye is a Medium Altitude Long Endurance (MALE) UAV designed and manufactured in the United Arab Emirates by Adcom Systems for strategic missions, including special operations and reconnaissance, as well as border surveillance and communications relay. (Adcom Systems)

The snake-like Smart Eye 1 is described by Adcom as "a high-performance UAV optimized for efficient cruise with high-aspect-ratio wings and laminar airfoils. The flying qualities are superb, it is very stable, good turbulence resistance and docile stall." (Adcom Systems)

types can each carry two gimbaled camera platforms and a wide range of payload sensors including infrared, thermal imaging, and electro-optical.

Early United 40 aircraft have a single hybrid engine driving a pusher propeller, but the Block 5 variant has two 115-hp engines beneath the forward wings driving tractor propellers. This variant is also confirmed to be an unmanned *combat* air vehicle. At the Abu Dhabi International Defense Exhibition (IDEX) in February 2013, Silvia Radan of the Dubai-based *Khaleej Times* spoke with al-Dhaheri, reporting that she had learned that the Block 5 variant, with "its futuristic aerodynamics . . . can carry 10 missiles on board, each one having a [37-mile] range and [621-mph] speed . . . It can fly more than 100 hours without refueling at a 30,000-foot altitude. It is very reliable, has twin engines, six fly control units, and over 400 channels of communications."

Six of the Namrood-1 missiles are carried internally on a rotary launcher and the other four are mounted on underwing pylons. It has been reported more recently that earlier United 40 variants were also armed in a similar way.

Also displayed in mockup form at IDEX in 2013 was Adcom's Global Yabhon, a 26,000-pound aircraft similar in configuration to the United 40 Block 5 that would be powered by a pair of underwing-mounted turbofan engines. As the name suggests, it would be a potential competitor to the Northrop Grumman Global Hawk, though it could also function as an armed UCAV.

The United 40 Block 6 aircraft, introduced at IDEX in 2015, is a naval variant that is equipped for anti-submarine warfare with sonobuoys and a single lightweight torpedo mounted on the centerline of the fuselage. This aircraft was developed in cooperation with Italy's Finmeccanica (now Leonardo), especially its Whitehead Alenia Sistemi Subacquei division.

Al-Dhaheri has also mentioned an aircraft called the Yabhon NSR, a probable variant of the Yabhon-R, that is not mentioned on the company's current website.

"It actually hunts the Yabhon United 40," said al-Dhaheri. "It is the first one in the world to hunt UAVs. It has an advanced auto-tracking system, being capable of image tracking and downloading video to the user, and also capable of automatic engage and destroy operation."

In March 2015, Chris Biggers of the UK-based investigative journalism site *Bellingcat* provided a rundown of some of the export marketing that Adcom had done for its United 40 UCAV, relating that "the Russian military reported the purchase of two Block 5s with a service entry date around 2016. . . . Beyond Russia, Algeria was considering the purchase of the aircraft for its intelligence, surveillance, and reconnaissance requirement. . . . Adcom has also offered several United 40 systems to the United Nations for use on humanitarian missions. Selex, a subsidiary of Adcom partner Finmeccanica, also supports United Nations border surveillance missions in the Democratic Republic of the Congo with the Falco system."

Biggers goes on to speculate that "possibly due to a lack of military sales for its flagship drone, teaming with Finmeccanica could have been a strategic move to follow the partner into a new market segment. In a presentation made at the Berlin Airshow 2014, Adcom reiterated the use of drones for NGOs engaged in wildlife conservation and governments requiring critical infrastructure monitoring."

In 2015, al-Dhaheri unveiled Adcom's small Flash 20 surveillance drone. "I call that aircraft a whale tracker," he said with tongue in cheek. "It flies for 60 or 70 hours, which would be nice for whale tracking."

Obviously, there are also a good many other things (*military* things) at sea that a drone with that kind of endurance could also track.

In November 2015 Angus Batey of *Aviation Week* reported that Adcom was in talks aimed at international collaborative efforts. They had already partnered with DO Systems Ltd., self-described as a "special mission solutions provider" based in Bournemouth aimed at

manufacturing and flight test operations in the UK, probably in Wales.

"Adcom Systems is a world champion now in UAVs," Ali al-Dhaheri told Batey. "I am very impressed with the Welsh government and the people there. They're eager to have the technologies of unmanned aircraft. It's progressing very well. . . . India has a big interest in all our products. We are now in the process of creating the company and working with the government there. And Saudi Arabia is coming along very well. These technologies have to be established in the country, and it's not simple. We need to educate and train people to set up manufacture. But we are very fast; we can set up manufacture in six months."

If (and that's an important qualifier) the UAVs and UCAVs being developed in the United Arab Emirates really do match the claims of technical sophistication third only to the United States and Israel, then it could be that Abu Dhabi may emerge as one of the world's leading and most unlikely centers of combat aircraft development.

Inside an Adcom "full luxury" Ground Control Station (GCS). Capable of operating multiple drones simultaneously, it is contained within a truck that is equipped with sleeping berths as well as a kitchen. (Adcom Systems)

The Adcom United 40 XP is a Medium Altitude Long Endurance (MALE) that is designed for reconnaissance as well as strike missions. This one, marketed for maritime operations, is shown armed with an air-to-surface missile, as well as a torpedo. (Adcom Systems)

UNMANNED AERIAL
COMBAT TECHNOLOGY IN CHINA

In no country on earth is the growth in UAVs and UCAVs mushrooming at a faster pace than in China. Indeed, that country is already emerging as one of the world's leading centers of all forms of combat aircraft development. In 2010, there were around 100 entities developing or manufacturing UAVs in China. Just five years later, that number had more than doubled, with two-thirds of them being private enterprises. Indeed, many (if not *most*) of the sophisticated drones being sold to the hobbyist market in the United States are of Chinese origin.

Large scale unmanned aerial vehicle research and development in China takes place within established industrial concerns, some state-owned, as well as at universities, where proof-of-concept aircraft are designed and built on a much broader scale than at western universities. In turn, military UAVs and UCAVs are further developed as well as being fielded by the Chinese military establishment, the People's Liberation Army (PLA), which incorporates the PLA Air Force, and the PLA Navy.

The state-owned Aviation Industry Corporation of China (AVIC) is one of the country's leading aerospace companies. AVIC dates to 1951 and was among the first aircraft manufacturing entities formed by the Communist government of the People's Republic of China. Based in Beijing, AVIC is now a major aerospace and defense holding company that ranks in the top third of the Fortune 500 list of global companies. A major subsidiary is the Shenyang Aircraft Corporation, also known as Shenyang Aerospace, based in the city of the same name.

One of China's first high-performance unmanned *combat* air vehicles was the Guizhou WZ-2000 (Wu Zhen 2000). The project originated in 1999 with the Guizhou Aviation Industry Group (GAIC), another AVIC subsidiary. GAIC is best known for its manned aircraft, including an upgraded variant of the Chengdu J-7, the Chinese-built version of the old Soviet MiG-21. Guizhou's eclectic activities include an automobile-manufacturing joint venture with Subaru of Japan. Making its first flight in December 2003, the WZ-2000 bears a striking resemblance to the Northrop Grumman RQ-4 Global Hawk.

Another Chinese jet UCAV program is the HW/WJ-600 series produced by the Beijing-based China Aerospace Science and Industry

A Cai Hong (Rainbow) CH-3 unmanned combat air vehicle armed with a pair of AR-1 laser-guided ground attack missiles flying a low-level maritime patrol mission. With a configuration similar to that of the manned Rutan VariEze, the CH-3 is a product of the China Aerospace Science and Technology Corporation (CASC). (Chang Hsiao-liang)

The Warrior Eagle (Zhan-Ying) is a stealthy, flying wing unmanned aerial vehicle with forward-swept wings that is reportedly capable of strike missions. It is part of the 601-S family of Chinese UAVs developed jointly by the Aviation Industry Corporation of China (AVIC) and Shenyang Aerospace University. (Chang Hsiao-liang)

Corporation (CASIC). Dating back to a predecessor that originated in 1956 as a producer of tactical missile systems, CASIC is best known today as a principal contractor for China's space program. As such, it produces both spacecraft and launch vehicles, while still remaining active as China's leading producer of both strategic and tactical missiles, including cruise missiles. The HW-600 is understood to be a reconnaissance aircraft, with the ground attack UCAV variant being designated as WJ-600, the prefix standing for Wu Jian, a shortened rendering of "Wu-Ren Jian-Ji-Ji," which means "fighter with no pilot."

The AVIC 601-S series of low-observable UAVs jointly developed by the Shenyang Aircraft Corporation in cooperation with Shenyang Aerospace University are among China's prominent drones. So varied are the aircraft within this family that Stephen Trimble of *FlightGlobal* has described the 601-S family as China's "internal pipeline of military aircraft demonstrators."

"Flying wings are a holy grail for aerodynamicists seeking to optimize lift, and for electromagnetic frequency experts seeking to minimize the structural corners that are easy reflectors of radar waves," Trimble writes in a May 2013 *FlightGlobal* article on Chinese unmanned aerial vehicles. "Chinese industry has been focusing on the problems of tailless, flying wing designs for several years. Shenyang engineers, for example, published an academic paper in 2007 entitled *Application of Flying Wing Configuration to UCAV for Recon-*

naissance, which concluded that such a tailless design is 'an optimal selection' for aerodynamic purposes."

The 601-S Sky Crossbow (Tian-Nu) was a small experimental proof-of-concept flying wing unmanned aerial vehicle design upon which the series was later built. With twin tails for flight stability, it was nicknamed *si duo-mian fei-yi jia shuang-chui-wei* (flying wing with twin tail). The Crossbow is 7 feet long, with a wingspan of 7.2 feet, and weighs close to 50 pounds. It is powered by an electrically powered ducted fan engine.

The Wind Blade (Feng-Ren) was essentially the same size as the earlier Sky Crossbow, but differed in that the twin tail was replaced by winglets. A variant of the Wind Blade design was adapted by the Nanjing University of Aeronautics and Astronautics as a flying wing demonstrator. The next step in the progression of AVIC 601-S designs was the Cloud Bow (Yungong). It was similar to the early aircraft except that the vertical control surfaces were now eliminated, given that flight control could be achieved entirely with the wing.

The Warrior Eagle (Zhan-Ying) was a departure from its AVIC 601-S predecessors in that it was much larger and had forward-swept wings. Though it remains a classified program and is said to be a demonstrator, there is a great deal of speculation in the Chinese aerospace media community that the Warrior Eagle may have been the first AVIC 601-S aircraft to be deployed on operational reconnaissance missions and to also have an unmanned combat capability.

The first AVIC 601-S drone to be *confirmed* as having had an operational role is the Keen Sword or Sharp Sword (Lijian) large, stealthy unmanned aerial vehicle, which was developed jointly by Shenyang in cooperation with the Hongdu Aviation Industry Group (HAIG). Having made its debut flight on November 21, 2013, at Nanchang in southern China, the Keen Sword is a tailless flying wing similar in appearance to the Boeing X-45A; but with a wingspan of 45.5 feet, it is noticeably larger. The Keen Sword is also often compared to the Northrop Grumman X-47B.

With some degree of overstatement, the Chinese daily paper *Global Times* noted "intense media coverage in the West" over the "sword of China's first stealth drone."

The Beijing-based *Science and Technology Daily*, less given to hyperbole, reported that the aircraft fuselage and wing are manufactured from composite materials, and that the Keen Sword's "belly magazine was specially designed with automatic tracking and surveillance functions." The paper adds that "China has included a new flight control and navigation technology, radio data-link technologies, dedicated power technology . . . automatic takeoff, autonomous navigation, automatic implementation of precision attack munition, and powerful features such as automatic landing."

As Li Xiaojian wrote for China's *Xinhua News*, the "blended wing body layout, extensive use of composite materials and processes, [provides] the Keen Sword with a very low radar signal so you can high-value precision strike ground targets deep behind enemy lines. . . . This 'trump card,' is not available in active duty fighters in China . . . [although] tail vent temperature leads to increased probability of infrared sensor detection by the enemy."

Stephen Trimble agrees, writing that the Keen Sword "does not appear designed for reduced visibility to radar in all aspects: the nozzle of a large, possibly afterburning, jet engine lies exposed and unshrouded on the aft fuselage, an easy target for detection by radar. Similar limitations appear on all of China's purportedly stealthy aircraft released to date, including the Chengdu J-20 and Shenyang J-31."

Li goes on to say that "in terms of unmanned combat aerial systems, development is also flying high, with high-resolution remote-sensing satellites that can obtain the key area of high-precision digital mapping to make unmanned combat aircraft capable of precision tasks and route planning."

The Keen Sword navigational interface is integrated with the BeiDou Navigation Satellite System (BDS), a Chinese satellite navigation system consisting of two separate constellations of satellites within a system that has been operating since 2000. Named for the constellation Ursus Major, or Big Dipper (BeiDou in Chinese), the system differs from the American GPS, Russian GLONASS, and European Galileo navigation systems in that it uses satellites in geostationary orbit, rather than satellites in medium Earth orbit. This allows for a system with fewer satellites, but it does limit coverage to a narrow geographic area, in this case China and parts of India, Japan, and Southeast Asia.

"Compared with manned aircraft, unmanned aerial vehicle bomb-carrying capacity is limited," Li Xiaojian writes, explaining the Keen Sword weapons capability. "The most suitable weapons are similar to United States' precision-guided small diameter bomb (SDB). At the Zhuhai Air Show, there were exhibited a number of small-diameter bombs, which can rely on the BeiDou navigation

Seen taking off is the Lijian unmanned combat aircraft, whose name is translated variously as Sharp Sword or Keen Sword. With a configuration similar to that of an American X-47B, it was apparently designed to be low-observable to radar, though its prominent engine exhaust, possibly an afterburner, ruins its stealth contour. It is part of the 601-S family of Chinese UAVs. (Chang Hsiao-liang)

system, especially the CM-506 small-diameter glide bomb, which uses terminal active homing guidance method, with a range of up to [80 miles]."

When Li asked about unmanned aerial refueling for the Keen Sword and the company's other unmanned aerial vehicles, AVIC's "experts said the technology was 'not a problem.'"

He went on to say that with aerial refueling "future UAVs can fly in the sky for several days, and their operational effectiveness will increase exponentially . . . with high stealth, long endurance, low cost, and other advantages, the Keen Sword would be suitable for a high risk area in silent reconnaissance and surveillance missions."

The AVIC Dark Sword (Anjian) unmanned aerial vehicle was developed in cooperation with the China National Aviation Corporation (CNAC), the state-owned company whose principal business is in airline operations. The Anjian utilizes earlier 601-S technology, but its airframe design differs greatly, appearing to have been inspired by a hypersonic research drone such as the American X-43 or X-51, rather than a flying wing form. Indeed, the developers have indicated that the Anjian is destined to be, or evolve into, a hypersonic demonstrator. In turn, it is seen long term as a step toward a hypersonic reconnaissance, or even a strike, vehicle. Also of note is the company statement that "high mobility of the drone is the greatest technical advantage." High maneuverability is noted as being provided by canards.

The shape-varying 601-S series unmanned aerial vehicle known as Bian-ti Wu-ren-ji is another flying wing intended to be a proof-of-concept vehicle. Its design, like that of the variable geometry aircraft of the 20th Century, allows inflight reconfiguration for differing flight environments. The theory behind the Bian-ti Wu-ren-ji is based on the principal that greater wingspan provides better stability at low speed.

The Dark Sword (Anjian) unmanned aerial vehicle was designed with speed and maneuverability taking precedence over stealth characteristics. It is part of the 601-S family of Chinese UAVs developed jointly by the Aviation Industry Corporation of China (AVIC) and Shenyang Aerospace University. (Chang Hsiao-liang)

Instead of a variable-sweep configuration, the wings can be folded to change the *shape* to adjust the aircraft. While this is similar in purpose to the familiar variable geometry concept, the degree of variation is greater. It has been suggested that the folding technology is ideal for aircraft carrier operations.

Aircraft carrier operations, long an interest of the Chinese PLA Navy, have become a higher priority in the second decade of the 21st Century. Beginning in 1985, China acquired four retired aircraft carriers, one from Australia and three from post-Soviet Russia. Of these, two became private tourist parks, while the former HMAS *Melbourne* (which had infamously collided with and sank an Australian and an American destroyer) was studied by the PLA Navy but was eventually scrapped. The former Soviet *Varyag* was recommissioned by the PLA Navy in 2012 as the CNS *Liaoning*. Thereafter, the PLA Navy undertook work on two Chinese-built carriers, the CNS *Dalian* and CNS *Jiangnan*. While the core complement of warplanes aboard these ships will be the manned Sukhoi Su-33s and Shenyang J-15s, unmanned aerial vehicle operations are considered an important part of future plans.

While many institutions are involved in potential carrier-based unmanned aerial vehicles, the Beihang University of Aeronautics and Astronautics is among a handful looking at submarine-based submersible UAVs. These are inspired by the early 21st Century DARPA program that led to the Lockheed Martin Cormorant folding-wing aircraft, which was tested extensively before the project was canceled in 2008.

The creation of the Cruise Sky (Xuntian) unmanned aerial vehicle design group, the Booby (Jianniao) was publicly revealed in 2012 as the first Chinese UAV capable of an *underwater* launch. First seen in 2012 is the XC-1 Flying Shuttle (Fei-Suo) underwater unmanned aerial vehicle, which was designed at the Civil Aviation University of China (CAUC).

Sometimes confused with the Beijing-based China Aerospace Science and Industry Corporation (CASIC) is the China Aerospace Science and Technology Corporation (CASC), a state-owned entity formed in 1999 and also centered in Beijing, which is active within a broad range of industries, including chemicals, communications, computers, environmental protection, medical care, and transportation equipment, which develop products and services primarily for the non-military market.

CASC is also known for its Rainbow (Cai Hong) family of unmanned aerial vehicles. The first two Cai Hongs were the CH-1 and CH-2, twin-boom, pusher prop surveillance aircraft with 14-foot wingspans. Created by designer Shi Wen, they made their debut around the turn of the century. The CH-2 was designed to be launched from a vehicle-mounted catapult using rocket-assisted takeoff.

The larger CH-3 and CH-4 aircraft also utilize pusher props, but have entirely different overall configurations than the earlier Cai Hongs, or each other. The canard layout of the CH-3 is obviously similar to that of the manned American Rutan VariEze and Long-EZ homebuilt kit aircraft of the 1970s. As with the Rutan aircraft, there are large winglets, but no vertical tail surfaces. The CH-4 has straight wings and a V-tail similar to that of the American General Atomics MQ-9 Reaper or the Turkish Aerospace Anka. What these two Cai Hongs have in common is that they started out as reconnaissance aircraft, and are now both being produced for the Peoples' Liberation Army explicitly as unmanned *combat* air vehicles.

As late as 2012, when the CH-4 was unveiled at the Zuhai Air Show, it was still assumed that the CH-3 and CH-4 would remain as surveillance aircraft and would be operated by the non-military sector. In the November 26 issue of *Aviation Week*, Bradley Perrett wrote that unlike AVIC, "which is working on combat drones, CASC's unmanned-aircraft specialist, the China Academy of Aerospace Aerodynamics in Beijing, concentrates on surveillance types. The CH-4,

fairly clearly, was not developed under a military contract, because the group has publicly exhibited it while it is still new."

He quoted Academy sources as saying that the CH-4 "suits such functions as border patrol, island protection, anti-terror missions and emergency communications. The aircraft can take off and land automatically and execute programmed flight."

When it came to weapons capability, CASC confidently told Perrett that "this is not a complex technology for us."

When the CH-4 made what was announced as its "maiden test flight" in September 2014, Li Pingkun, CASC's CH-4 project leader, told *ChinaNews.com* that "the test flight was very successful today. During acceleration and deceleration, the drone kept taxing on a central line on the runway. It's well-positioned to carry out the subsequent missions."

The aircraft carrier CNS Liaoning *was originally built in 1988 in the Soviet Union as the* Riga. *She was sold to China in 1998, later completely refitted, and commissioned into the PLA Navy in 2012. The Chinese are actively developing a large range of unmanned aerial vehicles that are compatible with carrier operations. (Simon Yang, licensed under Creative Commons)*

Meanwhile, *Airforce Technology* reported that the debut flight included "simulation target practice at an undisclosed location."

The CH-3 has a wingspan of 26 feet, a 12-hour endurance, and a payload capacity for offensive armament of up to 175 pounds. The CH-3A variant, meanwhile, can carry up to 400 pounds of ordnance, though its endurance with a full load is reduced to 6 hours. The armament can include AR-1 laser-guided ground attack missiles, as well as YC-200 guided bombs. The CH-3A also has an improved satellite datalink control system.

China's first known export customer for the CH-3 UCAV was the Nigerian armed forces, with whom they were soon being used in striker against the Islamic militant group Boku Haram. The crash of a CH-3 in January 2015 was reported by international media (including photos of the inverted wreck complete with missiles mounted on its underwing pylons) before Nigerian authorities were able to secure the largely intact remains.

The turboprop-powered CH-4, CASC's largest operational unmanned aerial vehicle, has a wingspan of 59.1 feet and a maximum takeoff weight of 2,930 pounds. It is produced in a reconnaissance configuration under the designation CH-4A and as a ground attack UCAV as the CH-4B. The former, classed as a Medium Altitude Long Endurance (MALE) UAV, has an endurance of up to 30 hours. The latter has an endurance of 14 hours with a payload capacity of up to 761 pounds. Ordnance that can be accommodated includes

air-to-surface missiles, such as the AR-1 and Lan Jian 7, as well as YC200 or TG100 guided bombs.

Like the American AGM-114 Hellfire or the Turkish Cirit, the AR-1 is a laser-guided, multi-purpose air-to-ground missile with an effective range of up to about 5 miles. The AR-1 is 56 inches long, compared to 64 inches for the Hellfire, and can accommodate a variety of warhead types, from high explosive to armor or concrete piercing. The AR-1 is one of a number of weapons that was developed from the Hong Jian (Red Arrow) HJ-10 air-to-surface missile series that was produced for use by Chinese attack helicopters, and which is seen as being the Chinese answer to the Hellfire.

SinoDefence reports that the CH-4 "sensor payloads include an electro-optical turret, which incorporates forward-looking infrared (FLIR), laser rangefinder, and laser designator functions. The turret has a maximum range of [9 miles], and provides target designation for the AR-1 missile throughout its flight. The UAV also carries a Synthetic Aperture Radar (SAR), which has a maximum detection range of [19 miles]. The CH-4 is able to deliver its weaponry from an altitude of [16,404 feet], and the AR-1 missile allows 20 degrees off-boresight launch, giving significantly increased flexibility and much reduced response time in operation."

Export sales of the CH-4B strike variant have been made to Egypt and Saudi Arabia, as well as to Iraq, where the Chinese-made drones have been widely seen operating out of al-Kut Air Base, 100 miles southeast of Baghdad. On October 10, 2015, the Iraqi Ministry of Defence announced what it said was the first use of one of its CH-4s against an Islamic State target in Al-Anbar province. At the same time, a video was released that showed Defense Minister Khalid al-Obaidi inspecting one of the CH-4s at al-Kut.

Nigeria was reportedly China's first export customer for the CH-3 unmanned combat air vehicle. This was confirmed in January 2015 when one crashed in northern Nigeria while in action against Boko Haram militants. (Mamman Vatsa)

A Cai Hong CH-4B unmanned combat air vehicle in service with the Iraqi armed forces. Developed by the China Aerospace Science and Technology Corporation (CASC), the CH-4B bears a strong resemblance to the American MQ-9A Reaper, which has not been exported to Iraq. The CH-4B has provisions for a half-dozen weapons and a payload capacity of up to 750 pounds. It can fire ground attack missiles from an altitude of 16,000 feet. (Iraq Defence Ministry)

A still larger CASC Cai Hong, the CH-5, made its first flight in August 2015. With a gross weight of more than 6,000 pounds, and a payload capacity of nearly 2,000 pounds, it is nearly triple the size of the CH-4.

At the opposite end of the spectrum is the CASC CH-802, a 14-pound reconnaissance micro air vehicle powered by a brushless electric motor driving a tractor propeller.

The CASC/ALIT CH-4 shares the name "Wing Loong" with a similar family of MALE UAVs from the Chengdu Aircraft Industry Group (CAIG). Now an AVIC subsidiary, CAIG was founded in 1958 in the Sichuan Province city of Chengdu as an assembly and modification plant for high-performance combat aircraft being supplied to China by the Soviet Union. Through the late 20th Century, CAIG developed its own combat aircraft and manufactured aircraft parts and subassemblies for others.

The CAIG Wing Loong series of aircraft, characterized by the Pterodactyl I vehicle, are strikingly similar in appearance to the CASC/ALIT aircraft, though they differ significantly in size and performance. Despite this, and despite their separate origins, they are occasionally referenced as being variants of the same aircraft, although because of the closely intertwined nature of the Chinese aerospace industry, they may be more closely related than is apparent.

The Pterodactyl I has a wingspan of 45 feet 11 inches, a quarter of that of the CH-4, while being 29 feet 8 inches long, about 2 feet longer than the CH-4. The faster Pterodactyl has a top speed of 174 mph compared to 146 mph for the CH-4, but its service ceiling of 16,404 feet is 40 percent less than that of the CASC drone.

The CAIG program got off the ground with the first flight in October 2007 by the Pterosaur I UAV. In turn, the program evolved into the Pterodactyl I, which entered service in 2009 and which became the standard variant. In turn, an armed attack Pterodactyl was introduced at the Zhuhai Air Show in November 2014 under the designation WJ-1, with the initials standing for Wu-Zhuang Wu-Ren-Ji, which literally means "unmanned combat air vehicle." Unveiled at the same time was the Pterodactyl GJ-1 (Gong-Ji Wu-Ren-Ji), which is a hybrid reconnaissance/strike aircraft possessing the weapons capability of the WJ-1, while being equipped with a dorsal pod containing reconnaissance and targeting equipment.

The strike Pterodactyls carry FT-series precision-guided bombs, such as the YZ-212, as well as AKD-10 air-to-surface missiles. Like the AR-1, which arms the CH-4, the AKD-10 is a derivative of the HJ-10 family of attack missiles.

Export customers who have acquired the Pterodactyl (at a reported unit cost of a million dollars) include Egypt, Nigeria, Saudi Arabia, and the United Arab Emirates.

Nanchang Hangkong University (NCHU) is home to one of the most interesting and forward-looking projects in the world of UAV propulsion technology. Dai Wei and Zhao Xue are developing their Owlet Hawk (Xiaoying) unmanned aerial vehicle to test the practicality of using a plasma laser to produce lift and thrust. As described by the University of Oxford Department of Physics, "Plasma accelerators utilize the enormous electric fields formed within plasma waves to accelerate charged particles to high energies in a fraction of the distance needed in a conventional particle accelerator."

This technology, which has evolved greatly in the second decade of the 21st Century, is also the subject of ongoing projects in the United States, such as those being conducted by the Plasma-Accelerator Group at UCLA and at Stanford University's SLAC National Accelerator Laboratory through their Facility for Advanced Accelerator Experimental Tests (FACET), where proof of the viability of plasma acceleration technology has been demonstrated. However, this technology is not known to be under development in the United States for powering unmanned aerial vehicles.

Meanwhile, a proof-of-principle plasma wakefield accelerator experiment using a proton beam from the Super Proton Synchrotron has been ongoing at the European Organization for Nuclear Research (CERN) center in Geneva. As has been shown in the Owlet Hawk program, plasma also has the capability of improving the stealth characteristics of future vehicles.

The CH-4B's baptism of fire with Iraqi forces came on October 10, 2015, when missions were flown against Islamic State terrorists in Anbar Province. Defense Minister Khalid al-Obeidi (foreground) came out to al-Kut Air Base to watch these aircraft on their first strike mission. (Iraq Defence Ministry)

Chapter 15

THE BEAST OF KANDAHAR, MYSTERY AND PEDIGREE

Had it not been for an incident in December 2011 when one turned up in Iranian custody, the Lockheed Martin RQ-170 Sentinel, also called, among other appellations, the "Beast of Kandahar," might have remained merely an obscure footnote. Instead, it became a luminary in the lore of the black world of clandestine unmanned aerial vehicles.

David Fulghum of *Aviation Week* magazine describes the Sentinel as "tactical, operations-oriented platform and not a strategic intelligence-gathering design," pointing out that the "RQ" designator implies that it is unarmed. However, this does not rule out a present or future MQ-170 variant that may or may never be officially revealed.

The Sentinel is a product of the Lockheed Martin Advanced Development Projects (ADP) component, better known as the Skunk Works, which operates in both Burbank and Palmdale, California. The Sentinel's roots can be traced back to earlier Lockheed Martin programs involving stealthy unmanned aerial vehicles such as the RQ-3 DarkStar and the P-175 Polecat. Like both of these aircraft, the Beast is essentially a tailless flying wing.

The DarkStar preceded it by nearly two decades, going back to the contract issued to the Skunk Works in July 1994. It called for the design and development of the fuselage, subsystems, final assembly, and systems integration of the unmanned vehicle, while Boeing, as the principal subcontractor, had responsibility for the wing and for wing subsystem development and testing.

Together, they completed the first RQ-3 aircraft in less than a year, and it rolled out at Palmdale in June 1995. The DarkStar prototype made its first flight on March 29, 1996, but was lost on its second flight. A second RQ-3 made its fully autonomous debut in June 1998, but the program was officially terminated just seven months later amid rumors of a super-secret successor that was dubbed "Son of DarkStar" by speculators within the world of black

This photo illustration by Erik Simonsen shows a Lockheed Martin RQ-170 Sentinel over a chaparral landscape such as is found in Southwest Asia. (Erik Simonsen)

aircraft enthusiasts. Unidentified aircraft that were encountered by U.S. Air Force U-2 pilots during Operation Iraqi Freedom in 2003 were identified by this term under the supposition that they were such a vehicle.

Aviation Week even quoted "a U.S. Air Force official" as calling this unknown aircraft a "DarkStar-like thing" built by Lockheed Martin.

In the meantime, the company was investing $27 million, described as a "significant" share of its research aircraft budget, in another unmanned "DarkStar-like thing" that carried the company model designation P-175 and was nicknamed "Polecat." This aircraft made its first flight in complete secrecy in 2004 and was not officially revealed to the public until July 2006 at the Farnborough International Air Show in England. No mention was made of the

mysterious member of the Skunk Works lineage that lay between the DarkStar and the Polecat. If it existed, and it almost certainly did, this would make the Polecat the "Grandson of DarkStar."

The Polecat had a wingspan of 90 feet, making it half again larger than the DarkStar. It was also said to have an innovative "twisting strut" inside its wings, which was designed to "flex in air and improve the laminar flow over its swept wings, propelling the aircraft to high altitudes."

Providing a possible clue to the construction of the later RQ-170, the P-175 was constructed 98 percent of composite materials, produced by a low-temperature curing process for composites developed by Lockheed Martin. The composites were cured at 150 degrees Fahrenheit, rather than the 350 degrees of a conventional autoclave.

Lockheed Martin Skunk Works personnel check out the RQ-3 DarkStar at Edwards AFB in California's Mojave Desert. The aircraft was built at the company's facility at nearby Palmdale. (Lockheed Martin)

Powered by two Williams FJ44-3E turbofans, the Polecat had an operational altitude of 60,000 feet, though its endurance was listed at a mere 4 hours. It had a payload bay between the wings that could accommodate a half ton of sensors, reconnaissance equipment, and potentially, weapons.

The sole Polecat aircraft, still a company-owned demonstrator, was lost in a mishap during high-altitude flight testing in December 2006 in the vicinity of Nevada's enigmatic Groom Lake, the well-known test facility that is so secret that it officially does not exist, the place known to both popular culture and the CIA as Area 51.

Lockheed Martin hinted in 2007 that the company might build a replacement, but nothing more was said. Lockheed Martin had moved on. The RQ-170 was already more than a gleam in the eyes of the Skunk.

What was perhaps the first public mention of the Sentinel came through an article in the December 19, 2009, issue of the South Korean *Joong Ang Daily* newspaper, which reported that a mysterious high-performance unmanned aerial reconnaissance vehicle was operational with the U.S. Air Force at Osan AB. It was later surmised that the RQ-170 was specially configured to detect and monitor ballistic missile tests and possibly nuclear tests. North Korea had conducted a series of ballistic missile tests earlier in 2009 and a nuclear weapons test in May 2009.

By December 2010, an official U.S. Air Force fact sheet confirmed that the Sentinel was operated by the 30th Reconnaissance Squadron, a component of the 432nd Air Expeditionary Wing (later 432nd Wing) at Creech AFB in Nevada, which is the umbrella organization that (among other things) was managing Predator and Reaper armed

The only officially released picture of the Lockheed Martin P-175 Polecat shows it over the Nevada desert of the Nellis AFB range, possibly during operations out of the Groom Lake facility at Area 51. (Lockheed Martin)

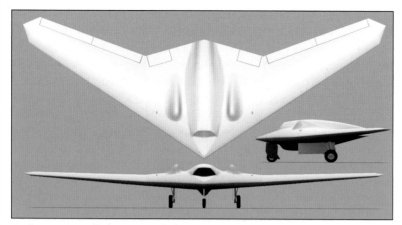

A three-view illustration of the RQ-170 Sentinel, the "Beast of Kandahar." It was created by Truthdowser "using 3D applications and basic photogrammetry techniques from the only three low-resolution photographs publicly available at time of completion." (Truthdowser, licensed under Creative Commons)

drones over Afghanistan. The 30th is a squadron with a lineage going back to 1943, which was reactivated in 2005 after having been deactivated in 1976. It is based at Tonopah Test Range in Nevada, a top-secret facility 65 air miles to the northwest of Groom Lake. Tonopah had been home also to the Lockheed Skunk Works F-117 Nighthawk "stealth fighter" program during the 1980s.

Virtually no details about the Sentinel have been released, but based on sightings, it is estimated to be about 14 feet 9 inches long, with a wingspan of around 65 feet 7 inches. Industry analysts have speculated that it is powered either by a single Garrett TFE731 or General Electric TF34 turbofan engine.

Operationally, RQ-170s have been seen at and confirmed to be flying missions out of the secured military side of the Kandahar International Airport in Afghanistan, earning its nickname as the Beast of Kandahar.

Among its operational missions were those in support of Operation Neptune Spear on the night of May 1–2, 2011, when the U.S. Navy's Special Warfare Development Group (SEAL Team 6) conducted

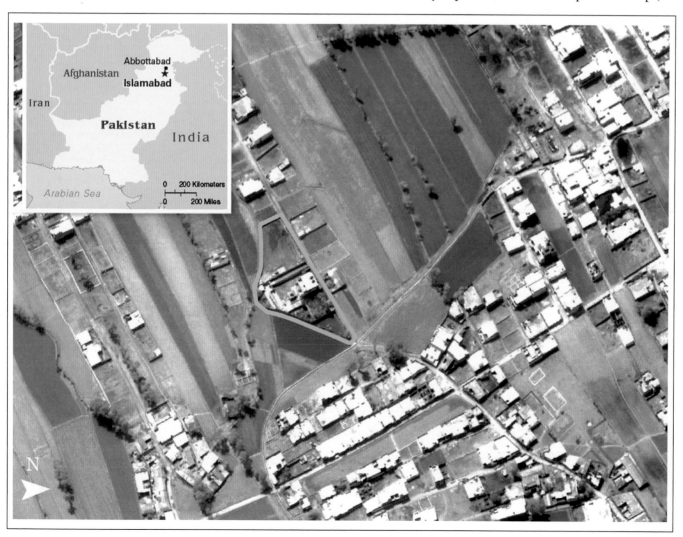

An aerial view, probably taken from an RQ-170, of Osama bin Laden's Waziristan Haveli compound (outlined in yellow) in the Pakistani city of Abbottabad. (CIA)

These images that appeared on Iranian state television appear to show the RQ-170 Sentinel that somehow crossed into Iran and was recovered. (Armed Forces of the Islamic Republic of Iran)

Iranian Supreme Leader Ayatollah Ali Khamenei, seated left and staring glassy eyed, listens to a narrator during his visit to the May 2012 aerospace exhibition in Tehran at which the Iranian replica of the RQ-170 was publicly unveiled. The uniformed man in front of the group on the right appears to be General Amir Ali Hajizadeh of the Iranian Islamic Revolution Guards Air Force. It seems that the original aircraft may be in the foreground, while a copy is in the background. (Office of the Supreme Leader of Iran)

These images show a reverse-engineered, though scaled down, Iranian copy of Lockheed Martin's RQ-170 Sentinel. (Office of the Supreme Leader of Iran)

their raid on the compound in Abbottabad, Pakistan, where terrorist mastermind Osama bin Laden was hiding. The radar-evading RQ-170s provided pre-assault reconnaissance data. It is believed that a real-time video feed was provided to the American National Command Authority in Washington, D.C., by cameras aboard at least one Sentinel orbiting high above.

Other missions have included officially confirmed flights over the Iranian-Afghan border area and unofficial missions over Iran itself.

In December 2011, seven months after the Abbottabad operation, an RQ-170 suddenly appeared on Iranian state television. The Iranians claimed that the aircraft was brought down near Kashmar in northeastern Iran, 140 miles inside the country, after Iranian technicians had successfully hacked the data link to its controls.

On December 8 Iranian television showed imagery of an aircraft resembling an RQ-170 being inspected by Iranian military personnel. It was noted by observers at the time that the lack of damage suggested the aircraft had neither been hit by an anti-aircraft weapon nor had it crashed.

The United States reported only that an unmanned reconnaissance aircraft "flying a mission over western Afghanistan" had been lost in that vicinity on December 4. The unidentified unmanned aerial vehicle was later confirmed to have been an RQ-170, and the CIA claimed that it had been operating the aircraft.

Retired Lieutenant General David Deptula, formerly the U.S. Air Force Deputy Chief of Staff for Intelligence, Surveillance, and Reconnaissance at Air Force Headquarters, and the man who had guided the development of unmanned aerial vehicles for many years, stated the obvious when he commented that "there was a problem with the aircraft and it landed in a place that it was not supposed to land."

Was the RQ-170 hacked? In an unrelated interview prior to its showing up in official Iranian custody, General Moharam Gholizadeh, the deputy for electronic warfare at the air defense headquarters of the Islamic Revolutionary Guard Corps, had told the Fars News Agency, "We have a project on hand that is one step ahead of jamming, meaning 'deception' of the aggressive systems . . . we can

define our own desired information for it so the path of the missile would change to our desired destination . . . all the movements of these [American UAVs are being watched, and] obstructing [them is] always on our agenda."

After the RQ-170 incident, that interview was pulled from the Fars website. On December 15, 2011, Scott Peterson of the *Christian Science Monitor* reported that "the relatively young Gholizadeh died of a heart attack, which some Iranian news sites called suspicious, suggesting the electronic warfare expert may have been a casualty in the covert war against Iran." He might also have run afoul of Iranian officials who felt that he had revealed too much.

On December 9, Iran had filed a formal protest with the United Nations Security Council claiming that its airspace had been violated. Meanwhile, the Obama administration waited until December 12, more than a week after the incident, to make a formal request for the return of the Sentinel. "We've asked for it back," said President Obama at a press conference. "We'll see how the Iranians respond."

The response was predictable.

"Instead of apologizing to the Iranian nation, [Obama] is brazenly asking for the drone back," said Ramin Mehmanparast, the Iranian deputy minister of foreign affairs. "It seems [Obama] has forgotten that Iran's airspace was violated, spying operations were undertaken, international laws were violated, and that Iran's internal affairs were interfered with. . . . Instead of an official apology and admitting to this violation, they are making this request."

Brigadier General Hossein Salami, deputy commander of the Islamic Revolution Guards Corps, added that "no nation welcomes other countries' spy drones in its territory, and no one sends the spying equipment and its information back to the country of origin."

In the United States, former Vice President Dick Cheney suggested that "the right response to [the incident] would have been to go in immediately after it had gone down and destroy it. You can do that from the air . . . and, in effect, make it impossible for them to benefit from having captured that drone. [Instead, Obama] asked nicely for them to return it, and they aren't going to."

In this picture we see what seems to be a pair of reverse-engineered copies of the RQ-170 Sentinel. In the background is an Iranian Shahed 285 light attack helicopter that is made in Iran with Russian parts, and which is itself a reverse-engineered aircraft based on the Bell 206 Jet Ranger. (Office of the Supreme Leader of Iran)

As Cheney intimated, it came as no surprise that Iran's next step was an attempt to reverse engineer the Sentinel. Iran is no stranger to direct copies of foreign UAVs. As noted in Chapter 11, their Karrar UCAV is patterned after the Beechcraft/Raytheon MQM-107 Streaker, while the Iranian H-110 Sarir, like many other smaller UAVs around the world, an obvious copy of an IAI Hunter.

The long-awaited Iranian replica was unveiled in May 2012 at an aerospace exhibition in Tehran attended by Iranian Supreme Leader Ayatollah Ali Khamenei. The Iranian unmanned aerial vehicle, which was displayed next to the captured Sentinel, was nearly identical in shape, but it had been scaled down by around 60 percent. The Western aviation media decided that the small aircraft was probably an unpowered static mockup aircraft, although in November 2014, Iran surprised the nay-sayers with the release of two minutes of video showing their reverse-engineered unmanned aircraft in flight, footage apparently shot from a helicopter. The FARS news agency reported that it had been flying for three months.

عاجل

صور تحليق طائرة RQ170 بدون طيار ايرانية الصنع

A screen grab from an Iranian television clip showing the RQ-170 replica in flight. (Iranian media)

Writing in *USNI News*, a publication of the U.S. Naval Institute, Dave Majumdar quoted unnamed industry sources who told him that "it seems their fiberglass work has improved a lot. It also seems that if it were a functional copy, versus a detailed replica, it wouldn't necessarily have the exact same landing gear, tires, etc. . . . They would probably just use whatever extra F-5 parts or general aviation parts they had lying around."

The Iranians announced that they would be mass producing their scaled down unmanned aerial vehicles for squadron service, and that they would be flying anti-ship missions against the U.S. Navy in the Persian Gulf. They also let it be known that they had received inquiries from China, Russia, and other countries who were interested in the secrets of the Sentinel.

In the ensuing few years, little has been forthcoming from official American sources regarding the RQ-170 and its activities as part of United States operations. Whatever software glitch caused it to be hacked has presumably been fixed, though it may well be years before any additional information is released. The Beast continues to be seen at Kandahar and is probably operational elsewhere.

The stealthy RQ-170 is an accidentally important element in the history of unmanned aerial vehicle technology. Like the F-117, it is a secret program that has captured the imagination of popular culture. It is also a reminder of the strict level of secrecy surrounding some elements of America's unmanned aerial vehicle programs that, had a Sentinel not gone down in Iran, the world might never have known anything more than what could be gleaned from a few grainy images. The story also tells us that, like the Son of DarkStar, there are probably other members of this family tree that will never be revealed.

An artist's conception of an RQ-170 Sentinel in flight. (Bill Yenne)

Chapter 16

THE X-47B, THE TIP OF THE UNMANNED SPEAR

In the first generation of high-performance unmanned combat air vehicles, the Northrop Grumman X-47 Pegasus program lasted longest and progressed furthest toward an operational configuration. Indeed, its importance was underscored dramatically on the eve of its retirement as a test program when U.S. Navy leadership made the bold paradigm shift to embrace a future in which manned aircraft would no longer be the tip of its spear. In April 2015, Secretary of the Navy Ray Mabus said publicly, "The F-35, as much as we need it, as much as we want it, as much as we're looking forward to having it in the fleet, should be and almost certainly will be our last manned aircraft."

A year later, a very enlightening revelation was made to the House Armed Services Committee by Rear Admiral Mike Manazir, the U.S. Navy's Director for Air Warfare.

"The United States Navy has been anxious to get an unmanned capability onto our CVNs for quite a while," he said. "Back in 2009 actually, [then-Chief of Naval Operations Admiral Gary] Roughead pounded a table in a secure space and said, 'I want unmanned on a carrier by 2018.' And that started a series of conversations in the Pentagon about unmanned capability on the aircraft carrier."

The aircraft that did as Roughead had demanded was the X-47. This aircraft had already been around long enough to be part of every stage of high-performance robotic aircraft development in the 21st Century. In the alphabet soup of the evolving DOD perception of drone warfare, the X-47 had its genesis in the turn-of-the-century UCAV program, then became the centerpiece of the U.S. Navy's UCAV-N program, and later it was the only aircraft under the J-UCAS program. In 2013, when the U.S. Navy announced the Unmanned Carrier-Launched Airborne Surveillance and Strike (UCLASS) program, its roadmap to future air combat operations, the lineage of the X-47 program naturally flowed into this as well.

For the old UCAV program, the X-47 was born at Northrop Grumman's Integrated Systems Sector (ISS), while Boeing's Phantom Works was developing the X-45 project. As the X-45A was being run by DARPA as a U.S. Air Force program, the X-47 was embraced by the UCAV-N study directed at similar aircraft for the U.S. Navy. This study examined the technical feasibility for a stealthy UCAV system to accomplish generally the same tasks that were planned for the Air Force UCAV, including surveillance, strike, and Suppression of Enemy Air Defenses (SEAD), but to do them while operating from an aircraft carrier. In answer to the UCAV-N requirement, Boeing submitted its

The U.S. Navy's X-47B unmanned combat air vehicle demonstrator flies up the port side of the aircraft carrier USS Theodore Roosevelt (CVN-71), underway in the Atlantic Ocean in August 2014. (U.S. Navy photo by Liz Wolter)

X-46 proposal, a variation on its X-45C, but Northrop Grumman went a step further with a decision to use company funds to build an actual flying aircraft as a demonstration of their UCAV-N proposal.

Designers at Northrop Grumman's Advanced Systems Development Center in El Segundo, California, drew on its considerable recent high-technology tactical aircraft experience, including the design and development of the B-2 Spirit and the RQ-4 Global Hawk. Though design work was done in El Segundo, the actual airframe was built mostly of non-metal composite materials at Scaled Composites in Mojave, California. Scaled Composites itself has an impressive pedigree, being owned and operated by the legendary Burt Rutan, the creator of numerous extraordinary aircraft from NASA's Proteus high-altitude research aircraft to Voyager, the first aircraft to circumnavigate the earth nonstop without being refueled. Named Pegasus and designated as X-47A, the Northrop Grumman aircraft rolled out at the Scaled Composites facility on July 30, 2001, 10 months after the debut of the X-45A. The first flight of the X-47A came on February 23, 2003, at China Lake, 9 months after the maiden flight of the Boeing X-45A.

Both the X-45A and X-47A were intended as demonstrator aircraft that evolved into later closer-to-tactical configurations that were designated X-45C and X-47B, respectively. The latter configuration was presented to DARPA on April 15, two months after the first X-47A flight. This included the kite-shaped aerodynamics of the X-47A Pegasus, but added short wings shaped rather like the outer wing sections of the Northrop B-2. As such, the kite shape was blended into a flying wing shape that increased the overall wing span by about a third.

As the company explained it, the kite design enabled "efficient integration of propulsion and weapons, while the wing extensions provide aerodynamic efficiency." The new design was also aimed at affording the tactical variant longer endurance, as well as "high survivability and the low-speed, aerodynamic flying qualities for precision landing and autonomous launch and recovery [aircraft carrier] operations." It was only two weeks later on May 1, 2003, that DARPA awarded Northrop Grumman a contract worth up to $160 million to produce and demonstrate two full-scale X-47B UCAV aircraft.

This formal approval of the X-47B coincided with DARPA's decision to merge the X-45 UCAV program and the X-47 UCAV-N program into the single joint project under its new Joint Unmanned Combat Air Systems (J-UCAS) Office. Administratively, the idea was to bring both the X-45, which was primarily a U.S. Air Force program, and the X-47, now a U.S. Navy project, under the same umbrella. Though the two separate programs had been directed toward service-specific needs, they had a great deal in common, and the Defense Department recognized the potential for "significant synergy" by combining them. Of course, merging two parallel columns of bureaucracy and redundancy was also presumed to reduce cost.

Boeing unveiled a full-scale mock-up of the X-45C at the Farnborough International Air Show in the United Kingdom in July 2004, and in October 2004 announced that DARPA had awarded

Chief of Naval Operations Admiral Gary Roughhead speaks to sailors aboard the Nimitz-class aircraft carrier USS Abraham Lincoln (CVN-72) in Everett, Washington. According to Rear Admiral Mike Manazir, the U.S. Navy's Director for Air Warfare, Roughhead had once "pounded a table in a secure space and said, 'I want unmanned on a carrier by 2018.' And that started a series of conversations in the Pentagon about unmanned capability on the aircraft carrier." (U.S. Navy photo by Mass Communications Specialist Seaman Adam Randolph)

Secretary of the Navy Ray Mabus addresses sailors on the flight deck of the aircraft carrier USS Ronald Reagan (CVN-76) as it arrives in Yokosuka, Japan. In April 2015, Mabus said publicly that the new F-35 strike fighter "should be and almost certainly will be our last manned aircraft." (U.S. Navy photo by MC2 Paolo Bayas)

A launch crew prepares a Northrop Grumman X-47B demonstrator for its first land-based catapult launch. This verified that the vehicle could structurally absorb the rigors of the aircraft carrier environment. (U.S. Navy photo by Kelly Schindler)

the company $767 million in funding "to continue the X-45C portion of the Joint Unmanned Combat Air Systems (J-UCAS) demonstration program over the next five years . . . to design, develop, and demonstrate three full-scale, flight-worthy air vehicles and two mission control elements." Having passed the Mid-Term Design Review with the X-45C in 2004, Boeing confidently planned a first flight in 2006.

However, in February 2006, the DOD's Quadrennial Defense Review brought down a decision to cancel the J-UCAS program, or at least the "jointness" of it, and to terminate the X-45C entirely. The program changed to a navy-only program, preserving the X-47, and the acronym changed, first to UCAS-N (alternately seen as N-UCAS) and later to UCAS-D ("Demonstrator"). The U.S. Air Force reportedly gave up the X-45C in exchange for budgetary support for a

Its wings folded, an X-47B unmanned combat air vehicle demonstrator is moved onto an aircraft elevator aboard the aircraft carrier USS George H.W. Bush (CVN-77) in May 2013. (U.S. Navy photo by MC2 Timothy Walter)

A Northrop Grumman X-47B unmanned combat air vehicle on the flight deck of the aircraft carrier USS George H.W. Bush. (U.S. Navy photo by MC2 Timothy Walter)

Preparing the X-47B unmanned combat air vehicle for its first catapult launch from the deck of the aircraft carrier USS George H.W. Bush in May 2013. (U.S. Navy photo by MC2 Timothy Walter)

new large *manned* strategic bomber program, then called Next Generation Long Range Strike (NGLRS) and later known by such names as Next-Generation Bomber (NGB) and Long-Range Strike-B (LRS-B). Undeterred, Boeing continued to develop the X-45C concept in-house. This evolved into the Phantom Ray program, which later re-emerged as a contender in the UCLASS program.

In December 2008, the first X-47B rolled out at Air Force Plant 42 in Palmdale, California. It was 38 feet long with a wingspan of 62 feet, compared 27.9 feet and 27.8 feet, respectively, for the X-47A. The U.S. Navy noted in a press release that it was about 87 percent the size of the F/A-18C Hornet aircraft operating aboard aircraft carriers.

The Northrop Grumman X47B demonstrator flies over the flight deck of the aircraft carrier USS George H.W. Bush. (U.S. Navy photo by MC2 Timothy Walter)

A helicopter-eye view of an X-47B unmanned combat air vehicle demonstrator launched from the flight deck of the aircraft carrier USS George H.W. Bush. (U.S. Navy photo by MC3 Brian Read Castillo)

This X-47B unmanned combat air vehicle demonstrator is a split second away from snagging the arresting cable with its tailhook on the flight deck of the aircraft carrier USS George H.W. Bush. (U.S. Navy photo by MC3 Kevin J. Steinberg)

Coming to a halt aboard the USS George H.W. Bush on July 10, 2013, this Northrop Grumman X-47B had just made the first-ever arrested landing at sea by an unmanned aircraft. (U.S. Navy photo by Alan Radecki)

A Northrop Grumman X-47B makes an arrested landing aboard the aircraft carrier USS Theodore Roosevelt in November 2013. The ship was the third carrier to be involved in tests of the X-47B. (U.S. Navy photo by Mass Communication Specialist Seaman Anthony Hilkowski)

It was intended that the first flight should take place in November 2009, but taxi tests did not even begin until January 2010, and the debut flight was delayed another year. The first X-47B demonstrator, Air Vehicle 1 (AV-1), made its first flight from Edwards AFB on February 4, 2011, and was joined by AV-2, which first flew on November 22, 2011.

In early 2012, AV-1 moved from Edwards to Naval Air Station Patuxent River, where the program made up for lost time. Known informally as "Pax River," the base is home to the Naval Air Systems Command (NAVAIR) and the Atlantic Test Range, as well as being the center of testing, evaluation, and systems acquisition activities relating to naval aviation. Here, AV-1 began a series of flight tests specific to carrier operations, such as arrested landings. Land-based catapult launches began at Pax River in November 2012. The plan had been for 50 test flights over three years, but the aircraft performed so well that the introductory phase ended after 16 flights.

Meanwhile, Northrop Grumman and the U.S. Navy were developing a suite of operator consoles, radio links, and software (the latter totaling 3.5 million lines of code) that could be installed aboard Nimitz-class carriers. The USS Harry S. Truman (CVN-75) was first, and by the end of 2012, all the U.S. Navy's East Coast carriers had received some or all of the equipment and modifications.

In June 2012, when AV-2 arrived at Patuxent River, it was delivered all the way from Palmdale by truck. According to reports on

The unmanned X-47B conducts night operations over Naval Air Station Patuxent River in Maryland. The U.S. Navy saw these as an "incremental step in developing the operations concept for more routine flight activity." (U.S. Navy photo by Erik Hildebrandt)

WRC-TV/News4, the NBC affiliate in Washington, D.C., this created quite a stir as it made its way along the Beltway surrounding the nation's capital.

"Beltway traffic is bad enough without adding extraterrestrial vehicles into the mix," wrote Thomas Tobin and Carissa DiMargo on the station's blog for June 14. "Facebook and Twitter users went wild over sightings of a saucer-shaped vessel being towed on local highways. The buzz called to mind the frenzy in 1947 Roswell, albeit in a much more modern way. Drivers spotted the craft on I-270 and on the Beltway as it was pulled behind a tractor trailer. But we can take the 'unidentified' out of 'unidentified flying object.' (And yes, we realize that it wasn't actually flying, either.) The military has confirmed to News4 that the 82-foot-long craft is an unmanned military aircraft, known as an X-47B drone. Maryland State Police towed it on a flatbed trailer from Garrett County, Maryland, to Naval Air Station Patuxent River—but even they didn't know what it was at the time, police said. The drone was towed by a series of vehicles all the way from California, and yes, it 'always attracts attention,' a military spokesperson told NBC4's Melissa Mollet. . . . The military is also cautioning people who may see the drones flying around in coming

The past and future of naval aviation? As an unmanned X-47B, left, is readied for launch, a manned F/A-18 Hornet conducts flight operations aboard the aircraft carrier USS Theodore Roosevelt. (U.S. Navy photo taken by Mass Communications Specialist Seaman Apprentice Alex Millar)

months—be careful and pay attention to the road if you're driving when you see them! 'Don't worry, that's not an alien spacecraft, just a flying military robot.'"

Even as the U.S. Navy and Northrop continued catapult verification and final flight software validation ashore at Pax River, the X-47B had made its first carrier "landing" in November 2012, although the aircraft was set there by a crane. Standing on the flight deck of the USS *Harry S. Truman* as the aircraft came aboard, Captain Jaime Engdahl, the navy's X-47B program manager, quipped, "This is a very important moment for the X-47B. The moment the aircraft set down on *Truman*'s deck was the moment it officially met the fleet. To operate large, unmanned aircraft off of a carrier, from anywhere in the world, will be a key capability for the Navy after these tests are successful."

In the meantime, the compatibility evaluations aboard the carrier over the ensuing three weeks included the more mundane activities of taxiing on the flight deck using the X-47B's arm-mounted control display unit (CDU) and testing its digital engine controls within environments pervaded by electromagnetic fields. Mike Mackey, Northrop Grumman's program director, commented that "we gained a lot of knowledge that we could never have gotten anywhere else except on a carrier. . . . The X-47B deck trials proved convincingly that the design and operation of the aircraft are fully compatible with the rhythm and operational requirements of the carrier flight deck."

Meanwhile, Don Blottenberger, the manager for the navy's N-UCAS program office, added, "We've learned a lot about the environment that we're in and how compatible the aircraft is with a carrier's flight deck, hangar bays, and communication systems. . . . Approximately 40 percent of our test team onboard had never been on a Navy ship before. I think it was eye-opening for the team to see the complexities involved in running and organizing a ship effectively. . . . I'm a believer that this is only the beginning."

BBC News noted on December 19, 2012, after the X-47B's first "deployment" that "as a fighter plane prepares to take off from a naval carrier at sea, the pilot and deck crew go through a tightly choreographed series of hand signals to tell each other they are ready to launch. It ends with a final 'salute' from the pilot to indicate that the aircraft is ready to be catapulted off the deck. But when the X-47B, the U.S. Navy's newest prototype combat aircraft, prepares for its first carrier launch early next year, there will be no salute. That's because there will also be no pilot. Instead, the X-47B will blink its wingtip navigation lights, a robotic nod to the human salute (and mimicking what the Navy does for night launches), before the catapult officer presses the launch button, and the robotic aircraft is flung off the front of the ship."

The Northrop Grumman X-47B, still being described by the U.S. Navy as its "Unmanned Combat Air System Demonstrator (UCAS-D)," touches down on the flight deck of the aircraft carrier USS Theodore Roosevelt on August 17, 2014. The Navy saw its flight operations as "demonstrating its ability to operate safely and seamlessly with manned aircraft. Theodore Roosevelt is underway preparing for future deployments." (U.S. Navy photo by Mass Communications Specialist Seaman Apprentice Alex Millar)

The first such catapult-launch "flinging" of an X-47B came on the morning of May 14, 2013, from the deck of the USS *George H.W. Bush* (CVN-77), underway in the Atlantic Ocean. Three days later, the unmanned aircraft, operating under the call sign Salty Dog 502, was conducting "touch-and-go" landings aboard the *Bush*. The first landing using arresting gear occurred in July, observed by a number of journalists who were invited aboard.

"We witnessed the capstone moment for the Navy UCAS program as the team flawlessly performed integrated carrier operations," Jaime Engdahl told the press. "We have been using the same [carrier] landing technology for more than 50 years now and the idea that we can take a large UAV and operate in that environment is fascinating . . . we have proven we can seamlessly integrate unmanned systems into the carrier environment."

However, the exercise wasnot without a glitch. Dianna Cahn, writing in the Norfolk *Virginian-Pilot* of July 12, reported that "the unmanned aircraft that made history when it achieved two tailhook landings aboard a moving aircraft carrier Wednesday [July 10] suffered a computer glitch on its third attempt and had to divert to shore, the Navy said Thursday. Instead of spending the next six days on board the aircraft carrier *George H.W. Bush*, the prototype X-47B 'waved off' the carrier landing and touched down at Wallops Island flight facility on the Eastern Shore of Virginia. The disrupted attempt came on the heels of success. Twice on Wednesday, the aircraft made automated landings on the carrier flight deck, witnessed by top Navy leaders and dozens of journalists who were brought on board for the event."

As Engdahl explained to Cahn and others, "We have a triple-redundant navigation system. That's what gives us the level of safety and the level of reliability to land on a ship. One of them had a software issue. The team looked at it and said the best thing to do is send the aircraft back to shore and recover it there. . . . The aircraft and the team. Everybody followed the procedures," he said. "The aircraft followed perfectly. It was actually very successful in doing what it had to do."

She reported that he went on to say that the X-47B team "was still looking at the data to determine exactly what happened, but expected that a simple reboot—turning the drone off and then restarting it—would remedy the problem."

Meanwhile, Sarah Sicard, writing in *National Defense*, observed that the "incident proved to naval officials that the X-47B was able to function autonomously." She quoted Engdahl as saying, "You have to design it with unprecedented levels of reliability and system safety. Everything went right. [When one of the three navigational sub-systems failed] the other two [subsystems] realized that. It exercised its already pre-planned logic and identified that sub-system anomaly, provided that indication to the mission operator who then made the appropriate choice to follow the procedures in the test plan. . . . What stuck with me was the ease with which everything happened."

Unfortunately, a fourth landing attempt on July 15 had to be scrubbed when the other X-47B suffered a "minor test instrumentation issue" while en route to the *George H.W. Bush* from Pax River. It returned and landed without incident at Patuxent.

In the wake of these successes and failures at the threshold of demonstrating an operational capability, the U.S. Naval Air Systems Command announced that the U.S. Navy would be *retiring* the two X-47Bs. A big part of this decision was the cost, which had grown to around $813 million after originally being funded at $635.8 million in 2007.

However, the cancellation announcement immediately hit a wall of criticism. On August 6, 2013, Dave Majumdar of *FlightGlobal* quoted Mackenzie Eaglen of the American Enterprise Institute who had reported a reversal of the decision: "Navy leaders are responding to criticism and probably the likelihood that sequestration will seriously hinder and/or delay UCLASS."

Two days later, Evan Ackerman, writing in the *IEEE Spectrum* publication of the Institute of Electrical and Electronics Engineers was a bit more direct when he observed, "Once everything was shown to work, the U.S. Navy was like, 'awesome job, now never fly those things again,' and the two X-47Bs were slated for permanent museum display. Fortunately for fans of big, expensive, scary-looking flying robots, the Navy has just changed its mind. The Navy is now planning to deploy the drones to aircraft carriers three more times over the next two years."

And so they did.

Flight testing resumed on November 10, 2013, aboard the USS *Theodore Roosevelt*, with evaluations of the X-47B in a digitized carrier-controlled environment. In June 2014, as reported by Beth Stevenson of *FlightGlobal*, the U.S. Navy paid Northrop Grumman an additional $63 million to carry out "post-demonstration" development under a Phase II contract.

In the meantime, in October 2013, the Naval Air Systems Command reassigned X-47B manager Engdahl as program director for NAVAIR's Precision Strike Weapons Program Office. In turn, he was relieved as X-47B manager by Captain Beau Duarte, who also became chief of the Navy's Unmanned Carrier Aviation office. Duarte had previously been NAVAIR's deputy program manager for Spectrum Dominance. Duarte noted that back in 1999 he had replaced Engdahl as "UAV project officer developing aircraft and technologies for the navy's nascent unmanned fleet [within Naval Strike Aircraft Test Squadron, VX-23]. At that time, our flight test workhorse was the BQM-147A Exdrone, a 90-pound fiberglass propeller-driven flying wing with a 6-foot wingspan and a two-stroke gas motor outputting a whopping 9 hp." Duarte contrasted the BQM-147 with the X-47B, whose accomplishments at sea in the summer of 2013 would have been "laughably unthinkable" in 1999.

The tests that began aboard the *Theodore Roosevelt* (CVN-71) in November 2013 expanded to the USS *Harry S. Truman* (CVN-75) in December and continued into 2014. As described officially, these

The U.S. Navy's unmanned X-47B demonstrator receives fuel from an Omega K-707 tanker while operating in the Atlantic Test Range over Chesapeake Bay on April 22, 2015. This test marked the first time an unmanned aircraft was refueled in flight. (U.S. Navy photo)

flights "demonstrated the X-47B's ability to integrate with the carrier environment. The aircraft performed precise touch and go maneuvers on the ship to generate data that characterizes the environment in close proximity of the carrier flight deck. In addition, the aircraft took part in flight deck handling drills, completed arrested landings and catapult launches. . . . A major objective for the UCAS-D program is to demonstrate a digitized carrier controlled environment to allow for robust communications between the aircraft and all carrier personnel involved with launching, recovering, and controlling the aircraft."

Coordinated air operations, including repeated launches and landings involving an unmanned X-47B alongside a manned F/A-18 Hornet, took place aboard the *Theodore Roosevelt* in August 2014. Beau Duarte commented that these flights "showed that the X-47B could take off, land, and fly in the carrier pattern with manned aircraft while maintaining normal flight deck operations. This is key for the future Carrier Air Wing."

Despite Duarte's apparent enthusiasm, it remains hard to imagine a time when the Hornets would be history and vehicles such as the X-47B would be the *only* combat aircraft on carrier flight decks.

In the meantime, the first X-47B night flight, which occurred at Pax River on April 10, 2014, earned the program the Collier Trophy, awarded by the U.S. National Aeronautic Association for the year's "greatest achievement in aeronautics or astronautics in America."

While press releases regarding the achievements of test air-craft are liberal in the use of the term "milestone," one can easily succumb to the attraction of the word when noting the events of April 22, 2015. On that date, the X-47B reportedly became the first unmanned aircraft to successfully conduct the world's first Autonomous Aerial Refueling (AAR). It was off the Eastern Seaboard within sight of Chesapeake Bay that the aircraft took on more than 4,000 pounds of fuel from a Boeing K-707 tanker aircraft operated by Omega Air Refueling, a civilian contractor that had been providing aerial refueling services under contract to the U.S. Navy since 2001.

In his official statement, Duarte pointed out that "in manned platforms, aerial refueling is a challenging maneuver because of the precision required by the pilot to engage the [hose and drogue refueling system] basket. Adding an autonomous functionality creates another layer of complexity."

In February 2015, as Secretary of the Navy Mabus was making it clear that the future of the U.S. Navy strike mission was in unmanned aircraft, the X-47B program was coming to the end. Paul Scharre, writing for *PilotOnline* on April 25, 2015, called the X-47B demonstration "a strategic imperative for the navy. Long-range anti-access weapons are threatening the carrier's ability to get close enough to an enemy's shoreline to effectively project power."

The X-47B had been the first important step toward an unmanned strike capability, and it served as Northrop Grumman's template for its next step into the UCLASS program.

Chapter 17

THE TRAVAILS AND TRIBULATIONS OF UCLASS

Through the middle years of the second decade of the 21st Century, it seemed to many that the future of unmanned combat aircraft might well be visible in the vehicle that the U.S. Navy imagined under its Unmanned Carrier-Launched Airborne Surveillance and Strike (UCLASS) program. Indeed, this program *seemed* as definitive and well-defined a picture of that future as the one painted by the Unmanned Combat Air Vehicle (UCAV) program 15 years earlier.

However, *neither* of the programs survived to embody that technologically and tactically promising future. UCAV had faded into J-UCAS, and then it just faded away. UCLASS, on the other hand, woke up one morning as something completely different. This is the story of the UCLASS program and its abrupt and surprising metamorphosis.

In January 2014, the notional UCLASS aircraft was described by Secretary of the Navy Ray Mabus as "an autonomous aircraft capable of precision strike in a contested environment, and it is expected to grow and expand its missions so that it is capable of extended range intelligence, surveillance, and reconnaissance; electronic warfare; tanking; and maritime domain awareness."

The transformational element in the UCLASS concept was that it was to be based on aircraft carriers. Other unmanned combat air vehicles, such as the U.S. Air Force MQ-1 Predator and MQ-9 Reaper operate from land bases in foreign countries, where their missions are subject to the acquiescence of foreign governments. Carrier-based aircraft operate from international waters.

As retired Major General Charles Dunlap told *USNI News*, a publication of the U.S. Naval Institute, in 2014, "Operating from a host country gives them the ability to put whatever restrictions they want on your operations. I'm talking about policy restrictions that they want you to follow. In terms of policy there are a lot fewer restrictions from a seabase."

An example came in January 2013, when French armed forces intervened in Mali at the request of that government to help defeat al-Qaeda in the Islamic Maghreb (AQIM) and other organizations who had beaten government forces and occupied much of the country. The French asked for help from American unmanned combat air assets, but Mali balked at the idea of basing them in-country. If carrier-based unmanned aerial vehicles had been available, that would not have been an issue.

Rear Admiral Mike Manazir, director for air warfare on the staff of the Chief of Naval Operations, said of the notional UCLASS aircraft that "they're big, heavy, capable airplanes that will fly for 14 hours." He is seen here in his previous role as commanding officer of the aircraft carrier USS Nimitz. (U.S. Navy photo by MC2 Matthew Hepburn)

As noted in Chapter 16, the UCLASS program evolved from the UCAV-N program, which itself evolved from the joint service J-UCAS program, which originated with the UCAV program at the turn of the century. The Northrop Grumman X-47 program passed through all three of the predecessor programs to become a UCLASS contender.

As aviation analysts Dave Majumdar and Sam LaGrone summarized in *USNI News* in 2014, it was originally assumed that "the new generation of carrier-based unmanned aerial vehicles would be built to extend the inland reach of carrier strike groups well beyond the reach of the current crop of manned fighters. In 2011, the Navy and the Pentagon moved to make a lower cost UAV to be quickly pushed into service to hunt terrorists, anticipating a world where U.S. forces could be restricted in flying land-based UAVs as well as act as an intelligence, surveillance, and reconnaissance (ISR) asset when the rest of the carrier air wing was off-duty."

Even before the UCLASS program officially began, this decision marked a milestone as the first of many lessening of expectations for the aircraft.

The program got off to a sluggish start. The U.S. Navy's request for proposals had been anticipated in late 2012, but after repeated delays it was not issued until June 2013. Two months later, the navy awarded four airframe development contracts, each worth $15 million, to Boeing, General Atomics Aeronautical Systems, Lockheed Martin, and Northrop Grumman. As expected, both Northrop Grumman and Boeing proposed familiar aircraft. The former was a development of the now-retired X-47 demonstrator aircraft, while Boeing proposed a variant of its Phantom Ray, which was based on the earlier X-45C variant of its X-45A UCAV aircraft.

Lockheed Martin proposed an aircraft based on its P-175 Polecat and its still-classified RQ-170 Sentinel reconnaissance drone, which would be known as "Sea Ghost." General Atomics proposed a naval version of its jet-propelled Avenger unmanned combat air vehicle that was naturally named "Sea Avenger."

As discussed by Amy Butler in the August 13, 2013, issue of *Aerospace Daily & Defense Report*, Lockheed Martin and Northrop Grumman were putting their emphasis on stealth designs, while Boeing

In January 2014, Secretary of the Navy Ray Mabus called the UCLASS vehicle "an autonomous aircraft capable of precision strike in a contested environment, and it is expected to grow and expand its missions so that it is capable of extended range intelligence, surveillance and reconnaissance, electronic warfare, tanking, and maritime domain awareness." (U.S. Navy photo by MC2 Armando Gonzales)

The Lockheed Martin UCLASS air vehicle concept integrated proven technologies from the F-35C, RQ-170 Sentinel, and other operational systems. The company said that "our approach leverages the experience of the Skunk Works and our cross-corporation team to meet the navy's requirements for a versatile and supportable carrier-based unmanned aircraft [for] any environment or threat scenario." (Lockheed Martin) and General Atomics stressed the importance of endurance and payload. Lockheed Martin's Bob Ruszkowski told Ms. Butler that his company's vision of a UCLASS aircraft was that it "needs to be a fifth-generation capability," stressing Lockheed Martin's background with America's two fifth-generation manned combat aircraft, the F-22 Raptor and F-35 Lightning II, as well as with the Sentinel.

There was a great deal of buzz in Washington that fall when it became clear that the U.S. Navy was planning to put a great deal of money into the program and to push it forward in resolute fashion. Hugh Lessig reported in the *Daily Press* on September 26 that in fiscal year 2014, the navy was planning to "spend $3.7 billion to develop, build, and field 6 to 24 aircraft as an initial complement of UCLASS. However, it does not plan to initiate a key review of the program until 2020, when the proposed aircraft would already be fielded."

The ambitious plan was to field four air wings of UCLASS strike aircraft during the technology development phase, but in early 2014, Congress put a stop to the idea of a contractor selection until *after* the preliminary design review was complete. Also now forbidden was the acquisition of more than six aircraft before the engineering and manufacturing development phase. It was originally assumed that the debut flight or flights of the aircraft purpose-built for the UCLASS program would take place in the second quarter of fiscal year 2017, but in March 2014, it was announced that this milestone would not occur until the third quarter of fiscal year 2018.

Technically, the concept for UCLASS was for an aircraft having the endurance to fit into an aircraft carrier "deck cycle" of 12 hours, the envelope of time that it takes for typical daily carrier operations to cycle through the confined deck space.

Rear Admiral Mathias "Mat" Winter, the executive officer for unmanned aviation and strike weapons at the Naval Air Systems Command standing in front of the Northrop Grumman X-47B demonstrator as he holds a press conference at Naval Air Station Patuxent River in Maryland. Said he of the UCLASS aircraft, "Its limited strike capability as the complementary force multiplier persisting capability will ensure the carrier strike group mission is even more effective than it is today." (U.S. Navy photo by Mass Communications Specialist Tristan Miller)

The Sea Avenger, the naval version of the Predator C Avenger, was the UCLASS proposal from General Atomics Aeronautical Systems. (General Atomics)

The available space on the flight deck and the hangar deck was also a factor in the overall dimensions of a UCLASS aircraft as they are with other aircraft. Originally, the aircraft was intended to be larger than a manned F/A-18, and about the same size as an F-14, but this idea was later scaled back. Operationally, the carrier deployed a sufficient number of UCLASS aircraft to maintain two orbits about 700 miles from the ship or a single orbit at a range of twice that distance.

As originally conceived, the armament plan was for the unmanned aircraft to accommodate weapons systems that are already deployed with the fleet for use on manned aircraft. These include GBU series Joint Direct Attack Munitions (JDAM) and were directed through multiple intelligence sensors, such as electro-optical/infrared and full-motion video, to permit detection and tracking of surface targets on land or at sea.

The UCLASS aircraft was intended to incorporate fifth-generation Active Electronically Scanned Array (AESA) radar. With its transmitter and receiver functions composed of compact solid-state modules, AESA is an active phased array radar that directs its beam through the emission of separate radio waves from each module that interface specific angles in front of an antenna. AESA radar is an improvement over older passive electronically scanned array (PESA) radar by spreading signal emissions across a band of frequencies. This makes AESA extremely hard to detect over background noise, which allows an aircraft to use powerful radar signals while retaining its stealthy characteristics.

In a January 29, 2014, interview with *USNI News*, Rear Admiral Mat Winter, the executive officer for unmanned aviation and strike weapons at the Naval Air Systems Command, told Dave Majumdar that "we will go forward and we will integrate UCLASS with its ISR, potential tanking, and its limited strike capability as the complementary force multiplier persisting capability that will ensure the carrier strike group mission is even more effective than it is today."

A month earlier, Majumdar had sat down with Rear Admiral Mike Manazir, Director for Air Warfare on the staff of the Chief of Naval Operations, who was also a naval aviator with more than 3,750 hours in F-14 and F-18 aircraft, a former squadron commander, the former captain of the USS *Nimitz* and of Carrier Strike Group 8. In short, he was a man who knew naval tactical air operations.

"They're big airplanes, they're not [General Atomics MQ-1] Predators," Manazir explained of the conceptual UCLASS vehicle. "They're big, heavy, capable airplanes that will fly for 14 hours, that can give away gas [act as an aerial refueling tanker]. We're going to put a refueling capability into them and they'll have an endurance package in them. They'll be able to give away something like 20,000 pounds of gas and still stay up for 7½ hours. If you take that UCLASS and you send it downrange, is it the sensor that gets the combat ID? I think with the designs that we're moving toward [we're] going to have an unmanned airframe that can operate in a non-permissive

Congressman J. Randy Forbes of Virginia, a staunch supporter of the UCLASS program, chaired the Seapower and Projection Forces Subcommittee of the House Armed Services Committee. (U.S. Navy)

Admiral James "Sandy" Winnefeld, vice chairman of the Joint Chiefs of Staff, testifies before the Senate Armed Services Committee in May 2014. Earlier, as head of the Defense Department Joint Requirements Oversight Council, he had written that "the numbers of available orbits [operational missions] provided as a fielded capability within total program budget is the Number One priority for UCLASS." (U.S. Navy photo by MC2 Martin Carey)

environment. . . . We're not going have JSF-like stealth. You're not going to have somebody that can go right over the top . . . of the threat capital city, but you're going to have something that can stand in somewhat."

Majumdar also learned that beyond the strike capability, which Winter had seemed to consider secondary to the ISR mission, UCLASS was intended to possess an air-to-air combat capability.

"Maybe we put a whole bunch of AMRAAMs [Advanced Medium-Range Air-to-Air Missiles] on it and that thing is the truck," Manazir said of the potential of the UCLASS vehicle. "So this unmanned truck goes downtown with as far as it can go with a [human] decision-maker [aboard an accompanying aircraft]."

Manazir went on to say that the UCLASS aircraft could be commanded remotely from a Northrop Grumman E-2D Hawkeye or even a Lockheed Martin F-35C Joint Strike Fighter flight leader, under the Manned-Unmanned Teaming (MUMT) concept that was emerging as part of Defense Department doctrine. Indeed, the U.S. Army was flying MUMT evaluations with AH-64 Apache helicopters and MQ-1C Gray Eagle UAVs at Fort Irwin even as Manazir and Majumdar were talking.

"The concept has a lot of merit," agreed Air Force Reserve Colonel Michael Pietrucha, a former F-15E weapons systems offi-cer, in a conversation with Majumdar. "This is not beyond the state-of-the-art. The difficulty is always that the aircraft itself has no judgment and no prioritization scheme and isn't going to have the systems onboard to do all things that a fighter does."

In describing the MUMT doctrine, Pietrucha pointed out that a fighter pilot in a manned aircraft could detect, track, and identify the target, then hand it off to the controller of the unmanned combat aircraft to engage hostile targets, adding that a "shooter can fire on a target that is being tracked by a sensor [so long as the target is within range]. If you solve that problem, then your missile caddy UCAV [unmanned combat air vehicle] wingman is a going concern. You can now target his missiles for him. . . . Under situations where I could theoretically get a missile off, it's going to waste a lot of energy making 90 degrees of turn, but my UCAV can point directly at the target. . . . In that case, his kinematics are better because his missile does not have to solve the turn problem."

Pietrucha and Majumdar went on to discuss how the robotic wingman scenario could be realized under the U.S. Navy's Naval Integrated Fire Control-Counter Air (NIFC-CA) concept in which common targeting data can be shared across multiple aircraft via a datalinks network. "The navy is ahead of the air force on this," Pietrucha admitted.

Vice Admiral Paul Grosklags (center), the commander of Naval Air Systems Command, and Rear Admiral Brian Corey (right) of the Naval Air Warfare Center Weapons Division, attend a briefing at Naval Air Station Point Mugu in California in October 2015. Grosklags had imagined great things for UCLASS, noting that the missions he had in mind would "include permissive airspace ISR and strike initially to start with. . . . As the program evolves, those missions would expand to more challenging contested littoral and coastal ISR and strike, to attacking an enemy surface action group." (U.S. Navy photo by Kimberly Brown)

Admiral Gary Roughead (right), then the chief of naval operations, speaks to Tim Clark of Government Executive Media Group during the Government Executive Leadership Breakfast at the National Press Club in Washington, D.C., in 2011. Later lamenting the lessening expectations of UCLASS, Roughead complained that "the less-survivable, less-endurance approach, although cheaper, is, to me, not transformational." (U.S. Navy photo by Chief Mass Communications Specialist Tiffini Jones Vanderwyst)

NIFC-CA operates through a sensor network with integrated fire control capacity that is known as Cooperative Engagement Capability (CEC). It is designed to improve battle force air and missile defense capabilities through the integration of multiple battle force air search sensors into a single, real-time, composite track picture to magnify fleet air defense by making jamming more perplexing. CEC as a component of NIFC-CA was already part of F/A-18, F-35C, EA-18G Growler, and E-2D Advanced Hawkeye air operations.

UCLASS had its boosters on Capitol Hill. The legislators who wanted to see it fulfill its ambitious multi-mission potential included Congressman Randy Forbes of Virginia, the chairman of the Seapower and Projection Forces subcommittee of the House Armed Services Committee. He saw the value in a carrier-based UCAV and did not want to see the strike mission downplayed in the program's development.

In February 2014, he wrote to Navy Secretary Mabus, insisting that "UCLASS must include a requirement for aerial refueling, survivability, lethality, and payload to have enduring utility in tomorrow's threat environment. . . . I place a premium on optimizing internal payload carriage capacity and versatility to support the simultaneous needs of both the carrier-strike group commander and the geographical combatant commander."

Forbes also stressed the capability of the aircraft to be aerial refueled. The X-47B demonstrated this in 2015, but it was still theoretical in the roster of UCLASS possibilities in 2014. He told Mabus that in his opinion, "Only through in-flight refueling can a UAS system sized for carrier basing achieve sortie endurances required for both responding globally to short-warning aggression irrespective of carrier positioning and, once in-theater, staging ISR and strike operations from outside the lethal envelope of an adversary's longest-range threats."

Forbes later said in a statement, "I strongly believe that the UCLASS program represents the future of our navy's carrier air wing and American power projection capabilities. Getting this program right today is essential to cementing our navy's advantages in the decades to come."

However, by 2014, Defense Department budget strings had tightened. The 10-percent across-the-board spending cuts mandated by the Budget Control Act ("sequestration") had gone into effect in early 2013, and a year later, this caught up to the UCLASS program.

Against this backdrop, there was a continued lowering of expectations with regard to the place of UCLASS in the Defense Department scheme of things. Range and payload were downsized and compromises crept in under the cloak of cost savings. Aerial refueling capability, a key feature in UCLASS as it was originally conceived, was deleted from the requirements. So, too, was low observability (stealth characteristics), an attribute most favored by Forbes and others.

In March 2014 it was revealed that on December 19, 2013, Admiral James "Sandy" Winnefeld, the Vice Chairman of the Joint Chiefs of Staff, who headed the Defense Department Joint Requirements Oversight Council (JROC), had written in a memo that "the numbers of available orbits [operational missions] provided as a fielded capability within total program budget is the Number One priority for UCLASS."

Dyke Weatherington, the director of Unmanned Warfare & Intelligence, Surveillance, and Reconnaissance (UW & ISR), Strategic and Tactical Systems in the Office of the Under Secretary of Defense for Acquisition, Technology and Logistics, was the man responsible for acquisition oversight of Department of Defense unmanned aircraft systems. Of UCLASS, he said that the Pentagon "can't afford to start programs that we can't finish. We can't afford to start programs that we get two or three into and we have to cancel and we have nothing to show for it." (DOD)

Bob Work, a former undersecretary of the navy and later deputy secretary of defense, observed in 2014 that "we have already more than 800 aircraft, like Reapers and Predators, that can operate in non-contested airspace. What you don't have is a lot of capability in stealthy type penetrators" like the original vision for UCLASS. (U.S. Navy)

The office of the Chief of Naval Operations put out a statement that explained the 2014 revisions, promising that "the UCLASS system will support missions in permissive and low-end contested environments and provide enabling capabilities for high-end denied operations. . . . The [downward revised] requirements were written to fill a long-standing gap in persistent, sea-based ISR and a review of the overall UAS portfolio."

The emphasis was now on ISR rather than strike missions and on operations within *"permissive and low-end contested environments"* rather than stealthy deep penetration.

In speaking of the potential of the UCLASS aircraft in air-to-air combat in February 2014, Michael Pietrucha had told Dave Majumdar that in an air combat situation, "my life cannot be replaced. It's not an abstract consideration in the cockpit and I'll expend unmanned airplanes left, right, and center in a way I wouldn't even consider using my own [human] wingman because the threat is too high. . . . The question is, are you actually saving any money or are you building a very expensive platform that is so less capable than a manned platform that it's not worth it?"

The concept of building a very expensive platform that is so less capable than a manned platform that it's not worth the price tag lies at the heart of many, if not all, interchanges between the armed forces and Congress whenever the subject of a new, untried weapons system is on the table in a congressional hearing room. The UCLASS program was such a program, and by the summer of 2014, it was reaching a turning point.

In July, Dave Majumdar and Sam LaGrone spoke with Vice Admiral Paul Grosklags for an article in *USNI News*. At the time, Grosklags was a military deputy to Sean Stackley, the Assistant Secretary of the Navy for Research, Development, and Acquisition, and the object of the discussion was to summarize the U.S. Navy's idea of the UCLASS program at a point in time at which the vision seemed to be changing from long-range missions against targets ashore to less ambitious short-range missions against targets at sea.

"It's very much part of our maritime package, as part of the carrier strike group," Grosklags said of the UCLASS. "The missions now in mind for UCLASS include permissive airspace ISR and strike initially. . . . As the program evolves, those missions would expand to more challenging contested littoral and coastal ISR and strike, to attacking an enemy surface action group."

Addressing the notion that a UCLASS vehicle was originally intended to have an endur-

ance of 14 hours, but that this could decrease as the aircraft was adapted for different sorts of missions, Grosklags replied that "14 hours of endurance is for the specific early operational capability mission, ISR with limited precision strike capability. . . . Once we expand into other mission roles with potentially more weapons or potentially more stuff on the aircraft, whether those be weapons, jamming pods, additional sensor pods, you name it, that 14 hours endurance requirement will no longer be in effect in those mission configurations. . . . The requirement for internal carriage is about a 1,000 [pounds]. There are requirements for two external 3,000 pound hardpoints."

Grosklags continued by explaining that "the whole [concept of operations] for this aircraft is that it will operate as part of the carrier strike group; it may also be tasked by the combatant commander for other missions. It is not designed to operate lone and unafraid, particularly in a hostile environment. . . . We have taken into account operations in the current threat environment in terms of jamming or loss of communications. We've not only looked at the current environment, but we've also looked at what we expect to see in the future environment."

On August 9, 2014, Dave Majumdar revealed in *FlightGlobal* that "concerns have been raised that the capabilities of the U.S. Navy's proposed Unmanned Carrier Launched Surveillance and Strike

President Barack Obama talks with General Martin Dempsey and Admiral James "Sandy" Winnefeld (center) at the White House. In 2014, the Pentagon denied speculation that Winnefeld had "relaxed" the "UCLASS requirements" at the request of the White House. (Official White House photo)

(UCLASS) aircraft have been so watered down from the original concept that the program is now vulnerable to cancellation by a cash-strapped Pentagon. . . . The lower requirements mean many are questioning the necessity of the program at all. As a result, there are some within the navy who believe UCLASS could be offered as a sacrifice as the Pentagon copes with a reduced budget."

Admiral Gary Roughhead, who had retired in 2011 as Chief of Naval Operations, and who was a champion of unmanned combat aircraft, lamented cynically that "the less-survivable, less-endurance approach, although cheaper, is, to me, not transformational. With the UCAS [the original dedicated unmanned combat aircraft program] you really do have a transformational weapon system. . . . The idea [of] a long-dwell, long-range, refuelable, survivable UAV coming off a carrier was extremely important. . . . The whole intent was to take that form, pursue refuelability (you get long endurance), and then use that and move forward on that. . . . By not having it refuelable I think it really changes what I would consider a transformational dimension of naval aviation."

Roughhead went on to point out that "aerial refueling would have allowed the navy to move unmanned assets from shore bases to a carrier at sea from across the globe. That would allow a carrier strike group commander to either reconfigure the air wing as needed or replenish combat losses. It gives you a tremendous amount of flexibility."

Airpower authority Rebecca Grant, the president of IRIS Independent Research, weighed in, complaining that "the current UCLASS

It was a lighter moment when Secretary of the Navy Ray Mabus congratulated Admiral Jonathan Greenert as he became Chief of Naval Operations in 2011. Three years later, however, Mabus and Greenert were not smiling. Dave Majumdar wrote in FlightGlobal that both men had become "upset with [Admiral James] Winnefeld and the [Defense Department Joint Requirements Oversight Council]'s decision to alter the UCLASS requirements." (U.S. Navy photo by MC2 Kevin O'Brien)

makes little sense to me. . . . A UCLASS as described by Roughhead would make sense. So would an armed UCAS vehicle if embarked in numbers adequate to provide [enough orbits to be] usable to a joint force commander."

Speaking for the Defense Department, Dyke Weatherington, the department's director of unmanned warfare and ISR, said that the Pentagon "can't afford to start programs that we can't finish. We can't afford to start programs that we get two or three into and we have to cancel and we have nothing to show for it."

Majumdar reported in his August 9 article that his sources told him that the "specifications for the UCLASS were diluted [by Winnefeld] at the behest of the White House."

Three days later, Majumdar was able to report that an unnamed "senior military official" had stated that "the vice chairman [Winnefeld] had no contact with the White House on the UCLASS requirements. And I would not characterize as 'relaxing' those requirements. . . . The requirements were shifted for UCLASS by actually increasing them in some areas and decreasing them in others to get a different mix. Everyone seems to be in agreement with the direction the program is heading, which should put an affordable, capable platform on carrier flight decks that will expand the navy's ability to project power within the full joint portfolio of unmanned systems. . . . Failing to have made the necessary trade-offs would have measurably limited UCLASS capacity in a number of critical mission areas,"

In the meantime, the Naval Air Systems Command responded that an aerial refueling capability *might* be added as a "future goal," though not as an initial UCLASS requirement.

In turn, Lieutenant Colonel Catie Hauge, speaking for Winnefeld, told Sam LaGrone of *USNI News* that "the White House had no input into the UCLASS requirement." When LaGrone asked White House national security staff spokeswoman Caitlin Hayden, however, she declined to comment.

LaGrone noted in *USNI News* on August 29 that his Defense Department sources had told him that the changes in focus of the UCLASS program were initiated by JROC "based on keeping costs down and a desire to keep unmanned counterterrorism missions as a U.S. military option without the need for foreign basing. . . . A camp in [the office of the Secretary of Defense] began to develop a concept that would gear UCLASS toward a cheaper version focused on counterterrorism missions that wouldn't operate in a heavily contested airspace."

Bob Work, the former undersecretary of the navy and now deputy secretary of defense, explained to LaGrone, "We have already more than 800 aircraft, like Reapers and Predators, that can operate in non-contested airspace. What you don't have is a lot of capability in stealthy-type penetrators. . . . The debate was still going on when I left the department [in May 2014]. I think that the Joint Staff was focused on the lower-end type of system and they were pushing that really hard. The navy was negotiating, saying, 'At least we need to have some growth capability in there.' The carrier is a $10 billion

asset with a $6 billion air wing. I don't see you plopping that off the coast of Africa reaching out and trying to find a high-value [terrorist] target. . . . The initial intent was to get an operational detachment for a carrier, as many of those as you can get. If you could get one or two, you would rotate those through the deployable carriers, those going to the Western Pacific or those going to CENTCOM depending on what you needed . . . if all this is going to be is about cost. You will inevitably be driven toward a lower end system, which I don't think the joint force needs."

At the end of September 2014, Dave Majumdar wrote in *Flight-Global* that both Secretary Mabus and Admiral Jonathan Greenert,

Defense Secretary Ashton Carter greets Senator John McCain before Carter's testimony at a hearing of the Senate Armed Services Committee on Capitol Hill in December 2015. Earlier in the year, McCain had publicly called the navy's then-current UCLASS requirements "strategically misguided." In a memo to Carter, he wrote, "I am concerned that the current requirements proposed for the UCLASS program place a disproportionate emphasis on unrefueled endurance to enable sustained ISR support to the carrier strike group, which would result in an aircraft design with serious deficiencies in both long-term survivability and its internal weapons payload capacity. . . . Our nation has made a sizable investment in this demonstration program to date, and both air vehicles have consumed only a small fraction of their approved flying hours." (DOD photo by U.S. Navy Petty Officer 1st Class Tim Godbee)

the chief of naval operations, were "upset with Winnefeld and the JROC's decision to alter the UCLASS requirements. In light of strong pressure from Congress, the industry, and a scathing new Government Accountability Office (GAO) report, sources say that there are indications the U.S. Navy is taking another look at the draft requirements for the UCLASS."

An unnamed industry source, meanwhile, had told Majumdar, "It's fairly obvious that the navy wants to run its own budget priorities, and the JROC is recommending otherwise with the UCLASS. I would also bet that the [Lockheed Martin F-35] Joint Strike Fighter versus future [Boeing] F/A-18E/F/G buys are being looked at with the navy wanting to delay or stretch out the F-35B/C buys."

The debate continued, and UCLASS languished for a year.

In March 2015, Senator John McCain, chairman of the Senate Armed Services Committee and a retired naval aviator, publicly called the navy's then-current UCLASS requirements "strategically misguided."

In a memo to Secretary of Defense Ashton Carter, he wrote, "I am concerned that the current requirements proposed for the UCLASS program place a disproportionate emphasis on unrefueled endurance to enable sustained ISR support to the carrier strike group, which would result in an aircraft design with serious deficiencies in both

Vice Admiral David Dunaway, commander of Naval Air Systems Command, receives a 2014 briefing at Naval Air Station Patuxent River. In October 2015 the Navy Times reported that Dunaway was growing impatient about the progress of UCLASS as he pointed out that "those "S"s stand for strike and surveillance, and there's some debate over which should take precedence . . . Can we bring an unmanned vehicle to the carrier much faster? Technically? Absolutely. Organizationally, it appears to be impossible." (U.S. Navy photo by MC2 Kenneth Abbate)

long-term survivability and its internal weapons payload capacity. . . . Our nation has made a sizable investment in this demonstration program to date, and both air vehicles have consumed only a small fraction of their approved flying hours."

The latter is a reference to the X-47B aircraft and to its not being used as a demonstrator after the completion of its prescribed test program.

In October 2015, when Meghann Myers, writing in *Navy Times*, raised the issue of its continued use with Phil Finnegan of the Teal Group, an aerospace and defense industry analysis firm, he agreed that "it makes total sense for current carrier crews to get some practice with the X-47B while they wait on UCLASS. . . . It's a desire for the Navy, which is the service which has least used unmanned systems and is behind the Army and the Air Force, to gain expertise. . . . And to gain expertise from the carrier makes a lot of sense when you're planning a major acquisition that would come from a carrier."

Finnegan went on to say that the navy and the Defense Department "don't want to use the X-47B [for continued evaluation flights] because they believe it would give an [unfair] advantage to Northrop Grumman in the UCLASS competition . . . [but] the requirements of the UCLASS competition themselves will very strongly determine which company has the advantage. . . . Northrop's expertise in strike and stealthy reconnaissance would put it at the head of the pack if the Navy decides to focus there, with Lockheed right behind it."

In her October 2015 *Navy Times* article, Myers added that Vice Admiral Dave Dunaway, now the head of the Naval Air Systems Command, complained that he was still waiting for congressional approval of the next round of requests for proposals from the contractors. As Myers wrote, "Lawmakers have been reluctant to get the ball rolling on UCLASS until the Navy figures out exactly what it will be; those 'S's stand for strike and surveillance, and there's some debate over which should take precedence."

"Can we bring an unmanned vehicle to the carrier much faster?" Dunaway asked rhetorically. "Technically? Absolutely. Organizationally, it appears to be impossible. There's a political battle going on with what kind of capability we need coming off the carrier."

In the meantime, in September 2015, the House and Senate armed services committees finally came to an agreement on the National Defense Authorization Act for Fiscal Year 2016, it included an allocation of $375 million for at least two UCLASS prototypes that would be an evolutionary step beyond the X-47B demonstrator. The two committees were displeased with the U.S. Navy for having requested only $134.7 million for the program.

John McCain's fingerprints were visible on a joint congressional statement that said, "The conferees believe that the Navy should develop a penetrating, air-refuelable, unmanned carrier-launched aircraft capable of performing a broad range of missions in a non-permissive environment. The conferees believe that such an aircraft should be designed for full integration into carrier air wing operations (including strike operations) and possess the range, pay-

load, and survivability attributes as necessary to complement such integration. . . . Although the Defense Department could develop land-based unmanned aircraft with attributes to support the air wing, the conferees believe that the United States would derive substantial strategic and operational benefits from operating such aircraft from a mobile seabase that is self-deployable and not subject to the caveats of a host nation."

In turn, Randy Forbes, the congressional champion of UCLASS, said that "as access-denied environments proliferate, the Carrier Air Wing of the future must contain a mix of manned and unmanned aircraft capable of striking in contested airspace. Integrating an unmanned aircraft fully into the Air Wing must be a priority in the years ahead."

When the 2016 National Defense Authorization Act finally passed both houses of Congress in December 2015, the heavily picked-over spending bill still included $300 million to move the UCLASS program forward, albeit with an operational date that was moved from 2020 to sometime in 2022 or 2023.

On February 1, 2016, however, everything suddenly changed.

UCLASS unexpectedly disappeared, only to be reborn as the Carrier-Based Aerial-Refueling System (CBARS) program. That which had just the day before embodied the future of unmanned aerial warfare had been repurposed principally as an unmanned aerial refueling platform!

It should be said that carrier-based combat aircraft were already being used to refuel other combat aircraft. Indeed, around a quarter

Shortly after returning from an inspection tour of Naval Air Station Pensacola in January 2016, Admiral John Richardson, the chief of naval operations, went out to personally brief the four companies that had been working on UCLASS proposals to alert them to change from UCLASS to CBARS. (U.S. Navy photo by Bruce Cummins)

of F/A-18 missions are said to be aerial refueling missions, and this capability had been a part, albeit a small part, of the UCLASS capabilities package. However, under CBARS, the primary strike mission was abruptly deleted from the requirements for the four aircraft that had been formally proposed for UCLASS.

The reasoning behind the program metamorphosis seemed to be an effort to take some of the refueling load off the F/A-18s so that *they* could be devoted to strike missions. As James Drew of *FlightGlobal* explained, "The changes shift emphasis from remotely controlled surveillance and strike missions to replacing overworked Boeing F/A-18 Super Hornets in the aerial tanking role."

This, however, runs contrary to the evolving U.S. Navy doctrinal move toward unmanned strike aircraft, a point of view strongly advocated by Secretary Mabus.

As with the F/A-18s, the notional CBARS aircraft transferred fuel from drop tanks hung beneath the aircraft, so it was apparent that the attachment points for the tanks of the CBARS aircraft *could* double as weapons pylons.

So that the startling news did not come as a complete surprise, Admiral John Richardson, the chief of naval operations, had gone on the road in January to personally call on the four companies that had been working on UCLASS proposals to alert them to the

After UCLASS became CBARS, Vice Admiral Joseph Mulloy, the deputy chief of naval operations for integration of capabilities and resources, promised that "the four competitors we had for UCLASS are still viable. . . . We want some of the other requirements in there, like we may expand the fuel requirement, but we know all four vendors have air-bodies that will meet those requirements." (U.S. Navy photo by MC2 Jason Graham)

coming change. He explained that a new request for proposals would be forthcoming to take the change of mission into account.

Vice Admiral Joseph Mulloy, the deputy chief of naval operations for integration of capabilities and resources, promised that "the four competitors we had for UCLASS are still viable. . . . We want some of the other requirements in there, like we may expand the fuel requirement, but we know all four vendors have air-bodies that will meet those requirements."

Writing in *USNI News*, Sam LaGrone explained that the metamorphosis of UCLASS into CBARS came "alongside an additional buy of Boeing F/A-18 E/F Super Hornets over the next several years and accelerated purchases and development of the Lockheed Martin F-35 Lighting II Joint Strike Fighter (JSF). The trio of budget moves seeks to blunt the Navy's looming strike fighter shortfall, move more stealth capability sooner into the carrier air wing, and create a development path for future unmanned systems onboard the service's fleet of nuclear carriers."

LaGrone reported on February 27 that Admiral Mulloy had told him, "We're probably going to drop some of the high-end specs and try to grow the class and increase the survivability [later]. It has to be more refueling, a little bit of ISR, weapons later, and focus on its ability to be the flying truck."

When it came to funding, Mulloy was quick to convey the impression that the U.S. Navy was sure that it could use the money that Congress had appropriated for UCLASS to pay for CBARS.

"UCLASS is dead, but the money that was appropriated by Congress in the line is still usable," Mulloy told James Drew of *Flight-Global*. "We headed to Congress and talked to all the lawyers."

As Drew wrote, "a multi-mission tanker is certainly not what Congress was expecting to come from the defense secretary's top-level intelligence, surveillance, and reconnaissance portfolio review, especially after successful ship-based demonstrations of the low-observable Northrop Grumman X-47B unmanned combat air vehicle."

By now, the U.S. Navy had even picked a name and designation for the CBARS aircraft. This was apparently because navy personnel were disgruntled with "CBARS" as a name for the program. Over the coming weeks, drafts of written testimony that would be submitted to Congress in advance of budget hearings were already referring to the aircraft as the "RAQ-25 Stingray."

Sam LaGrone reported on February 27 that "Navy officials" had told him that the service was less than enthusiastic about the name "big Pentagon came up with for the RAQ-25." He cited the name as "indicative of the churn surrounding the restructure of the Naval Air Systems Command (NAVAIR)–led program in the last year. . . . It's also unclear if the name "Sting*ray*" is a reference to [Navy Secretary *Ray*] Mabus, an advocate for unmanned aviation who said in 2015 the Lockheed Martin F-35 Lighting II Joint Strike Fighter would likely be the last manned strike fighter the Navy would ever buy. Subtle honorifics in Navy program designations are not new. The

retired Grumman F-14 Tomcat, in part, pays homage to the late Vice Admiral Thomas F. Connolly who crafted the requirements for the interceptor. During development of the F-14, some on the program refer to the fighter as 'Tom's cat.'"

In March 2016, the notional "Reconnaissance Attack" RAQ-25 nomenclature was superseded in the narrative by mention of the vehicle as a "Multi-role" aircraft, with the terms MQ-XX and MQ-25 being circulated. On July 15, the CBARS appellation was officially terminated, and it became official that the aircraft would be the MQ-25A Stingray. However, it was also announced that it would be designated as ZMQ-25A until a contractor was selected.

It was assumed that the contractor would be chosen from among those who had developed proposals for the abandoned UCLASS. In any case, Sam LaGrone has noted that, "the requirements for the tanking mission put wing-body-tail designs developed by Boeing and General Atomics more in line with the [current] mission as opposed to offerings from Lockheed Martin and Northrop Grumman, which focused on developing aircraft that would be better suited for operating in a more contested air space."

Thinking ahead to the changes he knew were coming under CBARS, Rob Weiss of Lockheed Martin's Skunk Works said on March 15 that his team was going to stay with a flying wing configuration in line with their Polecat, RQ-170 Sentinel, and UCLASS proposal.

"We believe [that a flying wing] will be just as affordable as a wing-body-tail configuration," he said. "But a wing-body-tail will not be able to fulfill the requirements for penetrating strike in the future. You can take the flying wing and not put on all the coatings and other capabilities in that initial version and be competitive on the cost but have a growth path forward, that same path to use that vehicle design to operate in a [contested] environment."

Congress, which had so recently appropriated more money than the U.S. Navy had wanted for UCLASS, was disappointed with the UCLASS-CBARS-Stingray evolution. In April 2016, members of the House Armed Services Committee, meeting for work on the Fiscal Year 2017 defense bill, let it be known that they wanted long-range strike capability retained in the aircraft. Nevertheless, they were apparently willing to compromise. Megan Eckstein reported in *USNI News* on April 20 that the committee "will not this year force the Navy's hand by withholding money [if] the Navy is not interested in starting out with strike as a primary mission."

It was during these hearings that Director for Air Warfare Rear Admiral Mike Manazir recalled that in 2009 then-Chief of Naval Operations Admiral Gary Roughhead had "pounded a table in a secure space and said, 'I want unmanned on a carrier by 2018.' And that started a series of conversations in the Pentagon about unmanned capability on the aircraft carrier."

He then went on to say that the navy wanted to focus only on a refueling and ISR capability in the interest of expedience, and that "we can accommodate those two missions on an unmanned system coming off the aircraft carrier more rapidly . . . what we've got to do is show we can use a platform to do two basic meat-and-potato missions on the aircraft carrier using the MQ-XX, and that will also provide a platform for us to go forward and do additional more advanced capabilities [such as long-range strike missions] in the future."

"Future" has always been a word that slips easily into any description of this series of unmanned combat air vehicle programs.

Two points can be gleaned from the long and winding tale of the metamorphosis of UCAV, as it became J-UCAS and UCAS-N, and then UCLASS and CBARS, then next, the MQ-25A Stingray, and onto possible later iterations. The first is that whatever name it has worn, it has *always* been called the future of unmanned aerial combat. The second point is that this future, once easily imaginable, has never turned out to be foreseeable.

Secretary of the Navy Ray Mabus speaks to sailors in the hangar bay of aircraft carrier USS George Washington (CVN-73) in October 2015. It has been speculated that the name "Stingray" was chosen for the MQ-25A vehicle as an homage to Mabus in the way that the F-14 Tomcat was said to have been named for Vice Admiral Tom Connolly. (U.S. Navy photo by MC3 Jonathan Nelson)

Chapter 18

THE FUTURE OF UNMANNED AERIAL COMBAT

In considering the future of unmanned aerial combat systems, a good place to start might be to continue with the congressional hearings of April 2016, a discussion of which in Chapter 17 led us to the conclusion that the future of unmanned combat systems is not foreseeable!

Rear Admiral Mike Manazir recalled a navy vision for that future, a vision that was rooted in the previous decade, but that had not evolved as planned. He spoke of how the U.S. Navy had come around to the idea of a Stingray with no sting, even after it had long been intended to have one. He spoke of the program that had once called for a stealthy strike aircraft ready to fly into contested airspace to destroy high-value targets, a program that now centered on an aerial vehicle that Vice Admiral Joseph Mulloy had called a "truck."

Manazir did, however, promise that the stingless Stingray had the *potential* for "more advanced capabilities in the future." This comment came a dozen years *after* a stealthy UCAV demonstrator, the Boeing X-45A, had first released ordnance on a simulated target.

As this disappointing anecdote illustrates, the future of unmanned aerial combat systems is as much about politics and budgets as it is about technology, and that above all, it is about vision. That which began as UCAV and evolved through UCLASS, like the Future European MALE program across the Atlantic, must be seen through the lens of *blurred* vision. Like so many aerospace programs through the decades, they are victims of confused goals, of corners cut, of a changing perception of the end product, and the cost of all these things, both in terms of budget and morale.

We are also reminded of how, even as high-profile programs chalk up more hours in conference rooms than on flight lines, lower profile programs are left in the hands of the people closer to the field of action, those whom Theodore Roosevelt famously called "the doer of deeds." It was here that the Hellfire missiles were first hung beneath the wings of Predator drones and *without* the benefit of a dozen years of costly feasibility studies.

This leads us to Lieutenant General Jon Davis, the Deputy Commandant for Aviation of the U.S. Marine Corps, who was also testifying at the 2016 hearings. When asked if his service had any interest in an unmanned strike aircraft, he replied, "We have tremendous interest." However, he was quick to point out that the Marines operate from amphibious assault ships and not from the much larger aircraft carriers of their sister service.

A solar-powered, lighter-than-air pseudosatellite operates, indifferent to weather, and indefinitely over the eastern seaboard of the United States. Could it be that the future of unmanned aerial combat will involve arming vehicles such as this with high-powered lasers for ICBM interception and other missions? (Lockheed Martin)

For the U.S. Marines, as for many applications in other services worldwide, the future is in smaller systems. The marines, like the navy, have long used the small Boeing/Insitu ScanEagle, as have the air forces of a dozen countries, including the U.S. Air Force. Since 2014, they have also used the Boeing/Insitu's RQ-21A Blackjack, a cousin to the ScanEagle.

For the marines, the future is also in rotary-wing systems, which can operate from amphibious assault ships and, indeed, from virtually any ship.

In the first dozen years of the 21st Century the U.S. Navy had pursued the Northrop Grumman MQ-8 Fire Scout program, though only a handful of aircraft were actually built. The MQ-8B variant was potentially a UCAV, with provisions for AGM-114 Hellfire missiles, GBU-44 Viper Strike laser-guided glide bombs, and the Advanced Precision Kill Weapon System (APKWS). In 2011, MQ-8Bs were deployed for operations over both Afghanistan and Libya, but only in a reconnaissance role. Beginning in 2013, some were equipped with RDR-1700 maritime surveillance radar for search and rescue. Under the APKWS program, the MQ-8B was also configured to fire Hydra 70 2.75-inch fin-stabilized ground-attack rockets. Normally, the Hydra 70 is unguided, but those first fired by a Fire Scout at the Yuma Proving Ground are among a new generation of laser-guided precision Hydras.

Beginning in 2013, the navy began flying the MQ-8C, also known as Fire-X, which matches MQ-8B avionics to the larger air-frame of a Bell 407 helicopter, the military version of which is the U.S. Army's OH-58 Kiowa Warrior which has an attack capability. During 2015, the navy tested the MQ-8C at Point Mugu, and in early 2016, the marines borrowed some of them for evaluation aboard their amphibious assault ships.

The marines had previously evaluated the Kaman/Lockheed Martin CQ-24 K-MAX unmanned helicopter and had deployed them to Afghanistan between 2011 and 2014 for use in transporting supplies to troops at remote outposts.

In 2016, as General Davis was discussing Marine Corps options in the wake of the metamorphosis of UCLASS, unmanned rotary-wing aircraft came up, and the capability of a drone such as the MQ-8C to be armed emerged as another potential scenario under the heading of unmanned aerial combat and one more expediently accomplished.

Will it be the United States leading the way tactically in operating unmanned combat air vehicles from ships at sea? Some form of the MQ-25 may or may not be the future unmanned strike aircraft that the U.S. Navy has said that it wants on its aircraft carriers. Some form of the MQ-8C may or may not be the future unmanned attack helicopter that the U.S. Marine Corps might use on its amphibious assault ships, but if it comes it will come sooner than that which evolves from UCLASS or Stingray.

However, in China, the development of shipboard drones already has a very high priority; one might even say that it is a higher priority than it is for the United States.

In the United Kingdom, meanwhile, the idea of a ship specifically designed as a "drone carrier" had been circulated. The "concept

Rear Admiral Michael Manazir, the U.S. Navy's director of air warfare, speaks to the New York Council of the Navy League on the topic of "Warfighting in the 21st Century." Manazir has observed that after having proven them capable of aircraft carrier operations, the state of the art in unmanned systems will "provide a platform for us to go forward and do additional more advanced capabilities [such as long-range strike missions] in the future." (U.S. Navy photo by Lieutenant Matthew Stroup)

Lieutenant General Jon Davis, the deputy commandant for aviation of the U.S. Marine Corps, said in 2016 that his service had "tremendous interest" in an unmanned strike aircraft like the X-47B, but he was quick to point out that the marines operate from amphibious assault ships and not from the larger aircraft carriers of the U.S. Navy, thus putting the emphasis on rotary-wing UAVs. (USMC)

ship" of such a class of warship is the UXV *Combatant*, which was based on the hull of the 8,400-ton Type 45 (or HMS *Daring* class) destroyers, six of which were built by BAE Systems Maritime and its predecessor, BAE Systems Surface Fleet Solutions. BAE Systems has described a vessel that would "launch, operate and recover large numbers of small unmanned vehicles for extended periods, [playing] the role of mother ship, a permanent base and control centre for the futuristic unmanned land, sea, and air vehicles before, during and on completion of their missions." By the time the last of the *Daring*-class ships was commissioned in 2013, the Ministry of Defence had decided *not* to acquire a vessel such as the UXV *Combatant* in the immediate future.

Although the British shelved their ambitious idea and the U.S. Navy parked its X-47B, the pace of Chinese unmanned carrier aircraft development has not slackened.

Micro UAVs are outside the parameters of this book, but the technology represented by them is certainly part of the future. One of the most interesting is the Lockheed Martin Samarai. A handheld vehicle, it weighs less than half a pound and streams live video from a camera that rotates around its center providing a 360-degree view without a gimbal. Perhaps most amazing is that it can be produced on a 3D printer.

"Our team has taken the basic shape and design of the naturally aerodynamic maple seed and harnessed it with flight controls and avionics," said Kingsley Fregene of Lockheed Martin's Advanced Technology Laboratories about the Samarai. "We've learned a great deal about biologically inspired vehicles that we can apply across the laboratory, including a better understanding of micro-robots and the devices that control their movement."

A recon bird becomes a UCAV. This MQ8B Fire Scout aircraft, at NAS Oceana in Virginia, is equipped with launchers for Hydra 70 2.75-inch fin-stabilized ground-attack rockets. (US Navy photo by PM2 Class Daniel McLain)

Another window through which the future of advanced combat aircraft can be seen taking shape is in the folklore of the aviation enthusiast community, where slivers of information are shared for speculation.

For example, one of the most fascinating aircraft among the secret and unseen is the Northrop Grumman RQ-180, generally described as having been designed for intelligence, surveillance, and reconnaissance (ISR) missions. However, in almost the same breath, the speculators often make mention of adapting it for combat missions, presumably under the MQ-180 designation.

The aircraft was revealed in the December 6, 2013, issue of *Aviation Week* by Amy Butler and Bill Sweetman, the latter being one of the aviation world's most prominent investigative journalists, a man well known for his work in pursuing the story of the mysterious hypersonic aircraft known only as "Aurora."

Sweetman and Butler noted that the RQ-180 "aircraft will conduct the penetrating ISR mission that has been left unaddressed, and under wide debate, since retirement of the Lockheed SR-71 in 1998." Naturally, any mention of the SR-71, the fastest air-breathing aircraft

in history, always brings a very high bar in terms of performance into the conversation.

Despite the extensive revelations, details of the RQ-180 remain secret, with the last official word on the project being the terse statement by air force spokeswoman Jennifer Cassidy that "the Air Force does not discuss this program," which confirms only that there *is* a program.

As is so often the case, it is not so much about what is said, but what is *not* said, and what is said about related things. It is like looking for the shadow cast by something that may be out of sight around a corner. For example, Lieutenant General Charles Davis, the uniformed deputy in the office of the Assistant Secretary of the Air Force for Acquisition, told the House Armed Services Committee that the air force wants to use money allocated for the RQ-4 Global Hawk for "much higher priorities," which he declined to discuss in an open congressional hearing.

Then, Lieutenant General Robert "Bob" Otto, the Air Force Deputy Chief of Staff for Intelligence, Surveillance and Reconnaissance, spoke openly about the need for an unmanned ISR aircraft that

An MQ-8C Fire Scout unmanned aerial vehicle takes off from Naval Base Ventura County at Point Mugu during initial testing in October 2013. The MQ-8C air vehicle upgrade provides longer endurance and range and greater payload capability than the MQ-8B. (U.S. Navy)

could operate in "contested environments," the way that the MQ-1 Predator and MQ-9 Reaper do in the uncontested skies over Southwest Asia.

"We will seek a more balanced fleet of both manned and unmanned platforms that are able to penetrate denied airspace and provide unprecedented levels of persistence," Otto has said publicly, describing performance in an aircraft that is very much like the popular perception of the RQ-180.

This perception, like that of so many top secret programs through the years, flows from a folklore fueled by leaks and rumors from which a reasonably accurate picture may be drawn.

As an ISR platform, a future air force RQ-180 (or a "multi-mission" MQ-180 UCAV) like those aircraft developed under the U.S. Navy's UCLASS program, would certainly incorporate fifth-generation Active Electronically Scanned Array (AESA) radar. With its transmitter and receiver functions composed of compact solid-state modules, AESA is an active phased array radar that directs its beam through the emission of separate radio waves from each module that interface specific angles in front of an antenna.

It is no stretch of the imagination to assume that, if there had been a competitive bidding process, both Boeing and Lockheed Martin would have contributed proposals. It is a safe bet that the latter firm based its proposal upon lessons learned from the RQ/MQ-170, which the aircraft identified as the RQ/MQ-180 would supersede. In turn, the RQ/MQ-180 would certainly be larger, faster, and longer ranging than the RQ-170.

Lockheed Martin has also long been rumored to be looking at concepts for hypersonic ISR aircraft (both manned and unmanned) that could be seen as a worthy successor to the SR-71. Indeed, the enthusiast folklore had long spoken wistfully of such an aircraft as being designated "SR-72," which would almost certainly not be the case, though one never knows.

In turn, the Boeing RQ/MQ-180 proposal leaned on lessons learned during the X-45A and Phantom Eye programs, and Northrop Grumman used the X-47B (and the manned B-2) as foundation technology upon which to build. It is widely believed that the RQ/MQ-180 has a "cranked-kite" flying-wing design similar in appearance to the X-47B.

An MQ-8B Fire Scout UAV shares the flight deck of the littoral combat ship USS Fort Worth *with an MH-60R Sea Hawk helicopter in May 2015 at Changi Naval Base in Singapore. (U.S. Navy photo by Lieutenant James Arterberry)*

It has been suggested that the RQ/MQ-180 might use a variation on the General Electric CF34 medium bypass turbofan engine, which has often come up in discussions of future variations of the Northrop Grumman X-47B, such as the one proposed to meet the operational requirements of the UCLASS program.

The RQ/MQ-180 would almost certainly need to be aerial refuelable in order to fulfill its mission of deep penetration of contested air space. Perhaps this requirement in the RQ/MQ-180 had as much or more to do with the X-47B refueling demonstrations in 2015 as it did with UCLASS, where the importance of an aerial refueling capability had been downgraded.

In looking into Northrop Grumman financial statements, Butler and Sweetman intuited that the RQ-180 contract would have been awarded in around 2008, given that it was in that year that "the company disclosed a $2 billion increase in the backlog in its Integrated Systems division. This is the operating unit responsible for building the B-2 bomber, Global Hawk, and Fire Scout UAS and X-47B."

Two years later, Northrop Grumman had begun a major expansion of its factory complex at Air Force Plant 42, the secure manufacturing facility at Palmdale, California, where they had built most of the above aircraft. Meanwhile, followers of publicly available satellite imagery also noted the construction of shelters and hangars large enough for aircraft with 130-foot wingspans at the officially nonexistent flight test center at Groom Lake, Nevada, that is known as Area 51.

The K-MAX Unmanned Multi-Mission Helicopter has been operational with the U.S. Marine Corps in Afghanistan since 2011. It was created by Kaman and has been developed jointly by Kaman and Lockheed Martin as a hazardous mission vehicle. As noted by the latter firm, "It can be used in combat to deliver supplies to the battlefield, as well as civilian situations involving chemical, biological, or radiological hazards." Might its future include a UCAV variant? (Lockheed Martin)

It was further ascertained that an unnamed Northrop Grumman aircraft "entered low-rate initial production" in 2013, meaning that the flight test program has concluded and that the company was awaiting a Defense Department go-ahead for full production.

Like Aurora, the RQ/MQ-180 may not wear the official designation ascribed to it, nor may it be exactly the aircraft that the speculators are sure it is. One thing that the two aircraft do have in common is that they are both useful allegories in the fluid, ever-changing conjecture about the future of high-performance military aviation.

Meanwhile, there has also been talk about a U.S. Air Force "Hunter-Killer" conceptual aircraft that has been associated with the Scaled Composites unmanned Model 395 and Model 396 airframes, the former an unmanned variant of the company's Proteus long-endurance manned aircraft and the latter a spin-off of the RQ-4 Global Hawk that was developed in cooperation with Northrop Grumman. When General Charles Davis told the House Armed Services Committee that the Air Force wanted to use money allocated for the RQ-4 for "much higher priorities," perhaps this is what he had in mind.

At the leading edge of weapons technology for future combat air vehicles (both manned and unmanned) is the use of lasers. In 2013, under the name "Project Endurance," DARPA awarded $14.6 million to Northrop Grumman and $11.4 million to Lockheed Martin to "develop technology for pod-mounted lasers to protect a variety of airborne platforms from emerging and legacy electro-optical IR guided surface-to-air missiles." The recollection of the loss of an RQ-170 over Iran (and the since-dispelled fear that it might have been shot down) was still fresh in the collective Defense Department memory.

Specifically, DARPA was interested in "miniaturizing component technologies, developing high-precision target tracking, identification, and lightweight agile beam control to support target engagement," as well as "the phenomenology of laser-target interactions and associated threat vulnerabilities."

We next turn to the stratosphere and the aerie of the High Altitude Long Endurance (HALE) drone. The potential for an extremely long-endurance drone, both as a reconnaissance UAV or an armed UCAV is broad. So too is the spectrum of vehicles that might be considered. The Boeing Phantom Eye is certainly an example, as are the vehicles developed under NASA's Environmental Research Aircraft and Sensor Technology (ERAST) program from the early part of the century. ERAST included a series of solar and fuel cell–powered aircraft such as the Centurion, Helios, and Pathfinder.

DARPA, meanwhile, has looked into a variety of winged, unmanned aircraft under its Very high altitude, Ultraendurance, Loitering Theater Unmanned Reconnaissance Element (VULTURE) program, which looks to develop an aircraft with an endurance that would be measured in *years*. Among the candidates for the program was the Z-winged Odysseus vehicle developed jointly by Aurora Flight Sciences and BAE Systems.

In the United Kingdom, the firm QinetiQ (pronounced "kinetic"), a defense technology spinoff of the former British government organization Defence Evaluation and Research Agency (DERA), developed its Zephyr vehicle. Built of lightweight carbon fiber, the 55-pound solar-powered Zephyr used solar-charged lithium-sulphur batteries for nighttime power and established endurance of record of two weeks aloft.

Another window into the future: Inspired by a maple seed, Lockheed Martin's Samarai monocopter handheld vehicle weighs less than half a pound, streams live video from a camera that rotates around its center providing a 360-degree view without a gimbal, and is produced on a 3D printer. (Lockheed Martin)

Of the future of unmanned combat air vehicles, Lieutenant General Bob Otto, the Air Force Deputy Chief of Staff for Intelligence, Surveillance and Reconnaissance, has spoken of the need for an unmanned ISR aircraft that could operate in "contested environments," the way that the MQ-1 Predator and MQ-9 Reaper do in the uncontested skies over southwest Asia. (USAF photo by Airman 1st Class Aaron Stout)

The basis for a near-term, long-endurance UCAV may be a vehicle such as the Scaled Composites tandem-wing Proteus that was used as a testbed for a series of UAV collision-avoidance flight demonstrations. (NASA photo by Carla Thomas)

Lockheed Martin's Integrated Sensor Is Structure (ISIS) system is a disruptive Command & Control, Intelligence, Surveillance, and Reconnaissance (C2ISR) platform with an extremely large dual-aperture radar capability integrated into a fully autonomous stratospheric unmanned airship. This solar and regenerative fuel-cell-powered, electric propulsion, extreme endurance stratospheric vehicle provides broad-area coverage using a dual-band radar capable of detecting and tracking air, ground, and maritime targets from dismounted personnel to ballistic missiles. (Lockheed Martin)

In 2013, the Zephyr program became part of the Airbus High Altitude Pseudo-Satellite (HAPS) program. The term "pseudo-satellite," or "pseudolite," was coined recently to describe something that is not a satellite but something that can perform a mission typically executed by a satellite. They include HALE aircraft as well as the likes of mountaintop GPS transceivers.

Another configuration being developed to meet the definition and requirements for a HALE UAV that has attracted the attention of the Pentagon's Missile Defense Agency, as well as the U.S. Army Space and Missile Defense Command (SMDC), is the unmanned lighter-than-air vehicle.

The SMDC's Composite Hull High Altitude Powered Platform (CHHAPP) program was initiated to develop a series of autonomous, long-endurance, solar-electric, stratospheric airships. The first of these was HiSentinel, a 146-foot technology demonstrator airship created by Southwest Research Institute, Aerostar International, and the Air Force Research Laboratory (AFRL). In December 2005, the HiSentinel was launched from Roswell, New Mexico, reaching an altitude of 74,000 feet.

Since the turn of the century, Lockheed Martin has been especially active in the lighter-than-air field, pursuing a lineage thread that goes back to the Aeronautics Division of the Goodyear Tire and Rubber Company that began manufacturing the famous "Goodyear Blimps" in 1912 and started using them as advertising vehicles in 1925. Having evolved into Goodyear Aerospace as the product portfolio grew, the division was sold to Loral in 1987, passed to Lockheed in 1993, and to Lockheed Martin in 1995. Lockheed Martin claims its Goodyear predecessor, especially the airships that Goodyear built for the U.S. Navy before World War II, as part of its lighter-than-air heritage.

The Lockheed Martin HALE-D demonstrated key technologies critical to the development of unmanned airships, including communications links, solar array electricity generation, and remote piloting communications and control capability. (Lockheed Martin)

Since 2004, the U.S. Army has been using the Lockheed Martin Persistent Threat Detection System (PTDS) as a long-endurance intelligence, surveillance, reconnaissance, and communications platform in Afghanistan and Iraq. The PTDS uses multiple sensors to link tactical and theater surveillance assets and to distribute threat data to operational forces. For the U.S. Army's Long Endurance Multi-intelligence Vehicle (LEMV) program, Lockheed Martin produced its P-791. It was a hybrid airship in which part of the weight was supported by aerostatic (buoyant) lift for the sake of payload capacity and part by aerodynamic lift for the sake of speed.

Lockheed Martin also developed a stratospheric airship under DARPA's Integrated Sensor is Structure (ISIS) program, whose unfortunate acronym was chosen in 2009 before the rise of the Islamic State. According to Lockheed Martin, its ISIS vehicle would be capable of tracking "dismounted enemy combatants" at a distance of 190 miles, cruise missiles at 375 miles, and ballistic targets at ranges as far as 1,000 miles, using a large, lightweight, phased-array aperture, stating that "this approach reverses the current technical solutions of fixed-wing C2ISR assets that rely on high power and are limited by aperture."

The Active Electronically Scanned Array (AESA) antenna would be bonded to the hull of an airship 500 to 1,000 feet long that would remain in position for long periods above the jet stream at altitudes of up to 70,000 feet.

It was the MDA, the organization that seeks to potentially arm the Phantom Eye HALE drone with deadly lasers, that contracted with Lockheed Martin for the High-Altitude Airship (HAA) program. The HAA vehicle would function as a pseudo-satellite in the equivalent of a quasi-geostationary, persistent orbital station at an altitude exceeding 60,000 feet. With a 300-mile observation radius, the HAA could function as a surveillance platform, for telecommunications relay, or to observe the weather. The operational aircraft would be 500 feet long, roughly two thirds the size of the famous German Zeppelin *Hindenberg*.

In reaching the point in this book where we are about to interrupt a narrative that we cannot truly conclude, we must reflect upon the past decades of unmanned aerial combat and upon the future of the same.

There is still much to be written, for we are at the threshold of an era of military aviation that is barely entering its formative years.

One thing is certain. Unmanned combat air vehicles are here to stay. Once considered a novelty (as aircraft themselves once were) they are now firmly established as part of both tactical doctrine and

Odysseus, the Aurora Flight Sciences proposal for the DARPA Vulture program, would have a folding, Z-shaped wing structure. Using solar energy to power the aircraft during the day, and stored solar energy to power the aircraft at night, Odysseus would fly in the stratosphere throughout its five-year mission. (Aurora Flight Sciences)

of the self-image of defense establishments in the United States and elsewhere. In their 21st Century *Unmanned Systems Integrated Roadmap*, the U.S. Defense Department noted that "as unmanned systems have proven their worth on the battlefield, DOD has allocated an increasing percentage of its budget to developing and acquiring these systems. With the transition from a handful of innovative experimental systems to normalized program developments, unmanned systems have received their share of inclusion in Congressional direction and are influenced by many acquisition initiatives and departmental policies."

Such a statement could not have been made in the 20th Century.

We are reminded also of the words of Vice Admiral James Syring, the director of the Pentagon's Missile Defense Agency (MDA), who told the Space & Missile Defense conference in Huntsville, Alabama, in August 2015 that the Defense Department was formally embracing the idea of using a laser-armed drone to attack ICBMs in their boost phase.

He spoke of the Boeing Phantom Eye, which had already established a flight duration of two weeks, and which was capable of flying into the stratosphere to 65,000 feet. He spoke of the role of such a HALE platform in missile defense, and he said, "If it had been easy we would have done it by now, but given the rapid progress in laser technology, it's not a huge reach."

To bring the narrative full circle, we return to General Atomics Aeronautical Systems, with whom we opened this book. In so doing we recall the company's High Energy Liquid Laser Area Defense System (HELLADS) weapons system program. The important thing about this program is that it is aimed at an order of magnitude reduction in weight when compared to those used in the YAL-1A Airborne Laser aircraft, or even in subsequent laser weapons systems.

The power in kilowatts of a laser is directionally proportional to the weight of the system. In a ground-based laser, this is of less significance, but in an airborne system of any kind, weight is highly critical. By comparison, the laser installed in the YAL-1A required 55 kilograms (121 pounds) for each kilowatt of energy delivered. The goal of HELLADS is for a ratio of 5 kilograms (or less) to 1 kilowatt, or just 10 percent of the weight of the YAL-1A system. General Atomics intends to put a 150-kilowatt laser weapon into one of its unmanned combat air vehicles, a weapon that would be capable of shooting down "tactical targets such as surface-to-air missiles and rockets." Such a weapon, at the intended weight of 1,650 pounds, could easily be accommodated by either an MQ-9 Reaper or a General Atomics Avenger.

Could an unmanned combat aircraft loitering over a battlefield or flying through a contested target area fire a laser to shoot down a surface-to-air missile?

Could an unmanned, pseudo-satellite, either a winged or lighter-than-air vehicle, loitering in a persistent orbital station high in the stratosphere watching ballistic missile launches a thousand miles away be able to take a shot at that missile or another high-value target?

One has only to recall the 20th Century RQ-1 Predator operators who watched their targets through the lens of a surveillance camera and who wondered the same thing.

To be continued . . .

Boeing's Phantom Eye technology demonstration aircraft climbs into a cloudless sky over Edwards AFB after takeoff from Rogers Dry Lake. (NASA)

Vice Admiral James Syring (center, in black jacket) chats with Rear Admiral Ron Boxall, commander of the Stennis Carrier Strike Group, aboard the aircraft carrier USS John C. Stennis in March 2016. The director of the Pentagon's Missile Defense Agency, Syring told the Space & Missile Defense conference in Huntsville, Alabama, in August 2015 that the Defense Department was formally embracing the idea of using a laser-armed UCAV to attack ICBMs in their boost phase. (U.S. Navy photo by MC3 Kenneth Rodriguez Santiago)

From Hellfire to HELLADS: Seen here is a General Atomics Avenger unmanned combat air vehicle armed with a General Atomics High Energy Liquid Laser Area Defense System (HELLADS). The goal of the HELLADS program is to develop a high-energy laser weapon system with an order of magnitude reduction in weight compared to existing laser systems.

Appendix A

SPECIFICATIONS FOR SELECTED UNMANNED AERIAL VEHICLES

Note: Data is drawn from various sources, should be considered approximate, and is provided for comparison purposes only.

International Joint Ventures

Barracuda
Manufacturer: European Aeronautic Defence and Space Company (EADS)
Powerplant: One Pratt & Whitney Canada JT15D-5C
Wingspan: 23.7 feet (7.22 m)
Length: 27 feet (8.25 m)
Weight: 4,983 pounds (2,260 kg)
Maximum takeoff weight: 7,165 pounds (3,250 kg)
Payload: 551 pounds (250 kg)
Speed: Mach .85
Range: 124 miles (200 km)
Armament: MBDA Brimstone air-to-surface missile

Harfang
Manufacturer: European Aeronautic Defence and Space Company (EADS)
Powerplant: One Rotax 914F turbocharged engine (115 hp)
Wingspan: 54.5 feet (16.6 m)
Length: 30.5 feet (9.3 m)
Weight: 1,448 pounds (657 kg)
Maximum takeoff weight: 2,756 pounds (1,250 kg)
Speed: 129 mph (207 km/h)
Ceiling: 25,000 feet (7,620 m)

Neuron (nEUROn)
Manufacturers:
- Dassault Aviation: Master builder, design, flight control system, final assembly, static and flight test
- Alenia Aeronautica: Weapon firing system, weapons bay, flight test
- Saab AB: equipped fuselage, avionics, fuel system, flight test
- Construcciones Aeronáuticas Sociedad Anonima (EADS/CASA): wing, ground control station, data-link integration
- Hellenic Aerospace Industry: rear fuselage, engine, missiles, communication system
- Rüstungs Unternehmen Aktiengesellschaft (RUAG): wind tunnel tests, weapons carriage
- Thales: data-link, command interface
- European Aeronautic Defence and Space Company-France (EADS)

Powerplants: One Rolls-Royce/Turbomeca Adour/Snecma M88 (8,992 pounds of thrust)
Wingspan: 41 feet (12.5 m)
Length: 31.2 feet (9.5 m)
Weight (empty): 10,803 pounds (4,900 kg)
Weight (gross): 15,432 pounds (7,000 kg)
Speed: 609 mph (980 km/h)
Ceiling: 45,900 feet (14,000 m)
Armament: Two 500-pound (230 kg) bombs

Austria

S-100 Camcopter
Manufacturer: Schiebel Group
Powerplant: Diamond engine (55 hp)
Main rotor diameter: 133.9 feet (34 m)
Length: 122 feet (31.1 m)
Height: 44 feet (11.2 m)
Maximum takeoff weight: 440 pounds (200 kg)
Payload: 110 pounds (50 kg)
Speed: 140 mph (220 km/h)
Range (maximum): 112 miles (180 km)
Ceiling: 18,000 feet (5,500 m)
Endurance: 6 hours with 75 pounds (34 kg) payload
Armament: None specified

China

CH-4
Manufacturer: China Aerospace Science and Technology Corporation (CASC)
Powerplant: Turboprop engine
Wingspan: 59.1 feet (18 m)
Length: 27.9 feet (8.5 m)
Height: 11.2 feet (3.4 m)
Maximum takeoff weight: 2,930 pounds (1,330 kg) (CH-4B strike variant)
Payload: 761 pounds (345 kg) (CH-4B strike variant)
Top speed: 146 mph (235 km/h)
Cruising speed: 112 mph (180 km/hr)
Ceiling: 26,200 feet (8,000 m) (CH-4A reconnaissance variant)
Endurance: 30 hours (CH-4A reconnaissance variant) 14 hours (CH-4B strike variant)
Armament (CH-4B strike variant): AR-1 or Lan Jian 7 air-to-surface missiles and YC-200 or TG100 guided bombs

Pterodactyl I
Manufacturer: Chengdu Aircraft Industry Group (CAIG)
Powerplant: Turboprop engine
Wingspan: 45 feet 11 inches (14 m)
Length: 29 feet 8 inches (9.05 m)
Height: 9 feet 1 inch (2.77 m)
Gross weight: 2,425 pounds (1,100 kg)
Payload: 220 pounds (100 kg)
Top speed: 174 mph (280 km/h)
Ceiling: 16,404 feet (5,000 m)
Endurance: 20 hours
Armament: FT series precision-guided munitions or AKD-10 air-to-surface missiles

WZ-2000 (Wu Zhen-2000)
Manufacturer: Guizhou Aviation Industry Group
Powerplant: One WS-11 turbofan with 3,800 pounds of thrust

Wingspan: 32 feet 2 inches (9.8 m)
Length: 24 feet 7 inches (7.5 m)
Maximum takeoff weight: 3,748 pounds (1,700 kg)
Payload: 176 pounds (80 kg)
Speed: 497 mph (800 km/h)
Ceiling: 59,000 feet (17,983 m)
Range: 1,491 miles (2,400 km)
Combat Range: 497 miles (800 km)
Armament: KD2 air-to-surface missiles and ZD1 precision-guided bombs

India

Rustom (Warrior) 1
Manufacturer: Defence Research and Development Organisation
Powerplant: One Lycoming O-320 4-cylinder air-cooled
     horizontally opposed engine, (150 hp)
Wingspan: 25 feet 11 inches (7.9 m)
Length: 16 feet 10 inches (5.12 m)
Height: 7 feet 10 inches (2.4 m)
Weight (empty): 1,587.33 pounds (720 kg)
Payload: 165.3 pounds (95 kg)
Speed: 140 mph (225 km/h)
Ceiling: 26,000 feet (8,000 m)
Range:
     Line of sight: 156.25 miles (250 km)
     Relay communication: 218.75 miles (350 km)
     Ferry range: 621 miles (1,000 km)

Rustom (Warrior) H
Manufacturer: Defence Research and Development Organisation
Powerplant: Two NPO-Saturn 36MT turboprops
     wing-mounted turboprops, (100 hp each)
Wingspan: 67 feet 7 inches (20.6 m)
Length: 31 feet 2 inches (9.5 m)
Weight (empty): 3,968.32 pounds (1,800 kg)
Payload: 771.6 pounds (350 kg)
Speed: 140 mph (225 km/h)
Ceiling: 35,000 feet (10,668 m)
Range:
     Line of sight: 156.25 miles (250 km)
     Relay communication: 218.75 miles (350 km)
     Ferry range: 621 miles (1,000 km)

Iran

Karrar (Striker)
Manufacturer: Iran Aircraft Manufacturing Industrial Company (HESA)
Powerplant: One Toloue-4 or Toloue-5 turbojet
Length: 13.12 feet (4 m)
Top speed: 559 mph (900 km/h)
Range: 621 miles (1,000 km)
Endurance: 1 hour (fully loaded)
Armament: Kowsar or Sadid-1 anti-ship missiles, 1,000 pounds of bombs

Shahed (Eyewitness) 129
Manufacturer: Iran Aircraft Manufacturing Industrial Company (HESA)
Powerplant: Wankel-type engine
Wingspan: 52.5 feet (16 m)
Length: 26.3 feet (8 m)
Speed: 87 mph (140 km/h)
Ceiling: 24,000 feet (7,315 m)

Range: 1,000 to 1,700 miles (1,700 to 2,700 km)
Endurance: 24 hours
Armament: Up to eight Sadid-1 anti-ship missiles

Israel

Eitan (Steadfast)
Manufacturer: Israel Aerospace Industries
Powerplant: One Pratt & Whitney PT6A-67A (1,200 hp)
Wingspan: 86 feet (26 m)
Length: 43 feet (13 m)
Maximum takeoff weight: 10,250 pounds (4,650 kg)
Payload: 4,400 pounds (2,000 kg)
Speed: 230 mph (370 km/h)
Ceiling: 45,000 feet (14,000 m)
Range: 4,600 miles (7,400 km)
Endurance: 70 hours plus

Heron
Manufacturer: Israel Aerospace Industries
Powerplant: Rotax 914 (115 hp)
Wingspan: 54 feet 5 inches (16.60 m)
Length: 27 feet 10 inches (8.5 m)
Maximum takeoff weight: 2,530 pounds (1,150 kg)
Payload: 550 pounds (250 kg)
Speed: 130 mph (207 km/h)
Ceiling: 32,800 feet (10,000 m)
Range: 217 miles (350 km)
Endurance: 40 hours
Armament: None specified

Harop (Harpy)
Manufacturer: MBT division of Israel Aerospace Industries
Length: 8 feet 2 inches (2.5 m)
Range: 621 miles (1,000 km)
Endurance: 6 hours
Armament: 51-pound (23-kilogram) warhead

Hermes 450
Manufacturer: Elbit Systems
Powerplant: UAV Engines Limited R802/902(W), Wankel-type engine (52 hp)
Wingspan: 34 feet 5 inches (10.5 m)
Length: 20 feet (6.1 m)
Gross weight: 992 pounds (450 kg)
Payload: 331 pounds (150 kg)
Top speed: 109 mph (176 km/h)
Cruising speed: 81 mph (130 km/h)
Ceiling: 18,000 feet (5,486 m)
Range: 186 miles (300 km)
Endurance: 20 hours

Hermes 900 Kochav (Star)
Manufacturer: Elbit Systems
Powerplant: One Rotax 914 4-cylinder piston engine (115 hp)
Length: 27 feet 3 inches (8.3 m)
Gross weight: 2,425 pounds (1,100 kg)
Payload: 770 pounds (350 kg)
Top speed: 137 mph (220 km/h)
Cruising speed: 70 mph (112 km/h)
Ceiling: 30,000 feet (9,144 m)
Endurance: 36 hours

Italy

P.1HH Hammerhead
Manufacturer: Piaggio Aero
Powerplant: Two Pratt & Whitney Canada PT6A-66B 850 SHP turboprop engines
Wingspan: 51.18 feet (15.6 m)
Length: 47.27 feet (14.408 m)
Height: 13.05 feet (3.98 m)
Maximum takeoff weight: 13,550 pounds (6,146 kg)
Top speed: 455 mph (732 km/h)
Cruising speed: 368 mph (592 km/h)
Ceiling: 45,000 feet (13,716 m)
Range: 5,063 miles (8,149 km)
Endurance: 16 hours

Sky-X
Manufacturer: Alenia Aeronautica
Powerplant: One Snecma Microturbo TRI60-268 turbofan
Wingspan: 19 feet 6 inches (5.94 m)
Length: 19 feet 7 inches (7.8 m)
Height: 6 feet 1 inches (1.86 m)
Weight (empty): 2,204 pounds (1,000 kg)
Maximum takeoff weight: 3,196 pounds (1,450 kg)
Top speed: 403 mph (648 km/h)
Ceiling: 25,000 feet (7,260 m)

Pakistan

Shahpar
Manufacturer: Global Industrial Defence Solutions (GIDS)
Powerplant: One Rotax 912 piston engine (100 hp)
Wingspan: 22 feet (6.6 m)
Length: 13.8 feet (4.2 m)
Gross weight: 1,060 pounds (460 kg)
Speed: 93 mph (150 km/h)
Ceiling: 17,000 feet (5,000 m)
Endurance: 7 hours

Uqab (Eagle)
Manufacturer: Global Industrial Defence Solutions (GIDS)
Powerplant: One Rotax 912 piston engine (100 hp)
Wingspan: 18 feet (5.5 m)
Length: 13.1 feet (4 m)
Height: 3.9 feet (1.2 m)
Gross weight: 551 pounds (250 kg)
Speed: 93 mph (150 km/h)
Ceiling: 9,842 feet (3,000 m)
Endurance: 6 hours

Russia

Skat (Manta Ray)
Manufacturer: Mikoyan Russian Aircraft Corporation
Powerplant: One Klimov RD-5000B turbofan engine
Wingspan: 37.7 feet (11.5 m)
Length: 33.6 feet (10.25 m)
Payload: 4,000 pounds (8,819 kg)
Top speed: 497 mph (8,000 km/h)
Ceiling: 39,370 feet (12,000 m)
Armament: Mix of weapons in internal bays

Turkey

Anka
Manufacturer: Turkish Aerospace Industries (TAI)
Powerplant: One Thielert Centurion 2.0, turbocharged piston engine (155 hp)
Wingspan: 56.7 feet (17.3 m)
Length: 26.2 feet (8 m)
Height: 11.2 feet (3.4 m)
Maximum takeoff weight: 3,527 pounds (1,600 kg)
Payload: 441 pounds (200 kg)
Top speed: 135 mph (217 km/h)
Cruising speed: 126 mph (204 km/h)
Ceiling: 30,000 feet (9,144 m)
Range: 3,024 miles (4,896 km)
Endurance: 24 hours

Bayraktar
Manufacturer: Kale-Baykar (Joint venture between the Kale Group and Baykar Makina)
Powerplant: One Rotax 912 piston engine (100 hp)
Wingspan: 39.3 feet (12 m)
Length: 21.3 feet (6.5 m)
Maximum takeoff weight: 1,433 pounds (650 kg)
Payload: 110 pounds (50 kg)
Top speed: 138 mph (222 km/h)
Ceiling: 22,500 feet (6,858 m); record of 27,030 feet
Endurance: 24 hours
Armament: Roketsan MAM-L Smart Munition

United Arab Emirates

Smart Eye
Manufacturer: Adcom Systems
Powerplant: 80- to 115-hp piston engine
Wingspan: 68.9 feet (21 m)
Length: 22.97 feet (7 m)
Height: 6.5 feet (2 m)
Maximum takeoff weight: 2,205 pounds (1,000 kg)
Payload: 154 to 1,212 pounds (70 to 550 kg)
Top speed: 138 mph (222 km/h)
Cruising speed: 40 to 80 mph (65 to 130 km/h)
Ceiling: 24,000 feet (7,300 m)
Endurance: 120 hours

Smart Eye 1
Manufacturer: Adcom Systems
Powerplant: Two 17-hp piston engines
Wingspan: 14.4 feet (4.4 m)
Length: 10.7 feet (3.26 m)
Height: 2.95 feet (0.9 m)
Weight (empty): 110 pounds (50 kg)
Maximum takeoff weight: 220 pounds (100 kg)
Payload: 44 to 88 pounds (20 to 40 kg)
Cruising speed: 93 mph (150 km/h)
Ceiling: 9,800 feet (3,000 m)
Endurance: 2 hours

Yabhon R
Manufacturer: Adcom Systems
Powerplant: 80- to 100-hp piston engine
Wingspan: 21.3 feet (6.5 m)

Length: 16.4 feet (5 m)
Height: 6.5 feet (2 m)
Maximum takeoff weight: 1,257 pounds (570 kg)
Payload: 132 to 463 pounds (60 to 120 kg)
Cruising speed: 75 to 150 mph (120 to 240 km/h)
Ceiling: 22,000 feet (6,700 m)
Endurance: 27 hours

United 40
Manufacturer: Adcom Systems
Powerplant: two 230-hp piston engines
Wingspan: 57.53 feet (17.53 m)
Length: 36.54 feet (11.13 m)
Height: 14.37 feet (4.38 m)
Maximum takeoff weight: 4,409 pounds (2,000 kg)
Payload: 1,058 pounds (480 kg)
Cruising speed: 75 to 125 mph (120 to 200 km/h)
Ceiling: 26,000 feet (8,000 m)
Endurance: 100 hours

United Kingdom

Watchkeeper WK450
(aircraft and data based on Elbit Hermes 450)
Manufacturer: UAV Tactical Systems (U-TacS); partnership between Elbit and Thales UK
Powerplant: UAV Engines Limited R802/902(W); Wankel-type engine (52 hp)
Wingspan: 34 feet 5 inches (10.5 m)
Length: 20 feet (6.1 m)
Gross weight: 992 pounds (450 kg)
Payload: 331 pounds (150 kg)
Top speed: 109 mph (176 km/h)
Cruising speed: 81 mph (130 km/h)
Ceiling: 18,000 feet (5,486 m)
Range: 186 miles (300 km)
Endurance: 17 hours
Armament: Thales FreeFall Lightweight Multi-role Missile (FFLM)

Taranis
Manufacturer: BAE Systems
Powerplant: One Rolls-Royce Adour, moderate bypass turbofan (10,000 pounds of thrust)
Wingspan: 32 feet 10 inches (10 m)
Length: 40 feet 9 inches (12.43 m)
Height: 13 feet 1 inch (4 m)
Speed: Mach .9
Armament: Mix of weapons in two internal weapons bays

United States

MQ-1B Predator
Manufacturer: General Atomics Aeronautical Systems Inc.
User classification: U.S. Air Force Tier II, Medium Altitude Long Endurance (MALE)
Powerplant: Rotax 914F 4-cylinder engine (115 horsepower)
Wingspan: 48.7 feet (14.8 m)*
Length: 27 feet (8.22 m)
Height: 6.9 feet (2.1 m)
Weight: 1,130 pounds (512 kg)
Maximum takeoff weight: 2,250 pounds (1,020 kg)
Payload: 450 pounds (204 kg)
Speed: Cruise, 84 mph (135 km/h); top, 135 mph (215 km/h)

Ceiling: 25,000 feet (7,620 m)
Range: 454 miles (730 km)
Endurance: 40 hours (maximum)
Armament: Two laser-guided AGM-114 Hellfire missiles

The long-range Predator XP export variant has a wingspan of 55 feet (17 m)

MQ-1C Sky Warrior
Manufacturer: General Atomics Aeronautical Systems Inc.
User classification: U.S. Army Tier III, Extended Range Multi-Purpose (ERMP)
Powerplant: Thielert Heavy-Fuel Engine (135 horsepower)
Wingspan: 56 feet (17 m)
Length: 28 feet (8 m)
Height: 6.9 feet (2.1 m)
Maximum takeoff weight: 3,200 pounds (1,451 kg)
Speed: 155 mph (250 km/h)
Ceiling: 29,000 feet (8,800 m)
Armament: Four AGM-114 Hellfire missiles

MQ-9 Reaper
Manufacturer: General Atomics Aeronautical Systems
User classification: U.S. Air Force Tier II, Medium Altitude Long Endurance (MALE)
Powerplant: Honeywell TPE331-10GD turboprop (900 shaft horsepower)
Wingspan: 66 feet (20.1 m)
Wingspan (Reaper ER Long Wing variant): 79 feet (24 m)
Length: 36 feet (11 m)
Height: 12.5 feet (3.8 m)
Weight (empty): 4,900 pounds (2,223 kg)
Maximum takeoff weight: 10,500 pounds (4,760 kg)
Payload: 3,750 pounds (1,701 kg)
Speed: Cruise, 230 mph (370 km/h)
Ceiling: 50,000 feet (15,240 m)
Range: 3,682 miles (3,200 nautical miles)
Endurance: 40 hours (14 hours when fully armed)
Armament: Combination of AGM-114 Hellfire missiles, GBU-12 Paveway II and GBU-38 Joint Direct Attack Munitions

X-47B
Manufacturer: Northrop Grumman
Powerplant: Pratt & Whitney F100-PW-220U turbofan (16,000 pounds thrust)
Wingspan: 62.1 feet (18.92 m)
Length: 38.2 feet (11.63 m)
Height: 10.4 feet (3.10 m)
Weight: 14,000 pounds (6,350 kg)
Maximum takeoff weight: 44,567 pounds (20,215 kg)
Payload: 4,500 pounds (2,040 kg)
Speed: High subsonic
Ceiling: 40,000 feet (12,190 m)
Range: 4,000 miles (6,500 km)
Armament: Two GBU-31 Joint Direct Attack Munition guided bombs

Avenger (Predator C)
Manufacturer: General Atomics Aeronautical Systems Inc.
Powerplant: Pratt & Whitney Canada PW545B turbofan (4,800 pounds thrust)
Wingspan: 66 feet (20.12 m)
Length: 41 feet (12.50 m)
Payload: 3,000 pounds (1,360.78 kg)
Speed: 460 mph (740 km/h)
Operational altitude: 60,000 feet (18,288 m)
Endurance: 20 hours (extra 2 hours with bomb bay fuel tank)
Armament: AGM-114 Hellfire, GBU-24 Paveway III, GBU-31 JDAM, GBU-38 Small Diameter Bomb

RQ-170 Sentinel
Manufacturer: Lockheed Martin
Powerplant: Unconfirmed, but possibly one Garrett TFE731 or one General
    Electric TF34[15] turbofan
Wingspan: 65 feet 7 inches (20 m)
Length: 14 feet 9 inches (4.5 m)

Appendix B

AMERICAN MILITARY UNMANNED AERIAL VEHICLES

As designated under the post-1997 "Q" Designation System.

RQ-1A/B	General Atomics Predator	RQ-14A	AeroVironment Dragon Eye
MQ-1B	General Atomics Predator	RQ-14B	AeroVironment Swift
MQ-1C	General Atomics Warrior	RQ-15A	DRS Neptune
RQ-2A/B/C	IAI Pioneer	YRQ-16A	Honeywell Micro Air Vehicle (MAV)
RQ-3A	Lockheed Martin DarkStar	XMQ-17A	MTC Technologies SpyHawk
RQ-4A/B	Northrop Grumman (Teledyne Ryan) Global Hawk	YMQ-18A	Boeing A160T Hummingbird
RQ-5A and MQ-5A/B (formerly (BQM-155A)	Northrop Grumman (TRW/IAI) Hunter	MQ-19	Aerosonde (AAI Textron Systems) 250 Mark 4.7 and G
		RQ-20A	AeroVironment Puma
RQ-6A	Alliant Techsystems Outrider	RQ-21A	Boeing Insitu Blackjack (originally Interrogator)
RQ-7A/B	AAI Shadow 200	XRQ-22A	AeroVironment Global Observer
RQ-8A/MQ-8B/C	Northrop Grumman Fire Scout	RQ-23A	NAVMAR TigerShark
MQ-9A	General Atomics Reaper	CQ-24A	Kaman/Lockheed Martin K-MAX
CQ-10A	MMIST SnowGoose	MQ-25A ¿	Stingray (contractor not yet selected)
RQ-11A/B	AeroVironment Raven	RQ-170	Lockheed Martin Sentinel
RQ-12A	AeroVironment Wasp	P-175	Lockheed Martin Polecat (company designator)
Q-13	Designation not yet assigned*	RQ-180	Northrop Grumman (?)

* The RQ-13 designation is associated with the imaginary Layartebian Defense Corporation Stiletto, a fictional "variant" of the Lockheed D-21 of the 1960s.

Note: Some operational UAVs, such as the Boeing Insitu ScanEagle have not received official designations in this series.

INDEX

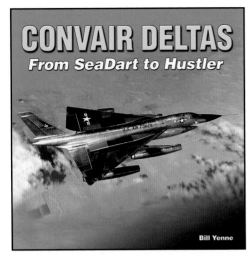

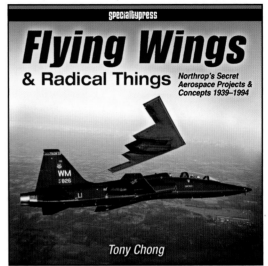
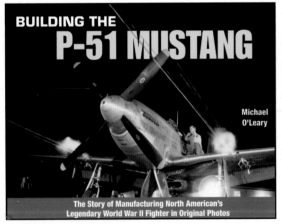
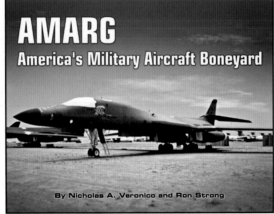